BEYOND CONTAINMENT

BEYOND CONTAINMENT

Alternative American Policies Toward the Soviet Union

Edited by
AARON WILDAVSKY

ICS PRESS

Institute for Contemporary Studies
San Francisco, California

Inquiries, book orders, and catalog requests should be addressed to ICS Press, Suite 811, 260 California Street, San Francisco, California 94111—415—398—3010.

Library of Congress Cataloging in Publication Data
Main entry under title:

Beyond containment.

    Includes bibliographical references and index.
    1. United States—Foreign relations—Soviet Union—Addresses, essays, lectures. 2. Soviet Union—Foreign relations—United States—Addresses, essays, lectures. I. Wildavsky, Aaron B.
E183.8.S65B49 1983   327.73047   83—12902
ISBN 0—917616—61—8
ISBN 0—917616—60—X (pbk.)

CONTENTS

IV

Conclusion

viii

PREFACE

Until very recently, American policy toward the Soviet Union has been premised upon the essentially defensive concept of "containment." In many respects, this policy has unquestionably served us well. But in the past few years, a series of ominous developments —the vast buildup of Soviet nuclear and conventional forces, the marked proliferation of Soviet-sponsored insurgencies, the unilateral deployment of over 350 new intermediate-range nuclear missiles against Europe, the suppression of Poland's Solidarity, and the brutal invasion of Afghanistan—has given us reason to rethink the long-standing assumptions of our foreign policy.

For all of its historical advantages, containment has been limited from the beginning by two drawbacks: its inherently defensive nature, and its dependence for final success on long-term changes in the fundamental character of the Soviet regime. It is partly on the basis of this latter promise that George Kennan sought to persuade Americans to adopt a containment policy in the wake of the Second World War.

Not only does this promise of change remain totally unfulfilled, but the defensive shield containing Soviet expansion has proved to be increasingly porous. The question has arisen whether our basic policy could not at least be supplemented by more active measures.

In an attempt to examine this question, political scientist Aaron Wildavsky gathered together six leading foreign policy experts in February 1983 for a weekend of seminars at the Claremont Hotel in Berkeley, California. The chapters of this book are based on papers prepared by the authors before the meetings and revised on the basis of discussion.

The final volume, while reaffirming the necessity for containment, explores a number of alternative strategies and tactics that could add up to a more "activist" policy stance designed to accomplish more without incurring notably greater risk.

Beyond Containment continues the Institute for Contemporary Studies' ongoing examination of U.S. options in this central area of foreign policy, treated in such volumes as *Defending America* (co-published with Basic Books in 1977) and *National Security in the 1980s: From Weakness to Strength* (1980).

It is hoped that this volume will make an important contribution to the reevaluation of U.S. foreign policy and strategy now under way.

Glenn Dumke
President
Institute for Contemporary Studies

ACKNOWLEDGMENTS

I would like to thank Don Collins for his interest in and encouragement of this project, and the Scaife Foundation for its financial support. Don Van Aatta, our research assistant, helped all of the authors by providing excellent material on the Soviet regime. Pat Glynn, of the ICS staff, attended our sessions and enlivened our discussions. My secretary, Doris Patton, kept us supplied with a steady stream of accurate communications. And LeRoy Graymer, president of the Institute for Policy and Management Research, arranged our meetings with his usual flair.

Aaron Wildavsky

I

Introduction

1

AARON WILDAVSKY

Containment: Indispensable Yet Unsatisfactory

This is the first of four projected volumes on alternatives to existing American foreign policy. The other volumes will consider American foreign policy in relation to our defense policy, to our allies, and to the Third World. Certain vital aspects of Soviet-American relationships—the compatibility of Soviet and American defense postures with the foreign policies of the two nations, the roles of allies and satellites, the relative importance of regions of the Third World—are reserved, therefore, for fuller future discussion.

This book begins with basic considerations affecting American foreign policy: chapter 2 deals with the dilemmas that make American foreign policy difficult; chapter 3 describes the Soviet system, which produces the problems with which American policy must grapple; and chapter 4 reviews the history of the doctrine of containment around which this policy has been organized since the Second World War. Chapters 5 through 10 are devoted to different levels of American foreign policy—from responses to attack against our vital interests to preventative measures, from the refusal to subsidize the Soviet economy to an attempt to pluralize their political system. Although the authors engaged in three days of intense discussion, during which time much mutual education took place, each is solely responsible only for his own policy proposal. Taking the proposals from the least to the most active, from minimum to maximum containment, I prefer, as my conclusion indicates, "all of the above." My objective is to help develop a maximal containment policy as an alternative to the existing policy of minimal containment.

There can be no doubt that the Soviet Union behaves aggressively, although it is hardly the only state that does so. But why do the Soviets act aggressively, and how aggressive are they? There are three alternatives: either the Soviet Union behaves essentially as other national states have in the modern world; or it is determined to attack, like Nazi Germany; or it is more aggressive than other nation-states but less so than Hitler's Germany.

Traditional nation-states have at times been quite aggressive, but their aggression has been rationally calculated and (at least in theory) limited in objective and time. In principle, such "normal" nation-states are constrained by the other nation-states, which by maintaining their own sovereignty prevent any single state from accumulating too much power and coming to mortally threaten the others. The mechanisms of the "balance of power," together with the common interest of all states in their own survival and hence in a minimal level of international cooperation, should ensure that international conflict is limited. If the Soviet Union is, in this sense, a "normal" state, then it can be dealt with by constructing an international system in which the balance of power constrains it.

But what if the USSR is *not* a normal state? What if, because of the way its internal political system operates, the Soviet Union must be endlessly aggressive? Or what if Soviet leaders use a different standard of rationality in calculating their moves, one that is predicated on the need of their state constantly to expand its control? What if the Soviet leaders feel it necessary to use any means, up to and including a nuclear first strike, to achieve these objectives? Then, clearly, the only appropriate American response is to declare an immediate state of national emergency and mobilize for war, as Britain and France should have done in the 1930s.

Perhaps the Soviet Union is aggressive for internal political reasons, but its aggressions are calculated and limited by a shrewd appreciation of the realities of international politics. If this analysis is correct, the sensible policy proposal is neither a return to the old European system of balance of power nor preparation for inevitable total war, but some form of containment. Such containment seeks to deny the Soviets gains from aggression. Within the consensus on the need for containment, however, there is disagreement about the relative importance of the aggressive impulse, and therefore about the level of American mobilization needed to counter the threat.

A policy of containing Soviet aggression remains indispensable. There is no alternative but resistance. But piecemeal resistance, at a time and place dictated by the Soviet Union, has proved infeasible. The original idea behind containment was that the containment of Soviet-aided and Soviet-sponsored advances would allow time for an internal evolution of the Soviet regime in a less aggressive direction. Rebuffed in foreign adventures, the theory went, the Soviet Union would be impelled to concentrate its attention on improving the position of its people. Thirty and more years later it is obvious that these expectations have proved unfounded. Containment by itself is deficient, yet there is no coherent doctrine with which to supplant (or, more accurately, supplement) it so as to guide foreign policy. Few, it is fair to say, are happy with the existing situation. Yet no alternative commands significant support.

New approaches, or at least moods—such as President Carter's extension of the olive branch—are followed by rapid retreats. New strategies, or at least catchwords like "linkage," end up riddled with inconsistencies. What prevails is a case-by-case approach, usually called "pragmatism," meaning that the United States does not know what to do; its policy is based on not having a policy. Indeed, even the administration of Ronald Reagan, except for accelerating the military buildup begun by Jimmy Carter, does not appear to have departed significantly from the policies of his predecessors. Some elements in the administration believe the Soviet Union cannot change its nature and, therefore, its foreign policy. This belief may account for the Reagan administration's emphasis on defense; but aside from early presidential rhetoric attacking the Soviet regime, this new emphasis has yet to lead to changes in foreign policy, which remains defensive, based as before on minimal containment.

Is this essential continuity, we may ask, due to circumstances imposing a very restricted range of choice on American decision-makers, or is it a result of a narrow vision? Both influences are important. The ultimate failure of the Nixon and Carter administrations to restrain Soviet behavior, whether in aiding North Vietnam or in invading Afghanistan, was not for want of trying. No one reading Henry Kissinger's memoirs would think containment (and its variant—a little more carrot, a little less stick, called détente) a deranged idea or its implementors evidently lacking in knowledge. As a recent reader of Jimmy Carter's memoirs, *Keeping Faith,* I was impressed by the number of issues—Soviet rearmament, the MX missile, the intricacies of Arab-Israeli affairs, the basing of nuclear weapons in Western Europe—that now recur in similar form and apparently with similar response in Reagan's time. Our attempt to devise departures from prevailing American foreign policy is not based on a "stupidity" theory of foreign policy.

The cacaphony of criticism itself makes it more difficult to gather support for existing policies or to risk trying new ones. It may well be that the only beating that hurts more than the one you take for defending current foreign policy is the one you get for proposing any (by definition, Dangerous with a capital "D") departure. Nevertheless, as encounters accumulate, there is more evidence on which to base consideration of different policies. As encounters remain unsatisfactory, there is better reason to consider novel ways of thinking and acting.

At a minimum, our efforts to appraise departures from existing policy should help better explain why the United States government, from the 1950s through the 1980s, regardless of party or personality, has pursued much the same sort of policy toward the Soviet Union. Nixon and Kissinger's policy of détente—cooperation with the Soviets for domestic development as an incentive for them to reject foreign aggression—was apparently based on the perception that the Soviet Union had changed enough to engage in traditional balance-of-power politics. Whether because the Soviets did just that but the American polity would not accept it, or because the premise that the Soviet Union had become a state like any other was faulty, the "Nixinger" policy eventually was reduced from cooperation to competition and finally to containment. That is where we are today: containment remains indispensable, yet unsatisfactory. Our task in this book is to appraise whether and to show how the United States might break out of this box.

Each author has been asked to keep one thing in mind: his preferred policy is to be one that could be implemented within the American political system as it exists now. Obtaining and maintaining domestic support is an integral aspect of conducting foreign policy. That is why a policy of appeasement and a policy of retaliation (they attack one place, we another) have been ruled out. Aside from the evident dangers these policies present, we judge that there would be overwhelming opposition to them both by preponderant majorities of the American people and by the elected and appointed elites engaged in foreign affairs.

In chapter 2 I shall discuss the dilemmas that a policy of containment creates for American foreign policy. Central to all these dilemmas is the slippery subject of assessing Soviet intentions. Despite the understandable inclination to reject this theme either as obvious (if only blockheads with different views could see the manifest truth) or as hopeless (since we cannot psychoanalyze Soviet leaders or otherwise see into men's souls), it is of vital importance. Advocates of opposing policies rationalize their harder or softer or different view in terms of a theory of Soviet intentions. So do the authors of this volume. In the conclusion, I shall draw together the various proposals in the book for fashioning as substantial a rival to present policy as a recalcitrant world permits.

II

Background

2

AARON WILDAVSKY

Dilemmas of American Foreign Policy

If there were new foreign policies that were unambiguously desirable, providing only benefits and no costs compared to old courses of action, there would be no difficulty in choosing the better way. Actually, however, policy choices are typically, if not inevitably, beset by dilemmas. Withdrawing all subsidies from trade and technology exchange with the Soviet Union, for example, as suggested later in this volume, appears to be an attractive policy on many grounds. The Soviets would thereby find it more difficult to reconcile the competing demands of their continuing military buildup, the expansion of their external empire, and the needs of their faltering economy at home. Yet such a policy would probably encounter serious opposition from our NATO allies, as well as domestic opposition in the United States from constituencies that rely on subsidized Export-Import Bank financing of exports to the Soviet Union or on export credit insurance from the Commodity Credit Corporation, or from those who believe that such action would be needlessly provocative.

To take another example, continuing to adhere to a policy of minimum containment — "staying the course," as proposed by one contributor to this volume — has much to recommend it. As always, we could do worse. Containment has not worked too badly in the past, and adherence to it would avoid or at least limit the opposition within the Alliance, as well as within the United States, that would ensue from more vigorous policies. Yet the actual working of containment appears to some to do no more than limit the rate at which Soviet external expansion occurs, not to reverse its direction. From this standpoint, containment should be supplemented by more intense competition, such as efforts to "disestablish the Soviet empire by all prudent means," as proposed by another contributor to this volume.

At some point an American arms buildup might do more harm than good. It could weaken the domestic economy and/or provoke the Soviet Union into more aggressive or, at least, more dangerous behavior. By doing too little for defense, however, the United States might encourage the Soviet Union to undertake offensive actions. Much depends on how Soviet intentions, as well as capabilities, are evaluated. Knowing that we may be mistaken in our perceptions, how should the United States proceed, by having "too much" or "too little" capability?

And so it goes: serious dilemmas accompany most foreign policy choices. Ambiguities, risks, and costs accompany both doing more and standing still.

Keeping Score

Differences over what American foreign policy toward the Soviet Union should be are mirrored by disagreements over the nature and success of our adversary. There is disagreement about not only what the United States should do vis-à-vis the Soviet Union but exactly how well it is doing. One might say that containment has been a mixed success, working in Korea but not Vietnam, in Zaire but not Angola, and similarly elsewhere in the Third World. But that is not the only view. Some observers see the Soviet Union on a progression toward world domination, with some twenty nations, beginning with the Eastern bloc, now under Communist rule and tied to the parent power in Moscow. Others, like Kenneth

Waltz, believe that "[the Soviet Union's] sporadic success should not obscure the fact that what the Soviet Union has done mostly since 1948 is lose. . . . Her successes have been . . . of little value . . . and evanescent."[1] George Breslauer adds that Soviet gains "have been largely in lower-priority areas (the Third World), while losses have been largely in high-priority areas (border security, the Middle East, trade, and arms control)."[2] Differences about score-keeping depend in part on the value the commentator puts on whatever the Soviets have acquired. Is Poland an asset or a liability? Is Cuba worth $3 billion a year of Soviet subsidy?

Valuation of ostensible Soviet advances also depends on which theory of international politics is being employed. Suppose one believes, with Waltz, that

in international politics, . . . the "domino theory" does not hold. In international politics, winning leads to losing. No country wants to be dependent on another. If a country becomes dependent because of weakness, its neighbors will resist suffering a similar fate. We have been misled by the vision of falling dominoes. The so-called domino theory rests on a profound misunderstanding of international politics. States try to balance each other off; they do not climb on the bandwagon of a winner. Contrary to the theory's counsel, we need not react to prospective victories for the Soviet Union unless they threaten vital interests.[3]

This view of world politics, in which there is seen to be a natural balance of forces that one needs do little to create or maintain, is certainly comforting. Yet if this view is mistaken — if gains for the aggressive side are cumulative, as the domino image suggests — the longer one waits to resist the tumbling of the dominoes, the worse things will become. Are we thinking of the First World War in which precipitate action ignited a conflagration inimical to the interests of all the combatants, or the Second World War in which timely intervention might have saved the day? The foreign policy chosen will be seriously affected by the theory adopted — "natural balance" versus "falling dominoes" — because one rationalizes letting things take their course and the other justifies early intervention. Keeping score is not just a game; recommendations regarding U.S. defense spending should depend heavily on estimates of the Soviets' current score.

No one doubts that during the 1970s the Soviet Union undertook a massive arms buildup that continues to this day, while military expenditure in the United States remained static or declined.

Nevertheless, informed opinion on the significance of this substantial increase remains divided. Is it offensive or defensive, a
drive to parity or an attempt at supremacy? If the United States
government believes that Soviet intent is aggressive, it must arm
to counter this potential; if the United States believes, as Seweryn
Bialer puts it, that "the unprecedented Soviet armament effort
may be in part a response to past nightmares, to traumas of past
insecurities that push the Soviets relentlessly toward . . . over-
security,"[4] then allowing the Soviets to catch up might mollify
them. Of course, if it is the very existence of the United States that
makes the USSR insecure, no American policy will alter Soviet
behavior.

It is not possible to say definitely what a trend means, because
that requires certain knowledge of the future. Hypothesis,
therefore, has to substitute for fact. Thus the controversy is carried on by asking whether the Soviet Union is a nation like any
other. The implication is that if it is just a run-of-the-mill great
power, its ambitions might be more easily satisfied. If it is not, if
Marxist-Leninist ideology and political practice dictate dominion
over others, then growth in arms is ominous. This is distressing,
for only continuous confrontation with Communism, if that, would
enable the United States to remain free. Norman Podhoretz does
not flinch from the consequences of this position:

> In advocating an anti-Communist strategy of containment, however, am
> I calling for an eternity of confrontation and the risk of war without let-
> up, without surcease, and without any hope of victory at the end? It
> would be dishonest and a species of cant to deny that this might indeed be
> the prospect. It is a horrifying prospect from which one's first impulse is
> to shrink. But the prospect from the other side is more horrifying still: a
> universal Gulag and a life that is otherwise nasty, brutish, and short.
>
> If, however, it would be cant to deny that an anti-Communist strategy
> holds out the possibility of an endless stalemate—a kind of cold-war
> equivalent of World War I—it would be conversely wrong to fall into
> what the late C. P. Snow once called "sentimental cynicism" by failing to
> acknowledge the possibility of a much brighter prospect as well.[5]

Which prospect lies in store depends not only on what America
does but also on the disposition of the Soviet Union to come to
terms. What are its intentions?

Is the Soviet Union, as Charles Bohlen once said, "a cause
rather than a country"? If it is a country, its desires may be

limited by a combination of preparedness and diplomacy; if it is a cause, only overwhelming force, if that, will suffice. But that is too easy. Suppose that the Soviet Union is both a great power and a "cause." How would the United States, in appraising Soviet intentions, know which of its actions to attribute to what motive—cause or country?

The Dilemma of Motives

Soviet intentions (or motives) are a dilemma in that either taking them seriously or ignoring them involves substantial risks. Does the Soviet Union expand for defensive purposes? Or does it seek to conquer others? Or both?

Some people believe that the Soviet Union acts aggressively because of fear of encirclement. In this they are half correct. The further the Soviets expand their borders, the more they come into contact with others who are then close enough to encircle them. Instead of being encircled by such mortal enemies as the Baltic States and Afghanistan, they move closer to potentially more powerful antagonists. Since conquest creates encirclement, the only situation that the Soviets would not need to fear would be global dominance, for then there would be no unconquered nations surrounding them.

Great powers, to be sure, are often defensively expansionist. The British empire was created in large measure out of defensive motives. The fear that foreign powers would fill the void provided part of the impetus for America's internal expansion through "Manifest Destiny." That the Soviet Union is not the only nation that has advanced under the claim of encirclement, however, offers small solace to those who must cope with the consequences today. Nor can historical comparisons tell observers whether there is a limit to Soviet ambitions.

The trouble for interpreters is that a pattern of aggression could be attributed to either a defensive or an offensive set of motives. Should the Soviet Union be animated by offensive motives, the risks it runs in taking active measures might well moderate its behavior. Even if its motivation were primarily defensive, the Soviet Union might still never feel fully safe; therefore it could well attack, thus making its behavior indistinguishable from that produced by an offensive motive. Even if it were to make a preemptive nuclear strike on the United States, killing most Americans, we would not be able to say for sure whether this cataclysm occurred because our destroyer feared it would be attacked first or because it just wanted to get rid of us. So far as designing a foreign policy is concerned, therefore, it might make no difference whatsoever which motive is attributed to Soviet behavior.

Indeed, the Soviet leadership might not know its own motives. They may lack insight of this kind or have reasons for obscuring their motives from themselves as well as from others. And as they act on the world and it reacts to them, they may change their motivation. An opponent's surrender may embolden them, whereas resistance may induce caution.

What we speak of as "true" motives really consist of rationalizations of behavior. The better the fit, the more episodes that can be traced to a given motive, the better we are able to explain the events in question and the more confident we feel in predicting future behavior. In other words, motives or intentions are equivalent to causes. Once the causes (George Kennan spoke of the "sources" of Soviet conduct) are known, the consequences become more predictable and, perhaps, more manageable. The search for the motives animating Soviet foreign policy stands revealed as the search for a theory on which to base a policy capable of controlling Soviet behavior. This is a tall order.

It is possible to embrace a theory about Soviet intentions that, if believed, would make a difference to American policy. Inherently hostile for ideological reasons, this theory goes, the Soviet Union will increasingly seek dominion until it compels the United States to capitulate or seeks a final nuclear showdown. If conventional and nuclear war are inevitable, preparations to prevail—to the extent that is meaningful—and to limit damage—to the extent that is feasible—are called for. Indeed, under such assumptions, an American first strike (a good example of the only defense being an offense) becomes thinkable. Yet though it might just be correct, almost everyone shrinks from the implications of so stark a theory.

The illustration is useful, however, because it reveals the close connection between theory and action: there is little agreement on intentions in large part because there is disagreement over what

American foreign policy toward the Soviet Union should be. If those who think the United States too aggressive downplay the harsh aspects of Soviet rule, that may be less because they approve of Soviet policies and more because they fear that criticism of Soviet conduct justifies an American military response of which they disapprove. The discussion of Soviet motives is a surrogate for the debate over American policy.

The Dilemma of Defensiveness

The dilemma of defensiveness the United States faces does not lie in any particular loss so much as in the perceived pattern of future losses. If the rules of the game are that I can take your marbles but you cannot touch mine, it is only a matter of time before I win. When all the United States does is react, it plays a losing game. Rebuffing a threat here or an incursion there leaves a great deal to be desired by those in charge of making foreign policy.

Containment calls for the United States to act at times of an opponent's choosing to defend regimes that may be distasteful and incompetent. Yet the U.S. political system makes it difficult to mobilize support over time on many issues without sign of success or evident moral probity. And since retaliatory measures are ruled out, the Soviet Union can afford to fail. So long as its side wins now and again, it is able to cumulate its winnings. Containment, pure and simple, is a losing game.

It is true, as is often said, that the Soviet Union is careful in choosing where to intervene; but it is not true, as is often implied, that the Soviets cautiously avoid angering the U.S. The care comes in calculating that the United States will not be able to intervene successfully or, if it does, that the Soviet Union can disengage itself without endangering its home base. The willingness to invade Afghanistan, to place medium-range missiles in Eastern Europe, to occupy Japanese islands, or to induce Cuba to send troops to Angola, does not suggest caution — unless caution means doing just enough to anger but not to enrage.

It is true enough that the Soviet Union has been rebuffed in Egypt, North Yemen, and other places where it sought to exercise its influence. But everywhere a full-fledged Communist-Leninist regime has been established, as in Cuba or North Vietnam, it has stayed in power by itself or, as in Poland, with the backing of the Soviet Union. Even a single reversal of Leninist rule would be important, for if it could be shown that regimes can change back again so that gains are temporary, the importance of particular Soviet victories would be diminished. If Afghanistan were to show that a Soviet invasion is reversible, and Poland that pluralization is possible, the temperature of temporary encounters here and there in the world would fall appreciably. So far, however, nothing of the sort has occurred.

When one party is mainly interested in starting fires and the other in putting them out, the balance of firepower is likely to lie with the instigator. Naturally, in seeking targets of opportunity, the Soviet Union is going to choose instances in which the United States finds it difficult to bring its power to bear. The Soviets may experiment with various options for supporting insurgency, dropping those possibilities that turn out to be difficult and leaving the United States to cope with what are, for it, the hard cases. The United States may then be faced with the choice of abandoning an ally or trying to defend it and risking defeat. In the first case the government is open to charges of cowardice, and in the second of incompetence; either way, the trust of citizens in their government may be shaken. Moreover, the facts in such cases are in dispute. The situations are murky. Maybe a given insurgent group is genuinely reformist—i.e., non-Communist—and maybe not. Since the answer lies in the future, no guarantee can be given. How, then, can the American government justify opposing small, poor, putatively well-meaning reformist groups? Short of the use of force, intervention is unlikely to be effective. With the use of force, intervention is likely to be considered immoral.

Containment imposes enormous coordination costs on the United States. Responding everywhere is exhausting; the American political system requires such widespread consultation and consent that it rapidly becomes overloaded. The government needs to have specific policies for all the places that are potentially vulnerable, but it also must demonstrate the existence of wrongdoing or a Soviet threat in each case. A chorus of criticism inevitably rises to the effect that the United States vastly overemphasizes the "military response" in El Salvador, Angola, Cambodia, or whatever territory happens to be involved at the moment. Whatever the merits of the critics' arguments, their prophecies of American failure tend to be self-fulfilling as the United States finds it increasingly difficult to gain domestic support for implementing so many different policies for different places. By virtue of its special form of organization, the Soviet Union suffers no such handicaps.

In light of such difficulties, various proposals have been made for reducing objectives to fit available resources. One of these is to confine containment to regimes considered democratic. This helps with the moral difficulty of supporting dictatorships but may exacerbate the strategic dilemma: democratic regimes may be weak (like Costa Rica) or may have enemies (such as the Arab states versus Israel) who are of strategic importance. Fragile democracies, like Colombia, may not be able to withstand hostile neighbors. Does containment of Communism in Trinidad, for instance, require that Communism be kept out of the Caribbean? And, to take a different example, Turkey does not have a democratic government today but its strategic value is immense, not least in regard to the Middle East.

Alas, "strategic value" is difficult to ascertain, being partly a matter of subjective judgment, partly affected by the actions of others, and partly based on estimates of a future that can be only dimly perceived. Are Ethiopia or Eritrea or South Yemen or Afghanistan of strategic value? That depends on whether the Soviets have merely responded to random targets of opportunity that just happen to enclose the Persian Gulf, or whether there is (or might later be) some larger scheme for putting pressure on oil-exporting nations. One could take the view that, given a nuclear deterrent, no other nations in the world (a Soviet attack across Canada or Mexico being hardly likely) are essential for American security. But this view might change, leaving an alternate perception of the United States alone in a sea of international hostility where it might one day be tempted to take dangerous measures to restore a margin of safety.

If most nations in the world are considered either potential democracies or places of potential strategic value, actual retaliation may be suggested. The usual way of countering actions one does not like, if one cannot respond effectively at the point of attack, is to attack elsewhere. But invading Cuba to win in Angola, or East

Germany to stop a Soviet move into Iran, would hardly command support. Moreover, retaliation is open only to those who have military might and the ability to use and sustain it. Nowadays that leaves America out. Experience suggests that the United States will be unable to find a clear and consistent set of criteria combining moral and strategic values so as to make containment effective abroad and supportable at home.

If American spokesmen believe what they say about the USSR, negotiations with the Soviets are a dubious proposition insofar as they foster, as they are bound to do, an image of Soviet reasonableness, conveying the impression that Soviet rulers are people with whom it pays to talk things over—people, presumably, like us. Negotiations over arms are doubly difficult because, given the underlying distrust, each side refuses to reduce those weapons in which it has, or thinks it will soon obtain, an advantage; thus each ends up with more in total force than before. The dilemma of negotiations is deep because no one wants to face up to the prospects for world peace if the Soviet Union and the United States become convinced that the survival of one requires the submission of the other.

In social life, the greater the complexity, the greater the urge to impose simplicity. And the simplest theory to explain our problems in foreign policy is that there are not many causes, but only one: the Soviet Union is to be held responsible. This may be true. Besides, by assuming what one wishes to be so, one may make it come true. Politicians are often held responsible for deeds not necessarily in the belief that they control events, but in the hope that they may learn how. Thus there emerged the strategy of linkage, whereby cooperation on any single matter came to depend on acceptable Soviet behavior in most matters.

Linkage leads to a double dilemma. On the one hand, the United States is not certain it has sufficient hold on the Soviet Union to make linkage work; if there are always things it wants from the Soviet Union, such as strategic arms limitation, the United States cannot insist on an all-or-nothing approach. On the other hand, a power that preaches pluralism might be better off to practice it. By blaming the Soviet Union where it is not directly involved, we may be helping the Soviets, in a way, to acquire influence.

An alternative to confrontation and linkage is condominium: a multipolar world (defined as one in which the polar powers cannot everywhere make their will felt) is divided into spheres of influence. The bipolarity of nuclear weaponry, in which no one else matters, leads to a division of influence in the various regions of the world, the USSR being accorded deference in this region and the U.S.A. in that. Having reduced the political temperature, the two great powers presumably would proceed to reduce the burden of armament in their economies and the risk of nuclear war by negotiating arms reductions.

The apparent reasonableness of such a policy makes it seem so easy. What the United States has to do, apparently, is give the Soviet Union equal status, recognize it as a superpower, and all will be well. Indeed, were the values of the two governments congruent, a superpower lovefest might well ensue. Were that really so, however, they would have long ago gotten together. The Soviet Union is a superpower whether the United States recognizes it or not; however, the Soviets have satellites, not allies. When cooperation becomes "condominium," the United States loses allies but the Soviet Union retains its satellites. The condominium arrangement that recognizes what the Soviet Union wishes to do with its superpower status—trying to take over non-Communist countries and, when successful, keeping them that way—is a form of preemptive surrender. But if the United States ought not to engage in condominium and wishes to avoid confrontation, all that is left is the regulated competition we call containment. Yet will it work?

The Dilemma of Deterrence

Containment can be reactive, responding after the event, or preventative, seeking to head off future difficulties. More active containment may be called deterrence. Balance-of-power policies, for instance, aim to deter by preventing any single nation from becoming strong enough to take over (or otherwise impose its will upon) others. The dilemma of deterrence in a democracy is that anticipatory measures require action before the evidence of the evil to be deterred manifests itself. When deterrence involves the use of force, by attacking (or threatening to attack) in one area to relieve pressure on others (perhaps Cuba for Poland), the dilemma becomes more painful; heavy casualties may be incurred without conclusive demonstration that the country America attacks is responsible, or that the evil in view will be mitigated. "Pearl Harbor" can hardly be invoked when there is no direct attack on the United States.

The concept of deterrence takes on a larger and more ominous cast when it is applied to nuclear warfare. The hope is that the United States and the Soviet Union have a sufficient number and variety of nuclear weapons that neither can contemplate a surprise attack without risking unacceptable damage. To some analysts the mere existence of a presently invulnerable underwater deterrent, together with the residual uncertainty provided by airborne and land-based missiles, is more than sufficient to provide deterrence. They tend to see the Soviet Union as hostile but not crazy—that is, as deterred by the risk of enormous damage. Other analysts see deterrence as more precarious and therefore in need of reinforcement by such methods as less vulnerable land-based missiles, improved command and control, better bombers, and the like. To those who are sufficiently worried, three hopefully invulnerable deterrent forces are clearly better than one.

Is it impossible for the Soviet Union to discover how to make the seas translucent, thus being able to detect and destroy American nuclear submarines? Might the Soviet Union not count on obliterating land-based missiles, neutralizing submarines by destroying their communications, and coping with the few bombers that, after the carnage of a first strike, would be able and willing to attack? Impossible? Barely possible? Likely, if safer alternatives are not available to Soviet leadership? Is this "worst-case" scenario a sign of American paranoia, as is frequently alleged, or of a pessimistic prudence? Should the United States seek, for instance, a war-fighting capability? The ability to fight a nuclear war may be rejected as aggressive. Better, in this view, for each side to hold the other hostage. But if a president were faced with an attack, knowing that all he could do was murder millions without affecting the enemy's ability to fight, would he give the order to retaliate? If the Soviet leadership imagines that the United States might not retaliate, deterrence as presently constituted might not ward off nuclear attack. Inevitably, we are forced back to the query about Soviet motives: is it a nation-state like our own or is it something fundamentally different? Judgments concerning what sort of deterrent force is necessary for the United States, how invulnerable our missiles have to be, and whether deterrence requires a war-fighting capability depend on estimates of Soviet intentions.

Intention interacts with opportunity. The United States would not much care if Albania or San Marino had internal structures tolerating no opposition. Is it true, then, that the Soviet Union, as aggressive as it might like to be, is guided largely by external constraints? Can it be controlled by foreign forces or is its behavior significantly shaped by the kind of political regime it is? Who would say of such a strong-willed regime that it is a passive reflector of external forces? A closer look at Soviet ideology and Soviet practice is in order.

3

AARON WILDAVSKY

The Soviet System

In order to prescribe American foreign policy towards the Soviet Union, it is necessary to consider why the Soviets pose a threat, and to what extent that threat is limited by the nature of life in a world of jealously competing nation-states.

One way to understand the problem posed for the United States by the USSR is to assume that the Soviet Union is motivated, directly and constantly, by an ideological commitment to world revolution, to remaking the world in its own image because the Marxist scripture demands it. This assumption is too simple for two reasons: First, the international Communist movement no longer has a single center, and many of the most ideologically committed revolutionaries in the world reject Moscow's ideas and definition of the situation (though not, perhaps, its funds) and scorn the USSR itself as "degenerate" or "revisionist." Second, few Soviets themselves believe any longer in the utopian goals of complete equality, world revolution, or the international workers' paradise. Those who do still believe are slightly pitied by their skeptical peers, who call them "red-asses" in Russian slang and dismiss them as, at best, hopeless dreamers.

A more sophisticated argument is that the Soviet Union seeks to defend its internal system of rule, a system that permits no opposition. Unfortunately for the United States, the doctrine that the Soviet Union cannot exist in the midst of opposition applies to the U.S. as well as to all other nations that do not recognize Soviet hegemony and are in a position to resist its sway. Like all other nations, the USSR seeks to defend its national interest; unlike other nations, this defensive interest requires offensive action against potential enemies.

This is not to assert that ideology is dead in the Soviet Union, but only that it is different from what is commonly supposed. For in the Soviet Union ideology is "both dead and influential as ever."[1] Irving Kristol points out that Soviet leaders are not theoreticians. They hardly cite Marx or Lenin anymore. Nevertheless, these are the only beliefs they know, the ones they use to legitimate "their very existence as leaders."[2] The utopian element in Soviet ideology, the belief in equality and world revolution, is gone, put off to a future so distant that it no longer matters.[3] What is left is the ideology as legitimation for inequality, for the rule of the privileged few. Soviet actions and this ideology do still fit together, as I will show, making study of the Soviet system essential for understanding and countering its foreign policy.

The living ideology of the Communist party is based on its political practice: rule from the top. Differences within the party are limited; those outside are prohibited. To find the functioning ideology, the shared values among the elite that legitimate its actual practices, we have to turn to Leninism.

The doctrines of "democratic centralism," with Party members recruited by cooptation, and of the monopoly of power, are mainly due to Lenin. Insisting that the Czarist regime could not be overthrown by a voluntary collective open to external manipulation, Lenin formulated the concept and perfected the practice of the disciplined organization run from the top. Leninism left no room for sharing power.

But how, given the Soviet propensity to use egalitarian rhetoric, can we claim that these are simply slogans, distinct from the leaders' operational beliefs? Uttering fine-sounding but vague phrases has limited utility. It is all right to talk about peace and brotherhood; such slogans do not commit anyone to anything at home, where it matters. However, in order to avoid encouraging undesirable behavior, official pronouncements cannot consistently contradict what people really want to do—and they don't.

Begin with equality. At home, the Soviet leadership does not preach equality and practice inequality; it both preaches and practices inequality. The Soviet Communist party cannot and does not say it is wrong for its members to have much more power and privilege than ordinary citizens. It can (and does) justify inequality. The Party does not even say it is wrong for some people to be paid more than others. On the contrary, it actively rationalizes discrepancies in pay and power as desirable in the interest of all. By the 1930s, Stalin attributed inequality of reward not to class division but to objective merit in contributing to economic construction. A resurgence of talk about inequality as a temporary phenomenon, lasting only as long as it took to complete the transition to Communism, was left behind with Khrushchev's demise.[4] Nowadays, inequality is an instrument of policy. Insofar as the Soviet regime depends on shared values to evaluate people and policies, institutionalized inequality is the norm.

Consider change. Marx spoke of change as the rule of life. Carried abroad, the rule of change, like the desirability of equality, has a certain resonance. Brought back home it would be intolerable, suggesting, as does the dialectic, that like all living things the Soviet regime is but a transitory phenomenon. In the debate about historical change concerning gradualism versus transformationalism, the official Soviet position is entirely fundamentalist: there was only one creation, the Bolshevik Revolution, and there will never be another. When it comes to talking about the rate of change, genuine ideological needs appear. Thus Stalin spoke against attempting to create socialism by "explosions" and Brezhnev came out for cautious advance.[5]

Of course, there are contradictions in the Party and therefore in its ideology. Party cadres want security of tenure but they also want important things to do. When spontaneity reigns, as in markets, there is no role for people who make things happen by brute intervention. Market mechanisms—because they make the Party redundant, because they upset the pattern of privilege (if cadres could make it on their own, they would not be dependent on their membership), and above all because they foster individual-

ism, i.e., independence from the Party — are antithetical to the existence of a Soviet-style society.[6] "Laissez-faire communism," as
Spielman calls Kadar's Hungary,[7] is a contradiction in terms, as
would become evident the moment Soviet military might was
removed.

What, then, is Soviet ideology? One way of stating it in specific
terms is to seek out, as does Bialer, "the most important legitimiz-
ing principles . . . of the Soviet political regime":

The commitment to a one party state and to the leading role of the party
within the state; . . . an interventionist psychology and . . . the need of
strong central government, of organization, of hierarchy, and of order;
the cult of national unity and the condemnation of individuals and
groups who threaten to impair that unity; . . . the radical decline of the
impulse to reshape society and a commitment to the basic structure
which Soviet society has attained.[8]

One can also attempt to sum up, in a short statement, the essence
of the leaders' beliefs by asking, with Daniels, what their ideology
most seeks to protect: "In reality the power of the Party apparatus
does not exist for any higher purpose: it is an end in itself. . . . The
controllers must maintain control in order that they continue to
be controllers."[9]

If we do not feel it essential to understand each and every
change in the Party line, still we know more than we think about
Soviet ideology — what is protected, who is protecting it, and how
the regime rationalizes this behavior. If the reigning ideology is
not full of pretty-sounding statements about a perfectly equal and
harmonious society, that does not make it "un-ideological" but
rather reinforces the conclusion that the social relations it is
designed to legitimate — rule from the top by self-selected elites
protected from the people — are inegalitarian.

It is one thing to have an ideology and another to make it stick.
A substantial point of agreement between democratic and Marxist
social science is that the maintenance of political power requires
an institutional structure devoted to that purpose. Victor Zaslavsky is correct in urging analysts of Soviet society to focus on its
critical connections, those *"structural* arrangements which encourage the persistence of ideas over time."[10]

Structure

The Soviet system seeks "to run all activities from a single center."[11] This structural arrangement, in the Communist party's quaint vocabulary, is called "democratic centralism"—democratic in that all party bodies are elected by the next lower unit, and centralized in that high organs control lower ones, "elections becoming ratifications of choices made by the permanent leadership."[12] Often "a party secretary or a union leader is a stranger to the organization that elects him."[13] The principle is one of cooptation, by which higher-level party officials choose the people below them so as to form a network of personal dependencies. Thus observers write about "patron-client" relationships that last over time so that "whom you know" is more important than "what you do." The best study of the subject concludes that, compared to those without the support of powerful patrons, "clients appear to be more susceptible to rapid upward and downward mobility."[14]

The structure is based on successive levels of Communist party secretaries, chosen by those above them, who ratify these choices until, at the National Party Congress, they elect to the Central Committee those whom it has selected. "Finally," Daniels concludes, "as the Central Committee elects the Politburo, the Party Secretariat, and the First Secretary, the circuit is closed: the First Secretary is confirmed in office by a circular process that ultimately he himself controls—or can control."[15]

Let us look a bit further into the main body of practices codifying cooptation, the *nomenklatura,* which the Party uses to recruit, reward, and discipline members. Every organization tries to narrow the gap between organizational and personal goals. If membership is viewed mainly (or entirely) as a means to live better, cadres will be less willing to sacrifice for the Party. Since "a party card is almost indispensable for advancement to a higher post in all walks of life," so that no one can expect to become a manager without it,[16] the Party has to try to guard against "careerism."

Literally, a *nomenklatura* is a list of jobs. Each party committee, from the district up to the Politburo of the Central Committee of the CPSU (Communist Party of the Soviet Union), has a *nomenklatura,* containing jobs that may not be filled without its consent. The more important the job, the higher the party organ that has the position on its *nomenklatura*. Taken together, the *nomenklatury* control "the most important leading positions in all organized activities of social life."[17] Since lower Party secretaries are on the *nomenklatura* of higher agencies, and the Party bodies collectively have all other social institutions' leading posts on theirs, hierarchical control is complete.

In the Soviet system, the merits of the Party member and of his patron are often the same. How, then, are elements of expertise to be introduced? Under Brezhnev, expertise was sought by placing greater reliance on formal education and by promoting mostly within ministries.[18] Among experts, of course, personal connections still matter most. The system stresses job security; the *nomenklatura* protects poor Party members in return for political reliability. As a Soviet citizen remarks:

> But unless they make a scandal by having an affair with the party secretary's daughter, they never get dismissed. Things may go downhill in their little factory or their theater but the plumbers (party members) simply get transferred to another job. . . . Being a party member, he is never demoted. . . . That is the way our system works.[19]

The system creates favoritism and nepotism. Thus it is difficult to recruit new blood into the Party. Perhaps a glance at the privileges of Party membership—privileges that rise with rank and are lost when it is taken away—will help us understand the ties that bind the people on the *nomenklatura* together.

Privileges

The privileges of the members of the *nomenklatura* consist of virtually everything that makes up a good life, except goodness itself: the food they eat (quality as well as quantity), the place they live (the region, the city, the neighborhood), the size of their apartment, medical care, entitlement to a cottage in the country (a Dacha), furnishings, Western technology, travel, vacations, access to cultural events, income, repairs, automobiles. In all these respects (and others too numerous to mention) the higher up you go the better off you are.

In many ways, members of the *nomenklatura* are more like a caste than a class. If money were the main difference, as in economic class, poorer people could still save up for what they wanted. If social status were the main difference, other qualities—education, income—could still provide equivalent benefits within their own strata. But many of the most desired objects cannot be bought; they can be acquired only through ascription, either by birth into a privileged family or by being listed on the appropriate *nomenklatura.* (There are exceptions in sports, arts, science, and literature but their numbers are few.) Thus the physical segregation between elite and mass becomes more well-defined with time.

The elite have special stores where they buy food unavailable elsewhere. This has been so well publicized that few pause over its significance: Brahmins won't let lower castes cook their food; *nomenklaturists* won't shop at the same stores as the masses. Even the potentially equalizing effects of higher education are vitiated by access to special tutors, inside information, and favoritism in admissions. To this should be added the famous "second economy" of bribery and the black market.[20] Ability to "wheel and deal" plus Party position plus legal income make up real purchasing power. Since income and opportunity for illegal action go together with membership in the *nomenklatura,* its participants parlay their opportunities manyfold. If state subsidies are counted in, and if such intangibles as competent doctors who pay attention to patients can be counted at all, inequality of command over resources between the *nomenklatura* and the "nobody" is immense.

The gap between those in the caste-like hierarchy of the Soviet Communist party and the ordinary citizen is so large that its members, knowing that any other mode of calculating merit would throw them back among the masses, would do almost anything— perhaps absolutely anything—to stay where they are.

In a society that shared power, the Communist party, as Henry Kissinger acutely observes, would have nothing to do. "The Party apparatus duplicates every existing hierarchy without performing any function."[21] It specializes in solving crises that would not exist were it not so internally rigid and externally hostile. In truth, the Soviet regime comes close to creating the world to which it responds, from the ubiquitous shortages manufactured by its command economy to the "imperialist encirclement" that confronts it when its latest aggressive act moves it closer to those who would rather not be its next victims. The Communist caste is autoerotic:

it stimulates itself by creating tasks where none need exist, a protection racket in which both the threat and the defense against it come from the same source.

Urging a modification of this view, Francis B. Randall, a historian of the Soviet system, writes that

> the Communists are in many ways parasites, but they are also the life of an otherwise inert body—a condition they have themselves brought about. Beyond the level of a novel, no one does anything for evil *or* good in the USSR save under Communist initiative. Take something all Russians and most Americans . . . would regard as good: their great B.A.M. railway construction in the Arctic wilderness. That is a Party enterprise in the original best sense of Stalinist idealism. Whatever is built or done, schools or prisons, ballet companies or germ warfare labs, the Communist guide, make possible, *do* as Diaghilev did the Ballets Russes. You can see the effect . . . among Russian exiles in Coney Island, who . . . complain that the state or the relevant refugee organization ought to find them jobs, tell them what to do, take them places, etc.—as the Party did in hated Russia.[22]

Leaving aside the informal and often illegal adaptations to Soviet life—bribery, black market, theft, private plots (including not only growing food but using state resources to provide private services, all of which, in some degree, overcome breakdowns in the formal system)—Randall's comments are correct. The initiative of the Communist party is, as he says, gained at the expense of inculcating passivity in the population. Gaining the initiative by denying it to others is, I maintain, a form of parasitism in that the labor of Soviet citizens provides the resource base that enables the Party to suppress their initiatives, leaving itself as the only possible source of action. Winning a race in which one is the only entrant leaves a lot to be desired.

Control

The Communist party is a parasite upon Soviet society, performing no socially useful labor. It serves only to oversee and alter the priorities of those who possess greater knowledge, either because they are better trained or because they are closer to the situation about which action is being taken. Its efforts to gain information about society are distorted (recall its recent insistence that it had control of a nuclear-powered satellite that proceeded to plummet toward earth) by the strong incentives to tell the polity only what it wishes to hear. Hence the multiplicity of controllers to ascertain the truth, which only independent, competent, and plural sources of information can approximate.[23] The major weapon wielded against the existence of plural centers of power, as all Soviet citizens are acutely aware, is the secret police, which is a parasite upon a parasite because it need not exist at all were it not for the Communist party's insistence on rule from a single center. Thus the Soviet Union has two states within a state, the Party living off the people and the secret police living off the Party.

Neither organ of control, police or Party, could exist without a strategic separation between the state and society. The other controls we shall discuss are also based on creating and manipulating boundaries between Soviet citizens. One of these, the slave labor camps—the ultimate boundary—begins but by no means ends the show of internal control.

Intellectuals and specialists with university degrees are controlled by Party, police, and privilege. Far more are produced than are necessary, and they know it. To become an Estonian or Moldavian specialist is to become a surplus product that has to be absorbed. Competition for position keeps such people divided; and the recognition that they would not survive competition by ability keeps specialists subservient.[24]

Only those considered trustworthy by Party and police, with rare exceptions, are allowed out of the Soviet Union with the right to return. Careful control of internal passports creates "impassible boundaries between nationalities,"[25] as national origin is entered in permanently.

Major cities, therefore, play a part in the stratification of Soviet society: they are called *closed,* meaning that access depends upon a special permit called a *propiska.* (Standards of living are much higher in the big cities, especially Moscow and Leningrad, where there is better food, clothing, cultural events, opportunities for higher education, and much else besides.) By issuing many temporary *propiskis,* pressure is placed on both present and would-be residents to conform.

A policy of closed cities goes hand-in-hand with the Russification of potentially dissident nationality groups, especially those, like the Baltic States, that have previously known independence.

The Soviets offer job and income incentives to encourage Slavic citizens to move to other ethnic areas, until Russian inhabitants rival or surpass them in population. By keeping these cities closed, the Party is able to control who is housed where.[26]

This distinction between *open* and *closed* is not an invention of the system's enemies but is integral to Party rule. Factories and whole enterprises are also distinguished by whether they belong to one category or the other. In closed or *regime* enterprises, dealing with military matters, high technology, or other Party priorities, workers are required to maintain strict secrecy. They are also held responsible for the political behavior of close friends and relatives, and no longer can leave jobs at will. Nevertheless, these positions are avidly sought because they pay much better, are more secure, and carry with them a number of perquisites, such as special shops. Naturally, managers try to have their enterprises classified as closed so as to improve labor discipline and their ability to secure resources. Zaslavsky cites survey evidence that workers in closed factories show greater support for the regime;[27] worker solidarity is split by the introduction of a new privileged stratum.

Unions are controlled by the Party. As Brezhnev said:

Our party's [the CPSU's] history has demonstrated with utmost clarity the absurdity of the concept of "independent trade unions," the unviability of anarcho-syndicalism which tried to present the trade union associations as the leading force of society, to substitute them for the state and to confer on them the functions of a political party.[28]

The fate of Solidarity in Poland reveals the resistance to forces independent of the Party. "Even under 'goulash socialism' of the Hungarian model," Baroch states, "there are no independent labor unions."[29]

In their own way, Soviet citizens fight back. Peasants who are controlled by being kept on collective farms, which most of them would like to leave, retaliate by slackening their efforts and concentrating on their private plots.* Workers begin late, leave their jobs, get drunk, steal, and otherwise perform badly. But they ordinarily do not struggle as a group; instead they engage in private

---

*Officially, peasants are now receiving their own passports. This reform is more symbol than substance, however, since they must still obtain the manager's permission to leave.

evasive behavior. "Limitchiks" marry to get a residence permit; others rely on relatives, do favors, engage in bribery.

The Soviet system of internal control, taken as a whole, is based on separation. The Party leadership is separated from its cadres by the principle of cooptation. The Party is separated from the citizenry by where they reside, what they eat, how much they earn, how they live. Citizens are separated from one another by police and Party surveillance, by open and closed cities and factories, by internal and external passports, and by differential access to education and medical facilities as well as to cultural and consumer goods. Separation at each level is strengthened by secrecy, not only of policy but of information about the condition of elements of society that might make a common cause. Where such strategies for separation fail, as in the case of the Crimean Tartars who were expelled from their homes during the Second World War, force is used. Tartars who attempt to return to Crimea are arrested, their houses are torn down, and they are sent back to Central Asia.

The importance of the ultimate mode of separating citizens from one another — the secret police — should be reemphasized. Political action is hardly possible without trust. (I know of a young man who, after being exiled for two years for telling an anti-regime joke, confined his conversation only to members of his immediate family.) It may well be that other controls would fail without the resort to constant intimidation.

Just as defending a single center of power domestically requires elimination of independent power centers before they can develop, so the Soviets seek the initiative in military and foreign policy. The observed pattern of Soviet behavior fits well with Uri Ra'anan's description:

Since the initiative provides much obvious advantage and because, in any case, Soviet literature has never ceased to emphasize this factor, it is a source of bewilderment why some Western observers continue to view the "action-reaction" model as appropriate for analysis of Soviet behavior patterns. The most simplistic version of this model suggests that "if we take step A, they will react with move B," or even more frequently, that "if only we refrain from act A, they will abstain from reaction B." This approach assumes, therefore, that Soviet leaders react primarily to *Western* moves or statements, whereas both Soviet publications and the history of Soviet moves in the international arena demonstrate Moscow's deep aversion to such a passive role.[30]

By getting there first, through seizing the initiative, the Soviets hope to create so favorable a disposition of forces that their adversaries must either give in or take responsibility for escalating the conflict to levels unacceptable to their people.

Because the Soviets cannot accept domestic diversity, their ideology stresses the undying hostility of foreign forces. Thus, as Henry Kissinger observes from experience, "they cannot defend conciliatory policies toward the outside world amid the struggle for power that characterizes the Soviet system except by emphasizing that objective conditions require them."[31] What might otherwise be regarded as coercive bargaining by threatening dire consequences may be the best (and, perhaps, the only) way that the United States can induce Soviet leaders to justify making concessions.

If analysis of the Soviet system can lead to a hard line, it can also be turned in a softer direction. In an innovative analysis of the Soviet regime, Kenneth Jowitt argues that in the past the Party has maintained its organizational integrity by imposing heroic tasks — revolution, consolidation of power, industrialization, defense against Nazism — upon its members. Once the Party was firmly in power, however, it became difficult to identify the proper tasks that would enable members to maintain their status in a legitimate way, i.e., by contributing to society. Without proper tasks, the Party turns into an organization for preserving the status, and hence the privileges, of its members.[32]

Is gradually giving in to Soviet desires, then, the surest way to soften them up? Should the United States accede to their demands so as to deprive the Soviets of the "combat environment" they need to keep themselves together? Or will a string of successes provide the regime with the only rationale it can offer its citizens for the parasitic part the Party plays in Soviet life — namely, that it gains victories abroad?

If the Soviets are merely trying to gain as much as they can without endangering their system, meeting with resistance should slow them down. If external aggression is a requirement of the internal Soviet system, however, mere containment only postpones the evil day; they will keep trying until they succeed or their system changes and with it their objectives. Either way, at least minimal containment — meeting aggression after it occurs — will be essential over a long period of time. As a prelude to developing policy recommendations, we turn next to an analysis of the history of the doctrine of containment.

4

PAUL SEABURY

Reinspecting Containment

Americans have no tractarian tradition of foreign policy debate —
no grand framework in which disputes can be carried on. Theories
play a crucial part in our policy discussion, to be sure; we are
awash with them. But there is no overarching system of beliefs
within which such theories take their place. Americans devise
theories in response to immediate exigencies; theorizing is stim-
ulated by real or imagined fears, problems, or emergencies —
even, sometimes, by opportunities. When disconcerting facts burst
upon our lives, we improvise. Such improvisions in turn supply a
world view that lends apparent purpose to our actions.

It is nevertheless true that one theory — that of containment —
served a whole generation of American decision-makers as
the foundation of our foreign policy. The tenacity with which
four-and-a-half administrations — from Truman through Lyndon
Johnson — pursued this strategy, and the persistence with which
bipartisan support was accorded it, challenged de Tocqueville's
conclusion that democracies, in purposeful dealings with the
world, cannot follow fixed designs. Until American political

resolve faltered in the Vietnam period, containment went virtually unchallenged for twenty years.

Kennan's Vision

As its author George Kennan saw it in 1947, containment was a strategy to check the outward spread of Soviet power by resisting it on its peripheries. In Kennan's formulation, containment did not foresee an immediate or even ultimate (or "inevitable") triumph of American liberal doctrine or of the principles of free societies (if by this was meant the political subjugation or conversion of the Soviet Union). Nor did Kennan envision a forced transformation of the USSR into a regime compatible with liberalism or capitalism. Indeed (as I shall discuss later) the doctrine was criticized by some Americans at the time of its original formulation for its supine acceptance of the Soviet system. In contrast, the Soviet leadership constantly proclaimed its goal of achieving the triumph of socialism and the liquidation of its enemies. Therein lay the heart of a difficult problem that containment sought to address. The premises of this policy, as spelled out in U.S. policy paper NSC−68 in 1950, were to be seen in the opposed purposes of the U.S. and the Soviet Union: for the Kremlin, world domination; for the U.S., a world environment in which free societies, ours included, could flourish safely. One cardinal supposition of containment was that Soviet expansion, checked successfully in one theater, would show itself in another, in a continuing series of challenges to America and the West wherever weakness was displayed.

When containment first became doctrine, the central theater was Europe, where the original confrontation took place. Europe remains the central theater, but it is quite important for us now to look back to the 1950s to see what then was the correlation of forces between the Americans and the Soviets, and how a European bipolar correlation related to the assets and capabilities of the two powers. In general, this was the picture:

In 1950, before the Korean War, the U.S. had virtually demobilized its army (its conventional ground forces); it had 2 combat divisions in Europe (as opposed to an estimated 160 Soviet divisions). The Soviets, who had not demobilized, thus commanded a gigantic army that, except for certain important considerations, could have rolled its way virtually unresisted to the English Channel in a matter of days.

From a broader perspective the picture was actually quite different from this. At that time the American economy was a giant cornucopia; through the Marshall Plan, America's vast resources contributed to Europe's economic recovery. The Soviet economy was ravaged by war; the Russians, anxious to rebuild it, looted their conquered territories. America gave to its allies, while the Soviet Union took from its satellites.

On the whole, however, the contrast between the U.S. and the Soviet Union, in both potential and actual power, was highly favorable to the United States. With its navy and air force, the U.S. had power projection capabilities that the Soviets could not then possibly match or even aspire to match. Even with its vast conventional forces in Europe, the Soviet Union remained what Russia had been historically: a landlocked colossus. It had virtually no navy; its submarine fleet was inconsequential; it had no strategic air force; and it had no nuclear weapons other than the bomb that it had just successfully tested in 1949. In short, it had no significant means by which to project its military power into regions other than those adjacent to it.

This aspect of Soviet military power was to change radically. The Soviet Union, originally a behemoth, was later to become both behemoth and leviathan, a force to be reckoned with on land, on sea, and in the air. While the ideological attraction of the Soviet system (seen from the outside) waned in the ensuing twenty years of the Cold War, its military power grew relentlessly. This massive though incremental change took decades of patient and unstinting effort, even as the internal character of the Soviet system remained essentially what it had been before. Because incremental change rarely creates surprise in the eyes of the beholders, it is understandable though not excusable that the Western public failed to take full notice of the implications of this transformation.

After more than a decade, Americans are reminded harshly that the Soviet problem is the heart of our foreign policy dilemmas. What can be learned from a second look at Kennan's containment policy now that might help in charting a new course of action in the 1980s?

The Idea of "Balance"

Containment's disintegration began with Vietnam, possibly at the time of the Tet Offensive and Lyndon Johnson's "abdication." But Kennan's doctrine had significantly altered even before our involvement in Vietnam began in 1964. Sometime before then the idea that the relationship between America and the Soviet Union was a "balance" of superpowers came into vogue and into official American discourse as well as the writings of journalists and theoreticians. The idea of balance exerted a subtle change in the meaning of containment: it suggested a parity in strategic power between the two countries (whether or not such parity actually existed) and also suggested a kind of "essential equivalence" between them.

What is important to note is the shift in emphasis and purpose implied by this new concentration on strategic balance. It became possible to think of Soviet-American and East-West relations as though the Soviet Union had actually become, or was becoming, a responsible part of a balanced structure in a stable world order. This new illusion took us far from the original containment doctrine, for a fundamental message in the 1947 *Foreign Affairs* article by "Mr. X" (Kennan) was precisely the opposite of this. According to Kennan's original doctrine, the Soviet Union was unnatural. It waged war against the rest of the world in every respect short of actual shooting; its leaders constantly proclaimed their intent to destroy all that they could not dominate. Later, eager to extricate himself from his 1947 analysis, Kennan repudiated this view, although Soviet leaders did not. Insofar as the "X" article assigned to the Soviets a prime foreign policy objective, it certainly was not the simple goal of seeking the security of Russia as a state. As Kennan saw the Soviet goal in 1947, the security of a Soviet totalitarian system required the subjugation of any significant power centers not actually under its control. Kennan's thesis distinguished implicitly between the Soviet Union and Russia, between the ideological movement-state and the nation, the first deriving its justification to rule from universalist principles having nothing to do with the interests of the Russian people. This movement-state prided itself on its sense of historical mission — which meant that it had to stand and move in opposition to the rest of the world. So while Kennan may never have owed an intellectual debt to Edmund Burke, the purport of the "X" article was not unlike Burke's in his reflections on the French Revolution. In the "Second Letter on a Regicide Peace," Burke wrote:

> I never thought we could make peace with the [Jacobin] system; because it was not for the sake of an object that we pursued in rivalry with each other, but with the system itself, that we were at war. As I understood the matter, we were at war not with its conduct, but with its existence; convinced that its existence and its hostility were the same.[1]

Kennan put it somewhat differently; here he was most at odds with critics such as Walter Lippmann:

> It is the Russians, not we, who cannot afford a world half slave and half free. The contrasts implicit in such a world are intolerable to the fictions on which their power rests. *The final establishment of communist principles can only be universal.* It assumes a Stygian darkness. If one ray of light of individual dignity or inquiry is permitted, the effort must ultimately fail.[2]

Kennan's original theory was thus thoroughly indifferent to the idea of a balance. In his version, the Soviet problem, given Western firmness, would eventually go away; the Soviet system would either disintegrate or undergo fundamental reform. Later, those who came to view a bipolar "balance" as normal and desirable would argue that the West had a vested interest in Soviet stability, in both the internal and external regions under its sway. Still others, looking in the mid-1960s at the strategic-military aspect of the relationship, began to argue that America should be a tutor to the Soviets in the ways of managing this balance; a Soviet Union ignorant of the principles of mutual assured destruction, for instance, might adopt a very dangerous strategic posture. Our task was thus to show the Soviets the technical means by which they could achieve a secure second-strike capability or verify the American deterrent posture. Whether U.S. policymakers ever recognized this new attitude or set of purposes as a drastic departure from Kennan's original prescription is a matter for conjecture; but the 1962 Cuban missile crisis and its resolution encouraged this way of thinking on the American side, and Secretary of Defense Robert McNamara became its chief proponent. According to this altered concept of containment, the power relationship between the two superpowers had become a permanent feature of world politics, and given the unaltered nature of the Soviet world view and the dangerous power they had at their disposal, Soviet leaders needed to be subtly enticed to become traditional members of the world's leadership. This view was further elaborated by some to include the notion that the Soviet leaders should be seen as insecure adolescents or envious *arrivistes,* and that they were, after all, animated by an all-too-human desire to be acknowledged as America's equal in the cultivated society of nations and to be accepted socially in the international family. The source of Soviet conduct, in short, was a deep but irremedial sense of inferiority. To be accepted, to be treated without contempt and condescension — so it was said — was not the least of Soviet expectations.

Détente as Therapy

It would be easy, then, for a therapeutic American foreign policy to induce the Soviets to fit harmoniously into the society of nations, joining with others in cooperative, constructive global tasks. For this to occur, a fixity of Western and American will of course would be necessary, but for reasons quite different from those pertaining to containment. By patient handling, the Soviets could be drawn, as it were, therapeutically into the society of nations. U.S. policymakers would accept the Soviet Union as an authentic world power, but at the same time resolutely persist in their commitment to the long-range balancing process. Thus the word "balance" introduced itself into the central discourse about the relationship. It became almost impossible to think in other terms: the U.S. should not under any circumstances accept a position of inferiority, and the Soviets should accept equality. The Soviets should be made to know that reciprocity and mutual restraint and respect were absolutely necessary for the balance to last.[3] With détente, a kind of codicil to this view, came the further notion that to become an acceptable member of the family of nations, the Soviet Union needed to be offered a stake and place in it. America and its Western allies should provide, for instance, strong inducements whereby the Soviet economy would be linked closely into the "normal world" by webs of interdependencies. The USSR might then come to recognize how its own interest lay in the international market economy and in the stability of the West. As bilateral superpower relations then relaxed in more intimate economic ties, outstanding differences could be adjusted in an atmosphere of mutual restraint and accommodation. Thus during much of the 1970s, the Soviet Union encouraged a vast inflow of Western capital, credits, technology, and managerial expertise to assist its own industrial development (and, as things turned out, to alleviate stresses on its economy as it pursued its relentless, escalating military buildup—the gravity of which long went unnoticed by Western publics).[4]

In retrospect, the best light that we can put upon the strategy of détente would be to call it "containment by inducements"—a strategy using carrots rather than sticks to encourage better Soviet international behavior. Carrots would be offered so long as the Soviets played according to Marquis of Queensbury rules.

We can now see one important attribute of détente in Soviet-American relations. In the Nixon-Kissinger period détente had great repercussions for the American public, which was weary of its international burdens. But détente did not promote a relaxation of vigilance within the Soviet Union, where policies of ideological vigilance (including greatly intensified repression of dissidents and intensified domestic propaganda) were stepped up. The Soviets made no bones about this and in this respect were hardly engaging in deception. In the Soviet understanding, "realistic" state-to-state relations were proper to a phase of history they called "peaceful coexistence," but such coexistence did not imply ideological change or abatement of efforts in the Third World, where the Soviets continued to pursue expansion via proxies. Furthermore, as U.S. defense capabilities withered in the course of détente and during and after the Vietnam fighting, Soviet military programs continued to expand yearly in an inexorable push toward strategic supremacy.

Viewed in the best possible light, the Nixon-Kissinger détente had some therapeutic uses. Premised upon a readjustment of both alliance and adversary relations, it helped to calm an America caught in the peculiar cultural revolution accompanying the Vietnam War. According to the Nixon doctrine, a phased retrenchment of U.S. overseas commitments would occur in tandem with the Allies' buildup of their own compensatory strength. But in

Nixon's mind détente was a unique world view. Kissinger's diplomacy sought to breathe life into this vision of a five-polar world structured around the U.S., the Soviet Union, Western Europe, Japan, and China. In Nixon's grand scheme, a balance among these five—a "pentagonal world"—would replace the bipolar system that had caused so much psychic misery to America in the postwar era. In this respect, the 1972 U.S. rapprochement with the People's Republic of China was envisioned by Nixon less as an alliance with one devil to countervail a greater one, than as part of a delicate system of statecraft through which further positive negotiations and agreements with the Soviets could be pursued. In short, a new multipolar global order would come into being, resembling that which Europe enjoyed in its heyday—an operating balance in which no one power could dominate the others. Furthermore, America could play a new role—not as manager of a grand coalition but as a balancer, much as England (in *its* heyday) had played in the European system. Needless to say, at the height of this brief experiment in statecraft, Europeans, warily noting that Kissinger's high diplomacy usually bypassed European capitals, began to fear the consequences of an even-handed implementation of the scheme.

There was a flaw in this vision of a pentagonal world, apparent in the sharp contrasts among the actors. Three were open societies, two totalitarian. But more important, pentagonalism could not disguise the enormous contrasts in the military capabilities and strategic intentions of the various players. The Americans and the Soviets were still unchallenged superiors. Japan had almost no defense capabilities; Europe, which did, was still a congeries of states, lacking the ability to act in unison for strategic purposes. Moreover, the Europeans, like the Japanese, loathed and rejected the prospect of playing *any* strategic role outside their circumscribed geographic area. China, whatever else it was, was militarily weak and severely damaged internally by its cultural revolution. However the pentagonal system might have worked, it could not conceivably have operated as the classic European one did—upon the cabinet diplomacy of essentially equal powers. In any event, the Watergate episode and the ensuing vigorous Soviet resumption of its expansive activities in Africa, Southeast Asia, Southwest Asia, Central America, and the Caribbean brought this quaint idea to an end. The renewed Soviet aggression—first manifest in Angola in 1975—came as a grim reminder: the only power capable of global resistance to Soviet global encroachments was the U.S. Yet in relative and absolute military terms America was far weaker after a decade of détente than it had been before. Détente had been an era of wishful thinking.

It is one thing to proclaim that world politics conforms to a particular view, and quite another to bring others to accept it and to act accordingly. The Soviets never for a moment accepted the American postcontainment world view. The very idea of balance was alien to Soviet thinking. Such an outlook remains unnatural to anyone who officially subscribes to Marxist-Leninist doctrine, and foolish to anyone who regards superior force as essential to political supremacy at home and abroad.

There has been far more continuity in Soviet foreign policy than might have been imagined in the early days of containment. Of course, Kennan took pains much earlier to point out how the operational characteristics of the Soviet elite affected their world outlook. He put the matter this way:

Being under the compulsion of no timetable [the Kremlin] has no compunction about retreating in the face of superior force. And being under the compulsion of no timetable, it does not get panicky under the necessity for such retreat. Its political action is a fluid stream which moves constantly, wherever it is permitted to move, toward a given goal. Its main concern is to make sure that it has filled every nook and cranny available to it in the basin of world power.[5]

The Original Debate

Since we have returned, in the Reagan period, to containment, and to the goal of ensuring the survival of the free world, it would be useful to review the controversies that originally surrounded the idea when it was advanced in the late 1940s. Containment was formulated as an alternative to two strategic options that, like antipodes, thoughtful Americans at the time concluded were dangerous and fundamentally incompatible with basic American interests: a deliberate U.S. withdrawal to its own hemisphere, or an active rollback of Soviet military power employing all means at our disposal, including the threat of all-out war.

For a few Americans in the 1950s, there was something emotionally attractive about the latter, dangerous option. The Soviets' blatant violation of the principles of the Atlantic Charter (particularly the right of national self-determination), Stalin's ruthless subjugation of the peoples of Eastern Europe, and the extraordinarily hostile advertisement of the Soviets' further intentions toward the United States and Western Europe all aroused widespread public animus toward both the Soviet Union and its proxies and satellites abroad. For some Americans, Kennan's call for a diligent, consistent policy of resistance to further Soviet encroachments was regarded as no less than a passive, tacit recognition of Soviet conquests. John Foster Dulles, then a private citizen, denounced containment as "immoral"; the Republican party platform in 1952 picked up and exploited his theme. Nonetheless, once in power, Eisenhower and Dulles accepted containment's logic, in deed if not in word.

But there were also Americans who, while rejecting both extremes of hemispheric isolation and rollback, still objected to containment. The most prominent of these was Walter Lippmann.

The first question on which Lippmann differed with Kennan was whether the political system would permit the kind of firm, unswerving public purpose necessary for such a grand design. Lippmann could not be blamed for being skeptical. His knowledge of American history and politics, especially when set beside the recent behavior of the U.S. in international affairs, was enough for him or for any well-informed American to doubt the capacity of this giant democracy to pursue a consistent design for any length of time. The retreat into isolationism in the 1920s, the repudiation of the League of Nations Covenant, the rejection of the Versailles Treaty, the refusal to underwrite, by commitment, the security of the Western democracies — these were the episodes of America's modern diplomatic history. In the view of many, including Lippmann, the role of public opinion and the American system of checks and balances made long-term strategy impossible. Indeed, at Yalta in 1945 Roosevelt had been so uncertain about the staying power of American influence in Europe that he told Stalin that American troops could not be expected to play a part in the policing of a postwar European order for more than a few years. And certainly it was true, at the time when Kennan and Lippmann wrote, that there were strong domestic pressures for American disengagement from a major international role. Military demobilization brought an extraordinary reduction of U.S. manpower; the ordinary pressures of a consumer society worked to eliminate most major wartime controls; and in the Truman period, the peacetime tug-of-war within the American constitutional structure created a confusing standoff in Washington between a Republican Congress and a Democratic administration.

Kennan was aware of these difficulties, so much so that barely two years after his "X" article catapulted him to fame, he wrote caustically in *American Diplomacy 1900–1950* of democracies:

I sometimes wonder whether . . . a democracy is not uncomfortably similar to one of those prehistoric monsters with a body as long as this room and a brain the size of a pin; he lies there in his comfortable primeval mud and pays little attention to his environment; he is slow to wrath—in fact, you practically have to whack his tail off to make him aware that his interests are being disturbed; but, once he grasps this, he lays about him with such blind determination that he not only destroys his adversary but largely wrecks his native habitat. You wonder whether it would not have been wiser for him to have taken a little more interest in what was going on at an earlier date and to have seen whether he could not have prevented some of these situations from arising.[6]

Kennan was describing, however, not prescribing; as he later remarked in the same book, "A nation which excuses its own failures by the sacred untouchableness of its own habits can excuse itself into complete disaster."[7] Lippmann assumed that these characteristics of American democracy were unalterable. In 1947 he took Kennan to task for believing that the American nation could sustain either will or purpose. Given the way America worked, he argued, any grand design was impossible—in particular any fine-tuned *Grosse Politik* encompassing the geopolitical maneuvers necessary to implement containment. Lippmann wrote, "A policy of shifts and maneuvers may be suited to the Soviet system of government, which, as Mr. X tells us, is animated by patient persistence. It is not suited to the American system of government."[8]

In retrospect, what can be said about this dispute? In the first place, events for a while proved Lippmann terribly wrong. The American system and the American Constitution did prove able to do what Lippmann said could not be done: containment was imple-

mented with great constancy of purpose. Four administrations —
Truman's, Eisenhower's, Kennedy's, and Johnson's — became
tenaciously committed to the fundamental ideas that Kennan initially espoused, and generally received strong bipartisan political
support. Congress authorized strategic-military resources to implement containment in many faraway places. From a broad
perspective, the success of containment during those years was
undeniable if one accepted the basic rationale for it in one respect:
the outward spread of Soviet power was generally checked. But in
Europe it was checked by a military system of countervailing force
that some Americans — Lippmann included — thought would be
wholly unacceptable to Europeans.[9]

Containment was criticized on two other grounds: first, the
geographic scope of the terrain on which it would have to be prac-
ticed; and second, its essential reactiveness — the fact that it
simply called for firmly responding to Soviet probes where and
when they occurred. The two features were, of course, related. Yet
if one assumed that Soviet strategy constantly, if usually
cautiously, probed outward, searching for targets of opportunity
and points of weakness — if the Soviets (as Dean Rusk later was to
say) were like hotel burglars trudging up and down corridors trying door locks — then what should one do? What was depressing
about such a prospect, as Lippmann saw, was the possibility that
the Soviets would most certainly probe at points of Western weakness, not strength; that they would habitually identify unpopular
regimes, despotic, tyrannical, or fearful ruling classes, and situations of turmoil; and that they would employ their all-too-familiar
organizational strategies to exploit such weakness to their advantage. Was the United States to be a fire brigade, always rushing
about to save ramshackle clients? Under such circumstances, the
U.S. would find itself constantly compelled to use, as Lippmann
put it, "satellite states, puppet governments and agents which
have been subsidized and supported, though their effectiveness is
meager and their reliability uncertain." To waste energies and
substance on such "dubious and unnatural allies" would be, he
said, to "neglect our natural allies in the Atlantic community and
to alienate them."[10] Lippmann's cautionary warnings in 1947 toll
sonorously in 1983; for as America repeatedly faced the Soviets at
remote geographic points, the "natural allies," the Western Euro-

peans, became "alienated" by the prospect of "faraway" wars in which they also might involuntarily become involved.

To Lippmann and to many other Americans both then and now, the Atlantic region, its peoples, and its civilization were the cherished prize, the core of America's overseas strategic concerns. If one accepted this priority, did that mean that America's only responses to the Soviet challenge should be within that region alone? Lippmann believed so. His answer was simple. Virtually ignoring Kennan's central thesis and explanation for Soviet behavior, he put forward his own solution to the challenge: to maneuver the Red Army, by diplomacy, out of Europe; and to fashion, with Soviet approval, a huge neutralized European zone including but not confined to Germany, thus assuaging legitimate Soviet fears of another invasion. Europe would be "evacuated" and would recover its "historic unity." The Western price for this evacuation of power, as he put it, would consist of "reparations" (to the Soviets); unspecified "concessions"; "trade agreements"; and finally, "ransom" (presumably economic). "If we were wise," Lippmann counseled,

and were more interested in settling the war than in making gestures of our disapproval of the Russians and of communism, we should offer to contribute our part of the ransom—if paying will achieve the main objective.

If, he concluded, the Russians rejected the ransom, or set too high a price, the situation could indeed become dangerous. But at least then, "our energies will be concentrated, not dispersed all over the globe."[11]

In retrospect, Lippmann's alternative prescription to containment might seem both facile and foolish. Indeed, within three years of Lippmann's suggestion, after the U.S. had retracted its strategic East Asian defense perimeter in a manner compatible with Lippmann's premises, came the Soviet-inspired invasion of Korea. By then Eastern Europe was firmly consolidated under Soviet rule. Of course, no "ransom" had been offered, unless one considered Secretary Marshall's generous offer of massive economic aid to Europe, including the Soviet Union (which Stalin brusquely rejected as a trick of American imperialism).

As the Korean War showed, the problem was exactly of the sort that Kennan had diagnosed. By 1950, Washington had given its solemn promise in NATO to sustain its European allies. But then the Russians probed with their proxies into a weak zone on their perimeter in a faraway place whose security was not guaranteed by America.[12] A major war resulted that could have been deterred.

The Hope of Soviet "Collapse"

Integral to Kennan's vision of containment was an element of hope. If a policy of containment were pursued with resolution and vigilance, and if the Soviet leaders became disillusioned in their own hopes and predictions of a Western collapse, then, Kennan argued, the chemistry of internal processes would work to transform their system. Such a transformation would in turn work fundamental changes in the international behavior of the Soviet Union.

Goethe said that in all things it is better to hope than to despair; the saying is no less appropriate today than when Kennan framed his doctrine. His hope lay in the conviction that Soviet totalitarianism was an anomaly that flourished upon abnormality, and that its fortunes would depend finally upon the success or failure of America and the West. Faced by an implacable, resolute West, Soviet leaders could not hope to justify their brutal rule. No people, not even the patient Russians, could long bear the perpetual high tension, the economic deprivation, the suppression of dissidence, the forced labor camps. The system would either collapse or undergo fundamental reform and moderation.

In arguing his case, Kennan invoked his famous *Buddenbrooks* analogy. It appeared, he surmised, that "the ideological power of Soviet authority is strongest . . . in areas beyond the frontiers of Russia":

This . . . brings to mind a comparison used by Thomas Mann in his great novel *Buddenbrooks*. Observing that human institutions often show the greatest outward brilliance at a moment when inner decay is in reality furthest advanced, he compared the Buddenbrooks family . . . to one of those stars whose light shines so brightly on this world when in reality it has long ceased to exist. . . . Who can say . . . that the strong light still cast by the Kremlin . . . is not the powerful afterglow of a constellation which is in actuality on the wane? This cannot be proved. And it cannot be disproved.[13]

"Breakup" or "gradual mellowing"—these different yet benign possibilities were held out by Kennan as an ultimate reward for American firmness and consistency. Ten or fifteen years, he predicted, was the time span required for such chemistry to work. Yet containment was pursued with some consistency for nearly twenty years, until 1968. Adding fifteen years to 1947 brought the world to 1962 and the Soviet nuclear offensive in the Caribbean. Another six years brought the world to 1968, the year of the Red Army's invasion of Czechoslovakia and the Soviet-fueled Tet Offensive, which broke the American will to contain. The sociopolitical promise of containment failed.

In Kennan's view (though he later tried to dissociate himself from this analysis), it was the very nature of the Soviet system that constituted the fundamental problem. This assessment contrasted with the view of Lippmann and those like him—that the cause of the confrontation was the friction and tension between Soviet and American basic interests in specific places. For Kennan, the fundamental problem lay in the fact that the Soviet Union regarded itself as necessarily at war with the West; the point here was, and still is, that even if Soviet leaders did not actually believe what they preached to the world, to acknowledge the permanent legitimacy of the Western democracies would be to strip the Soviet system of its central claim to legitimacy and to nullify its claim to monopoly of power. Thus the display of unremitting hostility to the capitalist world was essential if only for domestic reasons. To recognize this obvious fact of Soviet power and conduct would be to say, as did Burke of revolutionary France, that it was the system that was the problem, and not simply its behavior.

In the bleak decade between the Tet Offensive in 1968 and the Afghan invasion of 1979, many American leaders—their will to contain now weakened—tried to act as though the truths described above were no longer valid, as though the central issue now could be redefined through détente as a "limited adversary relationship," a "cooperative-cum-competition relationship," or even an "interdependence relationship." The contention was that the challenges of coexistence in Soviet-American relations was, and should be, the careful management of a relationship between equals; the Soviets, accepting U.S. recognition of their status of parity, would then behave as partners in peace. Through trade concessions, the Soviets, so it was argued, could be enticed to play a normal part in a normal world; and through diplomacy, as in the Helsinki agreement and in a resolution of the German question, points of tension could be reduced. In SALT negotiations, the arms race could be brought under control, while through patient understanding and positive economic transactions, including the transfer of massive American technological aid, the Soviets would become more dependent on the West. The capstone of this process of détente was achieved in June 1973 when the Soviets agreed to a Camp David communiqué, which required that both governments advise each other in advance of major threats to peace. Scarcely weeks later, the Soviets, aware of Egyptian plans for a new Arab-Israeli war, betrayed the pledge and withheld this information from Washington, urging a widening Arab participation in the war once it began.

What was lost sight of in this decade of self-deception was the fact that the Soviets modified neither their basic world view nor their strategy. While many Americans and Europeans embraced détente as a goal of diplomacy, the Soviets regarded it (or its Marxist-Leninist counterpart, peaceful coexistence) as a mere instrument of policy, to be used or discarded like any other.

How was such American self-deception possible? The current widespread circulation in the United States of bizzare revisionist histories of the Cold War (to the effect that it had been an imperial America that had fanned the flames of rivalry from the beginning) is inexplicable unless one assumes that the soil of public opinion already has been prepared for it. Certainly the emotional exhaustion induced by the experiences of the Vietnam War and America's own "cultural revolution" combined to make this possible. For a time, anti-Americanism became as American as apple pie.

The Soviets, at least, cannot be blamed for deception regarding their aims and strategies. In their theoretical literature, little of which penetrated the American media, as well as in *Pravda*, in speeches, and in announcements and analyses, the Soviet leaders never, even at the height of détente, attempted such deception. Détente was accepted in strictly bilateral state-to-state relations with the United States. But at the same time, the Soviets engaged in intensified ideological offenses abroad, particularly in the Third World; covertly, through proxies, they engaged in destabilizing measures of terrorism in vulnerable target areas in the West— notably in Italy, Turkey, Northern Ireland, and the Basque region of Spain; they heightened ideological vigilance at home (to be seen particularly in the savage suppression of dissidents); and they accelerated their military buildup to dimensions that official Washington took little public notice of until the late 1970s.[14]

The fault in Kennan's thesis and prophecy was not that his prescriptions were wrong; they were correct and necessary. But they were not sufficient. His hopeful prediction was not borne out. Fifteen years after the "X" article, the Soviet Union remained in essence the same system that it had been, though considerably more powerful than in Stalin's time; it had the same ideology; it was run by the same men—or kinds of men—who were at Stalin's side in the 1940s. The Soviets' implacable stance toward the West was tempered only in their operational style and by their desperate need for Western help to improve their ailing economy.

To be sure, some Pollyannish American students of the Soviet system even then, as now, believed that there were processes at work that would bring about the system's transformation. By sleight-of-hand, the system of Soviet politics could be made to appear little different from the American one, with plural power centers, hawks and doves, and contending interests. It could be argued, and was, that the Soviet system was simply another somewhat different advanced industrial society, plagued as the others were by stresses of industrialization, modernization, pollution, urban blight, and minority problems. Perhaps America and Russia as postindustrial societies might converge in a technotronic age. In any event, America might lend its own managerial experience in helping the Soviets to overcome some of the difficulties they experienced in running their complex economy; after all, it had been Iowa farmers, notably the Garst brothers, who enabled Khrushchev to develop maize-growing in the virgin lands (although Brezhnev in his memoirs later took credit for this accomplishment).

It is true that in the period discussed some of the worst features of Stalin's terror were abated. Khrushchev's de-Stalinization put an end to the foulest of abuses, and thanks to him some relaxation occurred in the system of totalitarian mind control. Yet the iron will and might of Kremlin leaders limited the effects of such modifications. The events of 1953 (in East Germany), of 1965 (in Poland and Hungary), and of 1968 (in Czechoslovakia) showed how resolute that will was. Anywhere within the Soviet orbit, open defiance of Soviet norms was ruthlessly suppressed. In America, 1968 was the year of the Tet Offensive and of Lyndon Johnson's retirement as commander-in-chief of containment. But it was also the year of the "Prague summer," when Red Army tanks stormed into Czechoslovakia, crushing another manifestation of disobedience. In Prague, then, Soviet leaders again showed how well they had learned the iron law so essential to their rule: in contrast to the laws of physics, in affairs of despotism the greatest danger of explosion comes not at peaks of pressure but afterwards, when the pressure is reduced.

Had Kennan still been convinced of his original doctrine in 1968, he might have noticed a sociological flaw in its practice: the Khrushchev period. The time when de-Stalinization was in fashion, when even Solzhenitsyn could be printed in the official publishing houses, and when "Goulash Communism" came briefly into style, was also the time of the greatest and most dangerous recklessness in the history of Soviet foreign policy. In the worst days of Stalin, as Kennan pointed out, Soviet orchestration of expansion characteristically was cautious though brutal. But in Khrushchev's time, what a difference! On four occasions in barely six years—first in Suez (1956), then in Berlin (1958 and 1961), and finally in Cuba (1962)—the new Soviet despot brought the world to the brink of the abyss by reckless nuclear threats, ultimata, blackmail, and (in Cuba) an ill-starred and fateful attempt to install nuclear weapons off the Florida coast.

In fact, in the occasional rises and falls in the intensity of Soviet domestic repression during the period from 1947 to 1968, there was no apparent correlation between international relaxation and domestic relaxation. If there was any correlation, it was negative: international recklessness was combined with domestic relaxation under Khrushchev, while greater international prudence ("peaceful coexistence") prevailed under Brezhnev, combined with a return to intensified domestic repression. It was, after all, the internationally reckless Khrushchev who personally endorsed publication of Solzhenitsyn's *One Day in the Life of Ivan Denisovich;* the internationally more prudent Brezhnev later carefully attended to Solzhenitsyn's persecution and subsequent exile.

As the need to recognize once again the centrality of the Soviet problem has grown, so has a very disconcerting déja vù in much current writing on the subject. An example is a recent article by Professor Adam Ulam, the distinguished Soviet scholar at Harvard, entitled "How to Restrain the Soviets." Ulam writes:

> It is indeed true that all of us must hope for changes to take place within the Soviet Union, changes which would persuade its leaders to liberalize their own society and to abandon their expansionist and destabilizing policies abroad. But such changes will not come of themselves.
> It is only if the democratic world recoups its strength and cohesion that it can expect that developments such as the recent ones in Poland will pass into history not as mere interludes in Soviet imperial expansion, but as harbingers of a new and better world.[15]

From the dim recesses of the late 1940s, an echo can be heard from Kennan:

> It is . . . a question of the degree to which the United States can create among the peoples of the world . . . the impression of a country which knows what it wants, which is coping successfully with the problems of its internal life and with the responsibilities of a World Power, and which has a spiritual vitality capable of holding its own among the major ideological currents of our time.[16]

Stark Alternatives

The Soviet problem remains the gravest issue for American foreign policy—indeed, for the destiny of Western civilization. The problem arises from the nature of the Soviet system, and the essence of the problem is that system's need to regard itself as being at war with us. As a consequence, we face three possibilities other than outright and unacceptable nuclear war: a collapse of the Western will to resist Soviet military growth and expansion, protracted continuance of international tension and military competition, or an erosion or collapse of the Soviet empire. These three possibilities are not mutually exclusive, but they need to be stated in the starkest terms in order for us to remember what we are up against.

To pose these stark alternatives is also to point out one unpleasant circumstance—namely, that the preconditions for a true peace are not attainable. The contest will continue, whatever we may wish or whatever gloss we may choose to put on the matter; thus the question is whether, as it continues, the Soviets may sooner or later attain unchallenged superiority in the global system.

For forty years, as the West has coexisted with the Soviets, the latter have persisted in systematically and deliberately destabilizing the free world and all regions outside their sway. The West, on the other hand, forswearing any forward designs, has kept up its guard; it has waited, like Mr. Micawber, for something to turn up. When nothing particularly encouraging came along, the unspoken assumption was that the Soviet system was here to stay, that it had become permanently entrenched. Having accepted that, it became easy for some to convince themselves that even if the Soviet Union were not so healthy as all that, or so permanent or durable or secure, nevertheless the West had a vested interest in Soviet stability and health. Finally, some came to the position of actually saying, as did former Secretary of State Cyrus Vance, that men like Brezhnev in their hearts shared the same hopes and longings for mankind as did the American president. Events have checked this line of thinking a good deal. But what may now replace it?

The return to containment should be welcomed as the return of a long-absent friend. But while necessary, it is not sufficient. The defect in Kennan's original formula lay in his confidence that the Soviet system, successfully checked in its outward thrust, would profoundly change in ways beneficial to the free world because of indigenous social developments. After all these years we should now admit that there are not automatic, inexorable laws of political dynamics of the sort in which Kennan placed his full confidence. Will and iron resolution, qualities that many social scientists fail to understand, play a formidable part. In the long history of the Soviet Union, its leaders have displayed extraordinary resolve in dealing with adversities within their vast empire, never forsaking their essential character and goals. There is no particular reason to suppose at present that the widely reported corruption within Soviet society in itself represents a more severe challenge to the Kremlin than did previous internal adversities.

Kennan's doctrine stopped short of encouraging contradictions within the Soviet system. In relations between the free world and the Soviet empire, there was a fundamental asymmetry: Soviet interference continued, while the West forswore reciprocation. The rules of the game should be changed.

Earlier on in this essay, when outlining Lippmann's critique of containment policy, I mentioned his dogmatic assertion that the American constitutional system was not capable of acting out the strategic role of "container" that Kennan prescribed. Further, I mentioned that events that ensued shortly after Lippmann made this assertion dramatically refuted his criticism: the American political system did prove capable of this, for a time.

But let me now again quote Lippmann at greater length on this important question, for his phrasing of the problem has a disconcerting relevance to our current situation:

> How, for example, under the Constitution . . . [is Kennan] going to work out an arrangement by which the Department of State has the money and the military power always available in sufficient amounts to apply "counter-force" at constantly shifting points all over the world? Is he going to ask Congress for a blank check on the Treasury and for a blank authorization to use the armed forces? Not if the American constitutional system is to be maintained. Or is he going to ask for an appropriation and for authority each time the Russians "show signs of encroaching upon the interests of a peaceful and stable world?" If that is his plan for dealing with maneuvers of a dictatorship, he is going to arrive at points of encroachment with too little and he is going to arrive too late. The Russians, if they intend to encroach, will encroach while Congress is getting ready to hold hearings.
>
> A policy of shifts and maneuvers may be suited to the Soviet system of government, which, as [Kennan] tells us, is animated by persistence. It is not suited to the American system of government.[17]

Oddly enough, later (after the Korean War broke out, that is) Lippmann came to have second thoughts on the matter of democracy and foreign policy. As he wrote in 1956, "The prevailing public opinion has been destructively wrong at the critical junctures . . . too pacifist in peace and too bellicose in war."[18] But we are left with a disquieting question, now that more than containment is called for: was Lippmann the diagnostician right or wrong *for the long haul* in his estimate of the American system? Was the first successful era of containment the norm rather than an aberration? If the answer to the latter question is no, we are in trouble; if yes, there is a lot of hope. A nation's vices cannot be its excuses.

III

Policy Alternatives

5

ROBERT W. TUCKER

Containment and the Search for Alternatives: A Critique

Since the outset of the Cold War the search for alternative policies toward the Soviet Union has been a recurring feature of the public dialogue on foreign policy. The initiation of the policy of containment in the late 1940s was marked by controversy; its subsequent history has been one of continuing controversy. In the thirty-five years since its adoption, containment has been given a number of quite different interpretations and has been implemented in a number of quite different ways. Yet it has seldom, if ever, been free of criticism. It has been considered either too aggressive or, more often, too defensive. It has been attacked for being too demanding of the nation's resources, or too threatening in its impact on domestic institutions and the quality of national life. Most often, perhaps, it has been criticized for failing to hold out the solid prospect of bringing the conflict between the United States and the Soviet Union to an early and satisfactory end.

The call today for alternative policies toward the Soviet Union thus follows a well-established pattern. To say this is not to dismiss, let alone to deride, the call. It is only to make the familiar point that as a nation we have never been quite satisfied with the policies we have pursued in responding to the Soviet challenge. This dissatisfaction has been apparent even when containment seems to have been most effective.

A consideration of possible alternatives to containment may be prefaced by a consideration, however brief, of present policy. The search for alternatives suggests the question "alternatives to what?" The answer presumably must be found in the policy of the current administration. Is the Reagan administration pursuing a policy of containment, its occasional professions to the contrary notwithstanding? If so, what kind of containment policy is it pursuing?

The Reagan Record

These questions cannot be clearly answered by pointing to administration statements of policy. More than halfway through its first term, this administration has yet to set forth a statement of policy toward the Soviet Union that possesses coherence in terms of interest and, perhaps even more, of the means whereby interest may be vindicated at bearable cost. There have been, of course, any number of statements asserting the intention to oppose further Soviet expansion and to reverse the trend, as the administration sees it, toward Soviet ascendancy. To this extent, the Reagan administration may be considered to have reaffirmed a continuing commitment to containment.

At the same time, this reaffirmation, if it is such, tells us very little. In its generality, it is compatible with almost any and every version of containment that has been pursued since the 1940s, as well as with versions that have not been pursued. The more specific interests and objectives of policy remain obscure, as do the strategic implications of policy—that is, the manner by which policymakers intend to relate means to ends. Nor have the infrequent attempts to elaborate policies been very enlightening. For the most part, these attempts either have consisted of rather empty exercises that told us what we already knew, or they have been statements that, if taken at face value as indicative of policy or strategy, have provoked skepticism and even incredulity. Former Secretary of State Alexander Haig's "four pillars"—restoration of American military power, reinvigoration of alliances, promotion of global economic growth, and achievement of a more satisfactory relationship with the USSR—belong to the former category. Unexceptionable in content, they told us nothing about the more concrete goals and strategies of the administration. Secretary of Defense Caspar Weinberger's statements of military strategy belong to the latter category, particularly his rejection of the "artificial constraints" of previous strategies with their commitment to 1½ or 2½ wars. In language reminiscent of a previous architect of containment, John Foster Dulles, Mr. Weinberger has spoken of the need to respond to Soviet aggression in one area by striking at points of Soviet vulnerability elsewhere.

Whereas Dulles's strategy proposed to meet a Soviet attack on the periphery by responding at or near the center, Weinberger's strategy apparently proposes to meet a Soviet attack at or near the center (the Persian Gulf?) by responding at "places of our choosing" on the periphery. In a period of American strategic superiority, the Dulles strategy was a credible one, whatever else may be said of it. The Weinberger strategy, however, would be credible only if this country possessed conventional forces sufficient to give it a multitheater capability superior to that of the Soviet Union. Clearly, the U.S. does not enjoy such capability today, and there must be considerable doubt whether it will enjoy it by the late 1980s. Even on the assumption that it may one day do so, the Weinberger strategy still evokes something akin to incredulity.

Whereas the Dulles strategy was intended to prevent small losses by threatening the adversary with a major loss, the Weinberger strategy appears designed either to prevent major loss by threatening the adversary with a series of small losses or to prevent a small loss by threatening him in return with small losses. The threat of major loss, however, would signal the dread contingency of a central war in which strategic forces would be employed. In this event, a response on the periphery would seem to be of marginal significance at best; the threat of such a response appears to be almost an inversion of any normal calculus of deterrence. The prospect of minor loss, on the other hand, may well be deterred by the threat to respond at several points of enemy vulnerability elsewhere on the periphery. But even if this threat of "horizontal escalation" avoided heightening sharply the prospects of vertical escalation—and it is very difficult to see how it would—it would assume a public willing to support not one "limited" war but two or three or more. In the light of our experience with such conflicts, this is quite an assumption.

Disparity Between Words and Actions

In sum, the statements on military strategy by Reagan administration officials have not been very reassuring. At best, they suggest an uncertainty over strategy that takes refuge in ideas about the possible uses of our military power that do not readily withstand critical analysis. At worst, they point to a disposition to employ military power on behalf of interests that at present do not enjoy the nation's support, and to do so in circumstances that may prove more adverse than any we have heretofore faced. When these statements are taken together with bland assertions about "prevailing" over the Soviet Union, it is not surprising that a growing number of critics have concluded either that the administration has been unable to fix upon a policy or that the policy it has determined to pursue is one of all-out confrontation, a policy that will require American military superiority. For the concept of "prevailing" either is a rather artless restatement of the premise underlying American containment policy from the outset (no administration has ever suggested that we should not aspire to, and would not ultimately, prevail), or it is a statement of intent to go well beyond the forms containment has taken since the years of the classic Cold War, and to do so in circumstances that are far less promising than the circumstances of an earlier period.

Administration officials have not infrequently seen fit to encourage the view that prevailing is more than mere containment. Whereas containment in their view meant living with the Soviet Union "as it was at any given time," prevailing presumably means putting an end to "Russian imperialism" and to the present Soviet empire. Prevailing, then, is not content with the status quo. Instead, it is a policy intent on convincing Soviet leaders to turn their attention and energy inward. And although prevailing is said to stop short of seeking to change the nature of the government in Moscow, that aim nevertheless appears implicit in the concept. If the Soviet regime draws its legitimacy today largely from foreign policy, as we are constantly told, what may we expect to happen to it when that foreign policy turns into a series of defeats, and Soviet control over Eastern Europe and other areas is steadily loosened and perhaps one day lost?

Experience has taught us that the watchwords of administrations are important as a guide to policy. To date, however, the watchwords of the Reagan administration have not been indicative of its actions. Between its more arresting statements on policy and strategy and its behavior there is perhaps a greater gulf than we have experienced with any administration since the Cold War began. One can only speculate why this disparity between word and action is so pronounced today. In part, no doubt, it responds to the need to appease domestic allies and supporters who are increasingly disillusioned by the behavior of this administration. Words may be a poor substitute for action, but they are better than nothing. They provide some reassurance about the spirit even though the flesh appears weak. The administration may also be in need of such reassurance. Only a superficial cynicism would find in its rhetoric a calculated sop for the faithful. That rhetoric is likely intended for the administration as well, for it too has need to believe that the vision and commitments with which it took office have not been compromised.

Reagan vs. Carter

Whatever the explanation of the striking disparity between rhetoric and action, the disparity itself is clear enough. Overall, the behavior of the Reagan administration to date has been quite moderate. Indeed, if we put aside its words, it is not difficult to make the case that the substance of its actions adds up to a policy that a second Carter administration, disabused of its earlier illusions, might well have followed. Certainly, a second Carter administration could hardly have reacted less forcefully to events in Poland than the Reagan administration has reacted. In its relations with allies, the preceding administration would have responded sooner to the need to set out a reasonable position on arms control in Europe. It would not have reopened the issue of the gas pipeline. Even so, it seems reasonable to speculate that the general tenor of policy toward allies today is not substantially different from the likely policy of a second Carter administration. The arms control proposals for Europe that the Reagan administration has made cannot be very different from the proposals made by any administration that did not intend to compromise its position on theater nuclear forces at the very outset. And the Reagan obstinacy on the pipeline, abandoned after a brief period, may have served some purpose after all, if only by dramatizing differences within the Alliance that, if not resolved somehow, would continue to erode it. These differences would have to be dealt with by any administration, as the Carter administration also recognized, even if the attempt to do so ultimately ended in failure.

In the other area of vital interest, the Middle East, the actions taken by the Reagan administration represent, on balance, no significant departure from its predecessor. The current administration has been more receptive to Israeli initiatives — or at least more passive in responding to them—than a second Carter administration is likely to have been. But this difference is subordinate in importance to the measures that have been taken—or, as some critics may insist, have yet to be taken — to insure access to the oil of the Persian Gulf. In this respect, the Reagan administration appears to have followed faithfully in the footsteps of its predecessor. The Carter Doctrine has in effect been reaffirmed, though the credibility of that doctrine continues to raise the doubts that it raised in an earlier period.

In Central America, a more persuasive case can be made for discontinuity. Yet the Carter administration was also hardening its Central American policy when it left office. The *modus vivendi* with Nicaragua was falling apart by the summer and fall of 1980, and the feeling of having been cheated was strong. Would the Carter administration have taken the course subsequently taken by the Reagan administration? The answer can be no more than speculative. It seems highly unlikely, though, that the preceding administration would have taken covert action against Nicaragua. At the same time, it does not appear implausible to assume that a second Carter administration would have supported the government of El Salvador by measures not dissimilar from those taken by its successor. Whether it would have seriously considered military intervention in El Salvador is quite another matter. Very likely, it would not have done so. It is not clear, however, that this must set it apart from the Reagan administration.

The Defense Program

It is in the area of defense that the Reagan administration is generally seen to have made the most dramatic break from the pattern of the preceding decade. This perception is not misplaced. In retrospect, the military buildup undertaken by this administration is likely to be judged more significant than any initiatives it has taken in foreign policy as such. Indeed, one may say that to date, at any rate, the defense program of the Reagan administration has been its most significant foreign policy action.

Even in defense, however, it is well to recall that the break from the pattern of the 1970s was made, however reluctantly, by the Carter administration. A second Carter administration would also have undertaken a military buildup, though its buildup promised to be markedly slower. (The last Carter budget projected a 5 percent real increase in defense spending as against a 7 percent real increase in the Reagan budget.) It is also the case that the Reagan administration has emphasized naval expansion to a degree that the preceding administration showed no disposition to do.

These differences cannot be dismissed. At the same time, their significance is often exaggerated out of all proportion. The additional increment of defense spending in the Reagan budget over the proposed Carter budget is scarcely of such magnitude as to transform a military balance that otherwise would merely have been redressed. The Reagan administration military buildup does not envisage strategic nuclear superiority; even if this were the intention, it could not be realized. The naval expansion that it is clearly intent on will confer an even greater naval superiority than the already marked superiority we possess today. But this expansion cannot materially affect the strategic balance. The two strategic programs to which the Soviets have voiced greatest opposition — the MX, and the Pershing and cruise missiles — are not the progeny of the Reagan administration; it may even be the case that they would have fared better in a second Carter administration. Certainly, they have not fared very well in the past two years.

Whether in foreign policy or in defense, the unavoidable conclusion is that the Reagan administration has not undertaken any striking, let alone radical, leap. Despite its failure, or perhaps simply its unwillingness, to articulate in reasonably specific terms a policy toward the Soviet Union, its actions so far indicate that it has such a policy, and that this policy may best be described as one of moderate containment. As such, the policy has focused on areas of heretofore undisputed vital interest—that is, on Western Europe and the Persian Gulf. Elsewhere, it has been notably cautious and restrained in reacting to Soviet involvement. It has shown little disposition to draw new lines in the Third World that could be crossed only at the risk of an armed response. Nor has it taken any measures seriously designed to loosen Soviet control over Eastern Europe or other Soviet satellites. This behavior, it is true, has often been obscured by a rhetoric that suggests much more than moderate containment. But even if that rhetoric is taken as evidence of a persisting disposition to follow a more ambitious policy, it does not alter the reality of the policy that is at present pursued.

Alternatives to Containment

What are the alternatives to present policy? In principle, there are three: confrontation, condominium, and withdrawal. Each of these alternatives has, of course, a number of possible variations. A policy of confrontation, for example, may range from an effort of only selective denial to an attempt to push a hostile and expansionist state back within its own borders through any combination of measures necessary to achieve this, short of the deliberate resort to war.

Even a policy of moderate containment, then, may be considered to fall within this category. It does so, however, only in the rather formal sense that any policy of containment will at some point have to oppose an expansionist adversary; that is, it will have to confront him, if necessary, by the threat to resort to armed force.

In the less general and formal sense, a policy of confrontation is one that seeks to frustrate an adversary at every turn—to deny him wherever possible every gain or advantage—to the end of compelling him to abandon the conflict and the objects over which the conflict has turned. A policy of confrontation falls one step short of war; although it may not end in war, in the past it has normally been regarded as the prelude to it. For a policy of confrontation normally seeks a favorable resolution of the conflict by requiring an adversary to choose between war and the sacrifice of interests he regards as vital. It is true that in the nuclear age, between nuclear powers, this choice is no longer as stark as it once was since the disincentive to go to war has increased so dramatically. Even so, a policy of confrontation cannot but present at least an attenuated form of the same choice, else it would become virtually indistinguishable from a policy of dissuasion (which may take any one of a number of different forms).

The objective of a policy of confrontation is to triumph, or to prevail, over the adversary, if need be through war. By contrast, the objective of a policy of condominium is to share victory with the adversary through an arrangement whereby both sides gain a part of the interests in contention. The agreement need not observe the principle of strict equality. Since great conflicts are generally marked by asymmetries of position and interest, as well as by disparities of power, any arrangement approximating one of condominium will not conform to a strict equality. At the same time, the putative agreement, which may be formal or informal, cannot deviate too far from a rough equality, else there would be little incentive to enter into it. The interests in direct contention must be compromised; if this cannot be accomplished by their division, it must be done by way of compensation.

The first stage of the process eventuating in condominium is normally one of détente. But détente is, as we have recently experienced, still very far from a condominial relationship. Although détente necessarily implies a relaxation of tensions—and of course the temporary cessation of behavior that gave rise to tensions—it need not imply agreement over any of the objects of contention that have either given rise to or sustained the underlying conflict. Quite apart from the motives entertained by one or both parties in undertaking détente, which may be to seek no more than a momentary respite for one reason or another, it is this ab-

sence of solid agreement that, at bottom, must give détente a tran-
sient and precarious character. Hence the conventional wisdom
that détente must within a reasonable period of time either move
forward to entente, which between great and imperial powers implies condominium, or give way to the conflict that preceded it.

Confrontation and condominium are radically different policies
for resolving conflict. Either can be achieved only in conjunction
with the adversary. In the case of confrontation, conflict is
resolved by compelling certain behavior. In the case of condominium, conflict is resolved generally through a mixture of
negative and positive inducements. In either case, though, the
resolution of conflict requires at least the minimal cooperation of
the adversary.

Conflict may also be resolved by avoidance. One of the parties
may choose to withdraw from the contest. Whether this will prove
possible without very great sacrifice of interest obviously depends
upon circumstance. Even if circumstance is such that it does permit withdrawal, there is of course always a price to be paid. Were
this not the case, the attractions of conflict would prove distinctly
limited, at least for any power that was not incorrigibly expansionist. But short of clearly placing core security in jeopardy, the
price of withdrawal must be weighed against the costs of continued involvement. The outcome of this calculation may well be
very different from what a prevailing consensus has decreed. Not
only may the interests at stake in the conflict be exaggerated, but
withdrawal may give rise to consequences that transform the conditions productive of conflict in the first place. A policy of withdrawal may be undertaken, in part at least, with the intent to
facilitate the creation of a new order, one that will displace the old
conflict through the emergence of a changed equilibrium of power.

These are the alternatives to present policy toward the Soviet
Union. There is no novelty in any one of them. Each has been discussed and debated many times, though the last—withdrawal—
has been taken rather less seriously than the other two. The demand today that we devise creative new approaches to the Soviet
Union appears to assume that there are alternatives other than
those outlined above. Unfortunately, there are not. One may manage a conflict in the hope and expectation that time and persistence will either change the behavior of the adversary or gradu-

ally alter favorably the environment in which the conflict is carried on. If that policy is rejected, however, it must be rejected for a policy that is intent on ending the conflict or substantially transforming it. One may end a conflict by forcing the adversary into submission. One may also end a conflict by mutual compromise over the objects in contention. Finally, one may end a conflict simply by withdrawing from it. Beyond these alternatives, though, our creativity in conflict resolution does not appear to go.

Condominium. Of the possible alternatives to present policy, the one that would seem to hold out the least favorable prospect is a policy of condominium. A global condominium presupposes that both the Soviet Union and the United States are disposed to enter into such an arrangement and that circumstances otherwise permit its effective implementation. These conditions of condominium do not obtain today, however, and it seems altogether unlikely that they will obtain in the foreseeable future. Indeed, while the prospects of a condominial arrangement were probably more meaningful in an earlier period of the Cold War, in fact they were never very meaningful. Although it is the case that in the years following World War II the objects of contention between the superpowers were far more passive than they are today, the comparison is still a relative one. For even in those years the world was surprisingly resistant to the superpowers.

This consideration apart, in an earlier period the United States had no disposition to enter into a condominial arrangement with the Soviet Union. The unscathed victor of the war, the U.S. enjoyed a power advantage over its emerging rival that was very considerable. Later, when this advantage began to decline, the world became far more assertive. Thus even if at a later and more mature stage of their competition, when their power had become more equal, the two great rivals had seriously entertained the idea of entering into a condominial arrangement, the requisite conditions for effectively implementing it were lacking. The years marking the high point of détente showed that our allies are almost as apprehensive over any understanding between the United States and the Soviet Union as they are over a relationship that points to confrontation.

These considerations do not rule out the prospect in the years

ahead of another détente, perhaps one that holds out greater
promise than its predecessor. A new détente would no doubt be
prompted by the deepened appreciation on both sides of the costs
and hazards incurred by an unregulated competition in arms as
well as by a common desire of both parties to give a greater degree
of stability and assurance to their relationship. A new détente, it
seems reasonable to assume, would not be entered into with the
expectations on this side that attended the old détente. Nor would
it be entered into, one must assume, in circumstances that marked
a significant shift of military power in favor of the Soviet Union.
On the contrary, this détente would be undertaken when American military capabilities were rising rather than declining. And it
would likely be undertaken in circumstances marked by continuing Soviet anxiety over the stability of its empire.

In these circumstances, a new détente might well take a form
and result in consequences quite different from the old. Even so,
there is little reason to believe that any new arrangement would
proceed beyond the quite narrow limits placed on it by the deep
and persisting aspirations of the parties, particularly the Soviet
Union, as well as by a world that is ever more resistant to great-
power control.

Confrontation. The prospects for détente, let alone for condominium, appear slight at present. More likely as a possible alternative to present policy is a policy of confrontation. Many critics of
the Reagan administration insist that we are already well into the
opening stages of a confrontational policy. Although, as I have
earlier argued, this charge is misplaced, it is so only if we judge it
on the basis of the administration's behavior to date. Judged by its
deeds, the current administration does not seek a resolution of the
conflict by forcing the adversary to make the critical choice between the sacrifice of vital interests and war. It may yet veer
toward a policy of confrontation, less because this policy responded to inner conviction than because the administration may
one day believe that its overall position had improved to a point
where a more confrontational policy could be undertaken from a
position of strength and of relative advantage. This perception
may even coincide with a crisis in Soviet-American relations, a
crisis that would put the administration's policy to its first clear-

cut test. We have no way of knowing how the administration would behave in one of those recurring moments of truth that have marked the contest between this country and its great adversary. It may behave in much the same way as it has behaved to date. Then again, it may not. The promise of the Reagan administration remains uncertain, and the prospect that this administration, or its successor, may yet turn to a policy of confrontation cannot simply be brushed aside.

In the circumstances of the 1980s, of what would a policy of confrontation consist? Clearly, it would consist in a return to the containment policy of the period preceding Vietnam. Instead of the moderate containment pursued today, we would again embrace a strategy premised on a "seamless web of interests" and view virtually every Soviet move, in however peripheral the area of the world, as a threat to our vital interests. A new policy of global containment might be based either on geopolitical considerations or on ideological grounds or, what is likely, on a mixture of both. Whatever the rationale, the policy result would be largely the same. The Soviet Union would be opposed, if need be by force of arms, wherever it might seek to expand its control or even its influence.

Proponents of a return to a policy of global containment often appear to assume that the implications of pursuing such a policy today would be substantially the same as they were in an earlier period. Yet the altered circumstances of the 1980s do not support this assumption. In the course of a generation, a momentous shift in the balance of power has occurred. The position of strategic superiority we once enjoyed has been lost and, in all likelihood, cannot be restored. For this and other reasons, the Soviet Union has achieved a status today that it did not possess in an earlier period. The attempt, in effect, to deprive it of what it now sees as the consequences of an equality achieved through considerable effort and sacrifice can be expected to provoke a severe reaction. This is why the meaning of a policy of global containment today cannot be equated with the meaning it may have once had. Though this policy may seek the same results, it does so in circumstances so changed that they virtually insure a confrontational outcome.

Nor is this all. Even a policy of global containment that re-

sembles an earlier containment is not likely to satisfy those intent
on bringing the great conflict to a successful issue. Earlier global
containment did not, after all, bear out the promise that supporters entertained of it. In 1947, George Kennan speculated that
"the United States has it in its power to increase enormously the
strains under which Soviet policy must operate, to force upon the
Kremlin a far greater moderation and circumspection than it has
had to observe ... and in this way to promote tendencies which
must eventually find their outlet in either the break-up or the
gradual mellowing of Soviet power." This promise entertained of
containment from the outset never materialized, even when the
strategy assumed its most ambitious form. Why should it be expected to do so as a consequence of adopting a new policy of global
containment? The question is indeed pertinent. Those intent on
avoiding the dilemmas of containment, while achieving the promise initially held out by it, have answered by calling for a policy
that goes beyond containment and actively exploits weaknesses
internal to the Soviet regime and its empire. Such measures are
considered by many today to be an indispensable concomitant of
global containment.

A policy designed not only to oppose any Soviet moves in the
world but to exploit any Soviet vulnerability, particularly in
Eastern Europe, must run considerable risks. For the message
conveyed by such a policy would quite clearly be that we no longer
intended to treat Moscow as an equal. At the very least, it would
require a position of military superiority in the possible areas of
contention, something that we do not possess at present and are
not likely to possess even when the military buildup now under
way is completed. Even if we did once enjoy so advantageous a
position, one we have never really enjoyed since the Cold War
began, the effort to turn the Soviet Union back to the status of a
regional power would risk meeting the kind of resistance that
might well eventuate in a fatal encounter neither side would find
possible to back away from.

Even in the comparatively far more favorable circumstances of
the 1950s and early 1960s, a policy of global containment proved
to be no more than a mixed success. Whether those circumstances
could be resurrected — and if not, then somehow compensated for
by a novel set of favorable conditions — seems more than doubtful.

Clearly, there is no basis for assuming that Allied support could be enlisted for the policy here considered. Quite the contrary, a policy intent on confronting the Soviet Union would be an almost certain prescription for breaking an alliance that is already in bad enough repair. If this were the result, the principal interest of postwar American policy might well be lost. Those who advocate a more ambitious policy toward the Soviet Union often shrug off this prospect and even intimate that, were it to materialize, we would simply have to face up to the consequences. But a fatal break with our major allies would not represent the jeopardizing of merely one interest among many. It would jeopardize the interest that, apart from the physical security of the country, constitutes the *raison d'être* of postwar American policy. That policy, we need periodically to remind ourselves, was not undertaken to defend those peripheral interests that have since taken so much of our attention and effort. Instead, the defense of peripheral interests must be justified primarily in terms of the security of our major allies. This is the case even for that greatest of "peripheral" interests, the Persian Gulf.

There is no evidence that a policy of global containment—in effect, a policy of confrontation—could command the domestic support required to sustain it. Instead, what evidence there is points to the conclusion that it could not do so. The experience of the first two years of the Reagan administration is quite clear in this respect. On defense, the administration has pushed to its outer limits the consensus in support of a military buildup, if it has not breached those limits.

The defense spending that the public appears willing to support (if by a considerably diminished margin) still falls far short of the effort that would be required to implement a policy of global containment. Even if the Reagan administration has not, as critics charge, destroyed the defense consensus by its failure to persuade the public that resources devoted to the current military buildup are being wisely spent or fit into a coherent strategy, it also has not created, and shows no signs of being able to create, a public disposition responsive to the sacrifices global containment would entail.

A policy of confrontation with the Soviet Union would be resisted by those on whose behalf it was presumably undertaken and would go far beyond the present, or any likely future, domestic consensus on foreign policy. This is quite generally appreciated today, more so than the public dialogue on foreign policy would often lead one to conclude. An awareness of the costs and risks attending the pursuit of a policy of confrontation is even reflected in the interpretations Reagan administration officials have given to the concept of prevailing. If prevailing means to win, it nevertheless is not interpreted to mean that we are to win through the pursuit of a policy of confrontation toward the Soviet Union. Instead, prevailing is to be sought through the exploitation of Soviet weaknesses, and particularly economic weaknesses. Although attacked by critics as part and parcel of a policy of confrontation, it is in fact a far cry from that.

To require the Soviet Union, in the words of administration officials, to bear the brunt of its own economic shortcomings and to feel the full burden of its own priorities, is to do no more than seek to discourage an arms buildup that has gone on without letup for the better part of two decades and that has been quite unaffected by the relationship of détente. It may be the case that the attempt to exploit Soviet economic weaknesses, even if enjoying Allied support, can have no more than a marginal effect. But this is a criticism of its effectiveness, not of its confrontational character. To contend otherwise is to argue that we are constrained to take no measures intended to hamper the growth of Soviet power, since these measures may be seen by the adversary as evidence of a confrontational disposition. If, however, the definition of confrontation is left to the adversary, one's course of action may readily become indistinguishable from what is objectively a policy of appeasement.

The real criticism of a policy designed to exploit Soviet economic weaknesses is that it cannot command Allied support. Though quite distinct from a policy of confrontation, it has met with Allied resistance and, in the case of the gas pipeline, has provoked yet another crisis in the Western Alliance. That crisis, in turn, may be seen as indicative of the extent to which since the 1960s the Alliance that has formed the cornerstone of postwar American foreign policy has unraveled. Committed as much to the détente that has grown up over the past decade and a half as it is to the Alliance, Western Europe is no longer willing to permit its transatlantic ally to involve it in a policy it does not approve.

It is against the background of growing differences with our major allies that once-unthinkable reconstructions of U.S. diplomatic and military strategy have appeared of late. What has become known as a policy of global unilateralism is largely the response to an Alliance that is increasingly found to hamper an effective American policy toward the Soviet Union while continuing to require a substantial portion of the resources this nation devotes to defense. A mood of increasing frustration and resentment toward our European allies has prompted the vision of a new policy of progressive detachment from Europe accompanied by a continued, or increased, active involvement elsewhere in the world. Indeed, it is presumably in the release from the burdens of our European commitments that we would be enabled better to secure our interests elsewhere, whether it be in the Persian Gulf, Asia, Southern Africa, or Central America and the Caribbean. In a reversal of historic proportions, the periphery of postwar policy would become the center while the center would become the periphery—but now the center would comprise much of the world beyond Europe.

This vision of a global unilateralism free from the constraints and burdens imposed by allies may gain increasing favor. It responds to deep roots in our past. It recalls the period when we were able to "go it alone," and when our fate was not tied to others. To the prospect of regaining an independence of action we have not enjoyed since World War II is added the attraction of a defense budget that would be free of the largest single charge made to it.

Does a policy of global unilateralism, however inchoate the vision of such a policy may remain today, represent an alternative to those already sketched out? It would not seem so. Although the mood this vision represents is indeed significant, the vision itself appears incapable of being transformed into a coherent policy. In abandoning Europe, we might free ourselves from the constraints of allies, but we would not free ourselves from the constraints of limited resources. Instead of needing less for defense, we would need more *if* we were to maintain, and perhaps add to, our position elsewhere in the world. The argument that the contrary would prove to be the case assumes that without our present commitment to Europe we would be in a much better position to close the gap between our commitments and our power elsewhere. But that assumption is well founded only if it is further assumed that while we withdraw our commitment and our forces from Europe, the threat the Soviet Union poses to our positions elsewhere would remain the same. This would be the case only if the Western European states proved able and disposed to do what heretofore they have not done—to defend themselves.

If we were to abandon our present commitment to Europe, and the Western European countries failed to fill the gap created by our departure, the Soviet Union would have much less to worry about in the theater of greatest importance to it. Freed from this concern, while progressively strengthened by the resource base Western Europe would then afford it, Moscow might be able to turn its attention elsewhere and to do so with far greater effect than it has had to date. Rather than closing the gap between our commitments and our power, Soviet ascendance in Europe consequent upon a U.S. withdrawal would have the likely effect of widening this gap. Having abandoned what had heretofore been the center of our interest for the periphery, we would find the periphery increasingly difficult to secure against the improved power position of the Soviet Union.

Nor is it quite apparent why we should continue to make the effort to defend the periphery, or at least most of it, against the Soviet Union. For the defense of peripheral interests takes on significance, for the most part, because of their relationship to the interests that compose the center. If our commitment is no longer to the center, why then to the periphery? When it is said, to take the most important example, that the abandonment of a Eurocentric policy would permit us to address more effectively our interests in the Gulf, the question arises: for what? To secure access to oil needed primarily by our allies? Why defend their extra-European interests, if we no longer care to defend their European interests?

Withdrawal. These considerations suggest that the current vision of global unilateralism either is a device, perhaps partly unconscious in design, for pressuring our allies into behaving in a manner more congenial to us, or it is indicative of a policy of withdrawal—not from the center to the periphery, though this is regularly intimated, but from the center *and* the periphery. The real alternative to a Eurocentric policy, then, is not a policy of global unilateralism, but one that resembles the hemispheric isolation of the past.

Since World War II it has been accepted as axiomatic that a return to a hemispheric policy is unthinkable. What has been unthinkable may become less so in the future, particularly if the erosion in Alliance relationships continues unchecked. Moreover, even if the reconsideration of a historic policy is occasioned by increasing frustration and resentment toward those who remain resistant to our will, once this reconsideration is seriously undertaken the attractions of a "smaller policy" may prove surprising. For if there are considerable risks run and sacrifices entailed by a policy of withdrawal, there are also apparent benefits.

Once we had abandoned our postwar interests and commitments outside this hemisphere our defense needs would diminish accordingly. We would still need naval forces sufficient to support a policy of hemispheric defense as well as to insure the security of our commerce. These needs, however (particularly the latter), are unlikely to prove onerous. Once accorded virtually a free hand in Eurasia, the Soviet regime would have little short-range interest in challenging our free use of the seas. Then, too, our commercial relations with most of the world are not, on balance, dependent on our present power and commitments. Only in one area, the Persian Gulf, can a contrary case be made, and given our largely abortive efforts to date to introduce our power there, it must be counted a very qualified case.

The chief attraction of a policy of withdrawal to this hemisphere is that it would avoid the principal risk a policy of global involvement, with or without alliances, must incur. It would avoid the risk of war and, above all, of nuclear war. Having withdrawn once again from the world beyond this hemisphere, though now possessed of a surfeit of deterrent power in the form of nuclear missile weapons, we would have little reason to fear attack, for an attacker would know with virtual certainty that he had far more to lose than to gain from so acting. To this extent, nuclear missile weapons give substance to the long-discredited isolationist dream. So long as it is clear that they will be employed only in the direct defense of the homeland, they confer a physical security that is virtually complete, and that the loss of allies cannot alter. Instead, alliances must *detract* from physical security, since it is the prospect of defending allies that may one day result in a war destructive of this security.

These attractions of a policy of withdrawal are not the only arguments that may be made on its behalf. The great objective of America's postwar policy has been the restoration of a more normal political world, a world in which those states possessing the elements of great power again play the independent role their power entitles them to play. Without such restoration, there has been no apparent alternative to a policy of containing Soviet power that did not hold out the promise of a world in which this power went without effective challenge. From this perspective, the logic of containment arises not so much from the nature of the Soviet regime or the specific conflicts of interest between that regime and this country as from the temptations — if not the compulsions — of a system that retains to this day an essentially bipolar character. It is the essential structural features of the conflict that must account for its persistence and its pervasiveness. Until such time as these structural features are substantially moderated, the logic of containment will appear inescapable and, indeed, the argument for global containment, whatever its costs and risks, will have a persuasiveness that has to be reckoned with.

The structural features cannot be moderated, however, so long as the potential power of our allies fails to find its full expression in the political-military as well as the economic sphere. So long as these states, possessing the elements of great power, refuse to play the role their power would entitle them to play, and so long as they are not seriously pressured into doing so, there can be no alternative to containment with all its dilemmas and frustrations. A policy of withdrawal, in the view of many of its proponents, would be undertaken with the intent of altering the structural features that have necessitated a policy of containment. Yet to accomplish this, it would not be sufficient to condition withdrawal upon a positive response to American incentive and encouragement. If a positive Allied response were made the limiting condition, a policy of withdrawal would not differ in substance from present policy: we have always insisted that our commitments to allies would become unnecessary once these states were able and willing to provide for their own security.

Thus the most persuasive case for a policy of withdrawal rests on the assumption that allies will respond to an American withdrawal presented as *fait accompli,* that a new political world will be called into existence, and that in consequence the conflict between the United States and the Soviet Union will be largely displaced. Clearly, this assumption is in the nature of a calculated gamble. The gamble may be won. Then again, it may be lost. We have no way of knowing how it will turn out. Should it fail, we will confront the very prospect that we have labored thirty-five years to prevent.

Desire for Decisive Outcome

What is common to the alternative policies considered here is that they seek directly to end the great conflict that has largely dominated the postwar system. Although they do so in very different ways and for very different ends, they share the conviction that we cannot continue indefinitely to shoulder the burdens and incur the hazards imposed by the conflict. Thus an end there must be, whether through accommodation and compromise, victory, abandonment or, finally, displacement.

Yet none of these alternatives would appear to hold out much promise. The best is withdrawal. Even that, however, appears promising largely in relation to the other alternatives. What may be said for it is that it remains clearly within our power to initiate and to carry through. The conflict with the Soviet Union may be abandoned. It may be abandoned without fear for our physical security. Indeed, a policy of withdrawal would result in the enhancement of our physical security, and it would do so while lessening the burden of defense. Withdrawal would not put to risk the nation's body. At the same time, it might well put to risk the nation's soul if the results were to lead to a Eurasia increasingly under the influence, and perhaps even the control, of the Soviet Union. For we would then find ourselves increasingly shut off from societies that begat and that continue to nourish our culture and institutions—societies our affinity to which has profound moral and psychological significance. The proponents of withdrawal regularly insist that these would not be the results and that those we abandon could be expected to assert themselves. Given their past behavior, though, we can have no assurance of

such an assertion. Instead, they might simply accommodate themselves to Soviet power. Moreover, once they had done so, there
might well be no way of reversing a situation we then would view
with growing dismay. At the very least, the attempt to recover a
position once abandoned would prove costly and dangerous.

Given these considerations, the question posed at the outset
must again be raised. Why the insistent search for alternative
policies toward the Soviet Union? Why the continuing dissatisfaction with a policy that, if its excessive expressions are only
avoided, has not served us badly? One answer is that containment
is inseparable from the continuing competition in arms with all of
the dangers this competition holds out. But the dangers attending
a policy of containment, dangers that persist even though this
policy is given moderate expression, cannot be radically reduced
save through either an overall settlement of the conflict or a withdrawal from it. And whereas the former alternative appears quite
impossible to achieve today, the latter can be undertaken only by
incurring other risks. Even if these other risks are somehow
avoided, we can still have no clear vision of what a postwithdrawal
world would be like and the necessities it would impose.

On the other hand, the dangers arising from the competition in
arms can at least be kept within tolerable bounds by a policy that
permits us to put a limit on them. If our interests are defined
restrictively, if we reject the notion that we must be able to
safeguard every spot on the globe and to counter every Soviet
move, we need not commit ourselves to an open-ended competition
in arms. Whether on the strategic or on the conventional level, it
will remain largely within our power to determine what is necessary for deterrence and for defense. A policy of moderate containment may prove quite compatible with measures of arms control
that substantially reduce those risks any rational foreign policy
must seek to diminish.

The more persisting indictment of containment, however, is
that from the outset this strategy has not lived up to the expectations entertained of it. These expectations, the argument runs,
largely justified the policy. Yet they have not been realized, and
they appear to hold out even less promise today of being realized
than they did in an earlier period. Containment has not led to the
mellowing, let alone to the breakup, of Soviet power that George

Kennan and others once held out as the great goal of policy. It has not forced the Soviet regime to become more inwardly oriented or to concentrate its efforts increasingly on improving the conditions of its people. Instead, the regime appears more expansionist today than in an earlier period. And if it is true that the ideological appeal of the Soviet Union has lost the attractions it once enjoyed, it is also true that this loss has been at least partly compensated for by the growth in Soviet military power. A strategy of containment presently incurs the same difficulties in coping with Soviet power that it has always incurred. The dilemmas of remaining on the permanent defensive are no different today from what they were yesterday. Nor are they less trying in the moral and material burdens they continue to impose.

This indictment of containment need not be labored. By this time, it is familiar enough. Moreover, it is in large measure true. The relevant question it must raise, however, is: what follows from it? Clearly, containment has not met all of the expectations that were widely entertained of it. To this extent, it must be judged a failure. But it does not follow that containment must otherwise be judged a failure, that the many consequences attending containment, which are at least in part the result of this policy, must also be seen as undesirable. Nor does it follow that there is an alternative policy that would at once redeem the failures of containment while preserving its successes.

The postwar order, we need to remind ourselves, is in large part an order inseparable from containment; with pardonable exaggeration, it may even be considered as the order of containment. It has not been an ideal order in a number of respects. Does this acknowledgment of its imperfection, however, thereby condemn it? For what will soon be four decades, it has brought a measure of prosperity and stability that, if not unprecedented, is quite remarkable. This prosperity and relative peace, it is true, has been achieved only at the price of some injustice. But the same must be said of all orders of which we have experienced.

If this judgment of the postwar order is well taken, why the insistence upon abandoning or even refashioning the policy that forms its principal foundation? It will not do to answer that we cannot go on indefinitely condemned to play a defensive role. We have now played that role for over a third of a century. The argument that we cannot continue to do so must at least show that there has been some intervening development that will now prevent us from doing what we have heretofore done. This development cannot consist of a material balance that has become increasingly unfavorable to us. For if the economies of Western Europe are added to our own, the material balance has instead become more favorable than before.

A defensive role admittedly carries with it certain liabilities, and nothing is gained either by denying this or by attempting to pass over it lightly. Despite its liabilities, a defensive role is the role we have occupied from the beginning, and it can be changed only at considerable risk to the very interests over which we have long contended with the Soviet Union. The issue, then, is not simply the liabilities incurred by such a defensive role but the risks of moving away from this role when weighed against the liabilities attending it. Those who worry over its dilemmas should also worry over the reaction of allies to the attempt to move away from a defensive role.

Exaggeration of Dilemmas

There is the added consideration that the magnitude and seriousness of the dilemmas of defensiveness depend in large measure on what one is defending. These dilemmas may prove quite severe, as we have already discovered, if a containment policy is followed that requires reacting to virtually every move of an adversary, without much regard for where the move occurs and the promise of an enduring gain. Then, indeed, almost any move appears ominous, and almost any loss seems to hold out a threat to the larger whole. But the perceptions of global containment need not be endorsed, and the calculus of interest informing it need not be accepted. From the perspective of a more modest form of containment, the dilemmas of a defensive strategy are at least attenuated. Occasional losses in peripheral areas of interest may be taken in stride, for there is no compulsion to see them either as posing a direct threat to vital interests or as signaling a pattern of losses that, by virtue of their cumulative effect, cannot be permitted. Nor is there reason to assume that we must prove incapable of taking advantage of such opportunities as may and will arise. Indeed, the history of our competition with the Soviet Union shows that we have exploited a number of opportunities, even if we have been on occasion rather slow in recognizing them. A policy of moderate containment must remain alert to those openings that will continue to arise in the contest with our great adversary. Soviet gains, we should by now appreciate, are not irrevocable.

The dilemmas of defending the postwar order have been regularly exaggerated both by critics and by supporters of containment. Yet the defense of this order does pose dilemmas that may seem very nearly intractable, and we can see them only too clearly in the current crisis of the Atlantic Alliance. The root cause of this crisis is as easy to diagnose as a cure is difficult to find. The American security guarantee to Western Europe has become increasingly suspect now that we no longer enjoy strategic superiority over the Soviet Union. In the circumstances of today, when the Soviet Union enjoys strategic parity with this country, the credibility of the American guarantee depends, in the last analysis, upon our complete identification with Western Europe. Yet such identification, assuming as it does a community of fate, defies experience. Nations have seldom, if ever, so identified with others, even though the consequences of doing so in the past were far less portentous than they are today. That they will make this identification today cannot but provoke a deep skepticism.

This skepticism defines the essential predicament of the Western Alliance. Although it may be moderated, there is no apparent way by which it can be resolved. Even its moderation must depend upon circumstances that are by no means within our control alone. It is now, and will remain, in the power of the Soviet Union to make members of the Alliance only too aware of their common condition. In a period of détente, this awareness may be subdued. In a period of rising tension, it may reach a level that proves very nearly debilitating to the Alliance.

Must one conclude that the security relationship we have entertained with Europe since World War II has now become unsustainable, or very nearly so, and that the capital the Alliance has lived on in the past is now reaching depletion? Not quite. What does seem clear is that the Alliance will prove increasingly difficult to maintain in reasonably good health and particularly in those circumstances where it is most apparently needed. If this is the case, we must recognize that, however necessary the Atlantic Alliance continues to be, we are now faced with the prospect of occupying an increasingly disadvantageous position in Europe with respect to the Soviet Union. A rising level of political intervention by Moscow in Western Europe, and particularly in West Germany, will be countered by the United States only with difficulty.

Even if the pessimists are right in contending that the Alliance is visibly disintegrating today and that the only serious question is the rate of disintegration and the period of grace left, the question of time is critical because it is also apparent that the Soviet empire in Eastern Europe is undergoing serious strain. This process of competitive decadence, as it has been wittily dubbed, may continue for some time to come. In the interim, the importance of defending the postwar order is clear.

A policy of containment must concentrate today on the same areas that initially formed its principal objects of concern. Western Europe (and Japan) apart, our vital interests extend no further than to the Persian Gulf. In the developing world, by contrast, we can afford to take a relaxed view of the competition with the Soviet Union. We can afford to do so not only because the disparate interests we have there are of a different order of magnitude, but also because the Soviet Union can seriously jeopardize them only by an effort that it has neither the resources nor the apparent disposition to make. The great fear of a generation ago, of a developing world that would fall under the increasing influence and even control of the Soviet Union, can no longer be entertained with any real semblance of plausibility.

Containment has not been significantly challenged in recent years by developments in the Third World. It has been challenged in those areas that have always formed its true centers of gravity. In the course of the 1970s, the military balance evolved in a manner increasingly favorable to the Soviet Union. How favorable this change was in fact, has been and continues to be a matter of considerable controversy and uncertainty. What is clear, however, is that the Soviet Union did substantially improve upon its military position relative to the West and that this improvement found a distinct response in Western Europe. At the same time, the power and position of the West in the Persian Gulf witnessed an erosion of striking proportion. The apparent vulnerability of this position by the close of the past decade was brought home — and with dramatic force — by two developments: the Soviet invasion of Afghanistan and the outbreak of war between Iraq and Iran. Whereas the former event was seen to point to the threat held to Western interests in the Gulf by Soviet military power, the latter event was seen to point to the threat held out by indigenous forces.

Implications of Recent Events

It was in the coalescence of these developments that the American security problem was defined in 1980 and must continue to be defined today. Yet in the course of only a very brief period, the dimensions of that problem have turned markedly for the better. They have done so, to begin with, because it is now apparent that the military balance is no longer moving in the direction it moved throughout the preceding decade. Although a present accounting of the balance might show little change since 1980, perceptions of the emerging balance have significantly altered in consequence of the burgeoning American rearmament effort. These perceptions are the "futures" on which present political capital is invested. Their effects are even now registered and they will be registered more apparently in the immediate years ahead.

Unless the Atlantic Alliance breaks apart as a result of the disagreements now wracking it, the Soviet Union faces the prospect of an emerging power balance that will eventually reduce its leverage in Western Europe. That leverage is also likely to be reduced by the weakened Soviet position in Eastern Europe. In 1980, the momentous developments that have since unfolded in Poland had only begun and their significance was still far from apparent. Even today, the full significance of these developments remains unclear. What is quite clear, however, is that the Soviet empire in Eastern Europe has been challenged as it has not been challenged since Yugoslavia's break in 1948. At the very least, the Soviet Union must now view with rising apprehension the security of its military forces and lines of communication in the area most critical to its European position.

In the Persian Gulf, the improvement in the West's position is even more apparent. In 1980, a combination of developments both internal and external to the Gulf presented a picture of almost unrelieved bleakness. Today, while the security of Western access to the oil of the Gulf is still far from assured, the threat to this vital interest has clearly receded. The international oil market has dramatically changed, and the power of the major Gulf producers has declined. Soviet arms have yet to subdue Afghan resistance, and the prospects are not bright that they will soon do so. The war between Iraq and Iran has not led to the interruption of needed oil supplies. Nor has it sparked another explosive increase in oil prices, though it has had a marginal effect in keeping prices from falling further than they have. The fear that the pattern of events in Iran would quickly spread throughout the Gulf has not been borne out. Despite a revolution and a war, the Gulf has otherwise been remarkably stable. Finally, the striking assertion in 1982 of Israel's continued military supremacy over the Arab world has combined with lowered expectations of the power conferred by oil to produce a much less assertive stance toward the West in most of the Arab world.

These are, in summary, the developments that have produced a marked improvement in the American security position since the turn of the decade. The decline in that position occurring throughout the 1970s has come to an end. Indeed, it now may even be moving in a reverse direction. If so, the threat to vital interests many of us perceived only yesterday has already begun to recede. It would be tragic if we were now to prove unwilling to leave well enough alone, particularly by attempts to speed up disintegrative processes that, though they hold out great hope in the long run, present considerable danger in the immediate period ahead.

Is there evidence today that the American public is prepared to leave well enough alone? The argument has been made against the policy of moderate containment urged in these pages that it cannot be sustained, if only because it does not respond to ingrained American attitudes toward foreign policy. In its cool appeal to interest, moderate containment, according to this argument, lacks the appeal required for a foreign policy that for all its "moderation" must still prove quite demanding. Then, too, in its need to come to terms with ambiguities, such a policy assumes a domestic environment that is more sophisticated and more compliant than in America. Whatever the abstract merit of moderate containment, this argument concludes, it cannot meet the domestic requirements of foreign policy.

There is much to be said for these considerations. The American experience in foreign policy does appear to underscore the need for a broader rationale for policy than moderate containment provides, if the public is to give its sustained support. Yet this broader rationale must threaten to turn into the kind of ideological crusade that is, in turn, incompatible with the temper and objectives of moderate containment. In this environment, policy becomes the captive of dogma until such time as political reality forces, at great price, its abandonment.

Yet this need not be the fate of American foreign policy and there is growing evidence that this analysis no longer defines the American tradition and outlook to nearly the degree it once did. In recent years, the public has supported neither withdrawal (and indifference) nor confrontation. Instead, the public has given a number of indications that it is not only prepared to accept a policy roughly approximating one of moderate containment, but that it does so for reasons not unlike those elaborated here.

Whether or not this estimate of the public's outlook today is overly sanguine, one thing does seem quite clear. There is no public consensus for a policy that goes beyond moderate containment. This being so, the effective choice at present is one between moderate containment, with all its difficulties and drawbacks, and a last fling at an activism that, in the great demands it must make and the great risks it must run, will lead again to disillusionment and the urge to withdraw.

6

ERNST B. HAAS

On Hedging Our Bets: Selective Engagement with the Soviet Union

America has sought to understand and come to terms with the Soviet Union for sixty-six years. We still have no agreed-upon understanding, and we have yet to come to terms with the Soviet phenomenon. It is almost a platitude to assert that American policy toward the Soviets has been both reactive and inconsistent, swinging from implacable hostility to the desire for mutual accommodation, and back again. If our Soviet policy were just a piece of our overall stance toward the world, this might be tolerable. Since the late 1940s, however, our overall posture toward the world has been largely shaped by our attitudes toward the Soviets; our foreign and defense policies have been subordinated to our shifting fears, hopes, and hatreds regarding Moscow's plans.

Toward a Strategy of Selective Engagement

I propose a global strategy of "selective engagement" for the
United States. This policy avoids the complete engagement with
all countries and issues that containment strategies have considered necessary for hemming in the Soviets. It takes for granted
that the expense and risk of containment are greater than the
benefits likely to be obtained. Selective engagement also avoids
the assumptions and implications of détente and entente, because
these strategies are based on the unprovable premise that Soviet
intentions are benign. It argues for doing what is necessary to protect democracy where it now exists and to work for a future world
less likely to be plagued by war and poverty. It scales down and
redefines some American world order values, recognizing that we
cannot, without risking our own ruin, continue the attempt to
mold the world in our image. Selective engagement aims at the
delinking of issues, at leading us into an international order in
which policies are no longer seen largely as means for containing
Communism in general and the Soviets in particular. Selective
engagement is a means for loosening up a system that is too
tightly coupled for safety.

This strategy must serve the values we profess. What follows is
my subjective ranking of the principles that ought to govern the
world in which, realistically, we can expect to live in the next
generation. Neither our values nor the world order they imply approximate the utopia of a denuclearized welfare world; the present
is not the time for crusades.

The avoidance of war, especially of nuclear war, heads the list.
However, an aversion to war does not imply unwillingness to wage
it if necessary for self-defense. Nor does it preclude toleration of
wars among other nations, preferably at some distance. Second, we
should be committed to the enhancement of basic human welfare
everywhere, particularly with respect to health, education, housing,
and food. Third, we should protect democratic institutions—civil
and political rights—in nations where they now exist, while supporting the growth of such institutions in nations where they show
promise. Fourth, we should be committed to the protection of the
global environment and to the better use of nonrenewable natural
resources. Finally, we ought to favor the economic modernization

of the underdeveloped countries while also managing the industrial adjustments necessary in the developed countries in order to accommodate the industrial growth of the South. The simultaneous transfer of resources to the developing countries and the protection of existing living standards in the North may call for policies of economic management at variance with our penchant for free markets and unrestricted private enterprise.

My argument for a different strategy toward the Soviet Union is based on certain postulates, or attitudes toward and judgments about our era in history, that go beyond values. I state them baldly here and justify them later in this essay. My prescription for a strategy of selective engagement depends entirely on the persuasiveness of these postulates:

- Because we have no agreed-upon understanding of Soviet plans and motives, we cannot be certain that there is a "Soviet threat." Yet we can no more be certain that there is no such threat.

- The undeniable growth throughout the world of various types of Marxism is not necessarily the same thing as Soviet expansionism. The Soviet Union is not "conquering the Third World."

- However, the future of democracy is very much in doubt in areas lacking the European cultural tradition (with certain exceptions to be explored). Apart from twenty-five or thirty countries, there is no "free world."

- A tightly coupled world is a dangerous world. If all issues on the global agenda—from nuclear weapons to environmental protection, from human rights to the rights of whales, from Patagonia to Greenland and from Beirut to Bali—hinge on our perception of Moscow's plans, then a crisis anywhere and over anything can trigger a full-scale war. A safer world requires the decoupling of issues.

- In a decoupled world, there is a chance for the survival of democracy even if the overall power of the Soviet Union or of Communism in other countries were to increase. Acceptance of Soviet equality need not mean surrender on the installment plan.

The survival of our values is threatened by two great perils: the presence of a superpower antagonistic to our beliefs and our dependence on weapons that will destroy us if we use them to defend our values. Selective engagement is a bet that we can survive despite these conditions because we are not sure about Soviet motives. But we would hedge the bet by decoupling policies, sacrificing pawns, and reengaging our energies on other issues elsewhere in the world by not betting everything on a containment that relies on nuclear deterrence. I begin my justification of these postulates with an evenhanded recapitulation of Soviet-American relations.

A History of Changing Moods

American policy toward the Soviets began with an effort to destabilize the revolutionary regime installed by Lenin. When this failed we moved to nonrecognition and moral condemnation, mixed with episodes of humanitarian relief and private investment in the rapidly industrializing Soviet economy. The advent of the New Deal brought diplomatic recognition and the settlement of outstanding financial claims while arm's-length relations continued to rule the day in other fields. World War II turned the cool atmosphere of mutual toleration into an overt alliance, an arrangement that lasted only as long as two common enemies provided an immediate threat. The Allies failed to agree on how to arrange the world after the defeat of the Axis and the Cold War followed, triggered by our view that Soviet hegemony in Eastern Europe meant the resurgence of Russian imperialism under Communist auspices, and by their impression that capitalist encirclement was being revived. Hot proxy wars in Greece and Korea followed, as did the formation of two tightly organized military-economic blocs. We denounced the Soviets as totalitarians bent on conquering the world, and they denounced us as imperialists determined to exploit the world. However, since by the end of the 1950s both sides possessed deadly nuclear arsenals, actual relations proved to be a good deal more cautious than the violent rhetoric suggested.

Serious efforts to limit and defuse the arms race began in the Eisenhower administration, as did tacit efforts to stake out and respect spheres of interests. Both sides, even while developing the missiles that were to create the condition of nuclear deterrence, sought to limit the likelihood of nuclear and of massive conventional wars. This trend was soon reversed, however, as Khrushchev reopened the German issue, exaggerated the Soviet missile buildup, demanded NATO's withdrawal from Berlin, and eventually installed missiles in Cuba. The Kennedy administration, at the same time, launched a massive new arms procurement policy while Khrushchev, despite the bluster, reduced the Soviet arms budget. The strong reaction of the Kennedy administration to the Cuban missiles brought about a Soviet retreat. It also created an atmosphere in which serious measures designed to prevent a repetition of this episode were launched. These included the first détente with its emphasis on arms control and increased professional and technical contacts between the two powers.

Johnson and Brezhnev continued these steps toward mutual accommodation, but they soon encountered a serious hurdle: the future of the Third World. America interpreted socialist revolutions and civil wars as evidence of continuing Soviet expansionism, a belief that led us eventually to embrace the domino theory and to fight in Vietnam—the third proxy war between the superpowers (not counting Arab-Israeli wars). For the Soviets, however, unrest in the Third World was said to express the continued unfolding of the contradictions inherent in capitalist society that would end in the overthrow of imperialism. Soviet leaders declared their commitment to peaceful coexistence with the West, *except* with regard to the duty of aiding Third World "liberation" movements.

While this disagreement slowed the progress of détente, renewed hostility never reached the rhetorical and diplomatic extremes of the 1950s. We sought to enlist Soviet aid in finding a negotiated solution in Vietnam; relations in Europe did not worsen; arms control agreements were concluded while massive military modernization programs were launched by the Soviets; and in the Middle East, where American and Soviet allies fought each other in 1967, 1970, and 1973, Washington and Moscow remained in close touch and probably moderated the policies of their clients. Moreover, the Nixon-Kissinger détente was launched while the United States intensified attacks on the Soviet Union's Vietnamese ally; the new détente, and the "linkage" policies designed to advance it, were fashioned in the midst of a proxy war. If war is the continuation of politics with an admixture of other ns, the Basic Principles Agreement of 1972, in which Nixon and Brezhnev sought to define the ground rules of détente, came to be the continuation of war moderated by a few notions of mutual abstention.

American withdrawal from Southeast Asia augured well for the second détente, but it ended over the same disagreement that bedeviled the first: disagreement over the Third World, this time in Africa. Still, before the Cold War resumed the second détente had resulted in the resurgence of Western agricultural and technological sales to Eastern Europe, deep financial involvement with the Council for Mutual Economic Aid (COMECON) countries, and spasmodic Soviet compliance with Western requests for the emigration of dissidents. But the promise of linkage proved illusory. President Carter's hesitation between continued accommodation and attacks on Communism (under the guise of the human rights campaign) was not resolved until the Soviet intervention in Afghanistan tipped the scales once more in favor of one view common since 1917—that the Soviet Union is determined to make the world over in its own image. Despite massive changes, American perception and policy seem to reenact older views and patterns. The wheel turns, but it does not advance.

Why does the Soviet Union, unlike any other major state, evoke reactions ranging from accommodation and acceptance as an equal to the desire to eliminate an implacable enemy? One answer is that Communism married to military power poses a threat to American conceptions of world order, a threat perceived as much more serious than the German and Japanese challenges in 1941. The second answer complements the first: we have never been able to decide whether it is Communism as such, Communism as an instrument of great power expansion, or the expansionism of that great power that threatens us. We are unable to decide in part because we cannot agree on an explanation for Soviet behavior.

Each of the following explanations of Soviet conduct is accepted by some segment of the American public. Many think the Soviets have a messianic faith in the mission of their country to spread Communism, peacefully if possible but by force of arms and subversion if necessary. Others argue that the Communist Party of the Soviet Union is a conservative bureaucracy, painfully aware of its lack of legitimacy in the eyes of its own population, and therefore eager to make up in foreign policy successes for its failings in domestic policy. Still others insist that Communism and domestic policy concerns explain little; that the Soviet Union is a superpower that behaves like any other superpower; and that its striving for security and empire is merely the mirror image of America's. And some revisionist historians argue that Soviet policy on the whole is no more than a defense against the encroachments of American expansionism since 1945—that is, against the neo-imperialism of late capitalism. The brutal fact is that we simply do not know with certainty why Soviet policy is what it is.

Six Strategies for Dealing with the Soviet Union

This essay is dedicated to the proposition that we ought to have a consistent strategy for living in a nuclear world. A strategy that could assure survival as well as the victory of our values would be greatly preferable to the bits of alternating strategies we have followed in the past. In the history of Soviet-American relations we can trace pieces of five separate strategies, each with its own characteristic attitudes and assumptions. A sixth one exists in principle. I label the strategies *rollback, containment, selective containment, détente with rapprochement, entente with mutual appeasement,* and *superpower condominium.*[1]

A strategy of *rolling back* Soviet power and world Communism is associated with implacable ideological opposition to the Marxist world view. It assumes that the global appeal of Marxism can be reversed at an acceptable cost by taking advantage of weakness, dissension, and unrest in the Soviet bloc and among the bloc's Third World allies. Many Americans professed such a commitment in the 1920s, the early 1950s, and again since 1980. Yet the strategy was never fully articulated, let alone implemented. The cost was not considered acceptable, not even in 1956, 1968, and 1982, when the opportunities for doing so seemed most promising, and not even under Republican administrations rhetorically committed to something approximating a rollback. As an overall strategy—as opposed to working for an occasional reversal of alliances in the Third World—rollback does not commend itself in a nuclear era.

Containment was American strategy during the early 1950s. It accepts the existence of the Soviet Union as a fact of history while deploring the implications of that fact. It seeks to freeze the boundaries of the Soviet realm by all appropriate means short of nuclear war, and hopes for the "mellowing" of Communism and of totalitarian institutions as the weaknesses of the system become apparent to its own citizens. The Reagan administration seems to espouse containment in this form and it adds a dose of rollback as well. "Project Democracy" aims to nurture democratic forces in Eastern Europe; by distinguishing policies toward Eastern Europe from the containment of the Soviet Union itself, the Reagan administration seeks to divide the Eastern bloc.

Selective containment moderates the strategy of complete containment by, in effect, sacrificing certain parts of the world because they are considered relatively unimportant to American interests. Selective containment reluctantly tolerates Third World populist-collectivist-totalitarian movements and governments when they do not directly threaten us. While the integrity of defenses and economic health in Western Europe and the Far East continue to be considered of the highest importance, the fate of specific countries in Asia and Africa is considered vital only if their adherence to the Soviet bloc also implies a threat to resources or military access. Whether all or parts of Latin America should be considered within the perimeter of selective containment is a matter of recurrent debate. Selective containment was American strategy from 1956 until 1963, and many advocate it today.

All three strategies imply a set of American beliefs that casts the Soviet Union as the chief enemy of world order. The international system is seen as unstable, polarized, and tightly linked. A setback in one area, or even in such functional fields as trade, money, and technology, is believed to diminish the power of the West in all others. International politics, in this view, is a zero-sum game. Every part of the "free world" is potentially important. All commitments to the "free world" must be honored lest the United States be seen as devoid of will. Negotiations with the Soviets must be conducted to prevent our being duped and to demonstrate American determination to be strong. All conflicts of interest with the Soviet Union are indivisible. In the long run, either the "free world" or Communism must win.

Détente and *entente* both imply a different set of beliefs. These strategies call for active measures designed to defuse confrontations, to transcend the Cold War, and to find means for peaceful coexistence between the two powers. The Soviets become a limited adversary as the international system is seen as multipolar and more stable, and as issues and geographical areas are no longer viewed as one seamless web of conflicting interests. Not all commitments are then considered equally vital. Third World countries are not necessarily "with us" or "against us." Negotiations with the Soviets become more businesslike, less designed to display American machismo. Issues are decoupled and dealt with separately even if they remain linked in the minds of key strategists. Détente, entente, and even a superpower condominium aim at the creation of ground rules for a more peaceful system of international relations.

Détente is not, however, designed to settle all outstanding quarrels or provide for a shared world view among the antagonists. It does aim at the systematic reduction of tensions that could lead to war. This requires rapprochement in the sense that timely agreements must be sought about specific grievances that might trigger war. Détente with rapprochement was America's objective from 1963 until 1976, although we did not abandon selective containment in Southeast Asia until our defeat in Vietnam. Nor did we forego the exploitation of targets of opportunity in the Middle East, which amounted to a rollback of the Soviets in Egypt. Some call the Nixon-Kissinger strategy of détente with rapprochement a path of "collaborative competition" because of the continued presence of zero-sum attitudes.

Yet it was the intent of that strategy to make even selective containment unnecessary in the long run. Détente was expected to lead to *entente with mutual appeasement.* The two superpowers were to recognize their joint stake in a peaceful world and live by a code of conduct for making it real. Kissinger knew that the competitive element in the détente strategy would not yield to the collaborative aspect unless the Soviets were gradually persuaded that they could be secure in the existing world order. Hence there had to be assurances and incentives in order to convince the Soviet leadership that the status quo could serve their interests, that a classical balance-of-power system would be preferable to the Soviet penchant for seeing the world as an unstable "correlation of forces" that could be made to tilt toward Moscow. These incentives took the form of a large number of agreements, ranging from trade and scientific exchange programs to the effort to spell out basic rules of international conduct to avoid confrontations. Mutual appeasement implied American acquiescence to some Soviet demands in exchange for similar concessions on their part. Fifty-eight understandings were concluded between 1969 and 1974, over half of all the Soviet-American agreements made since 1933.

Entente with mutual appeasement was American strategy between 1934 and 1945; it was also the elusive goal of Nixon and Kissinger. Why did it fail to come to fruition? The answer is that appeasement was seen as one-sided by each participant. American leaders increasingly felt that the United States made the concessions and offered the incentives while the Soviets rearmed, expanded into Africa, and encouraged the Vietnamese. The Soviets apparently felt similarly about American forays into the Middle East and about our unwillingness to agree that aid to national liberation movements is consistent with détente. Successful entente requires *mutual* appeasement; by 1975 even Henry Kissinger had conceded his failure to persuade the Soviets of his vision.

Still another, quite different, strategy is possible: an agreement between the superpowers to split the world into two spheres of interests and to rule it jointly — a *condominium*. The bipolar division of the world would be made final and peace assured by the agreement of the two rulers not to challenge each other's realms. Concomitantly, the two would agree not to permit the emergence of a third bloc or power. Nuclear proliferation in particular would be repressed and controlled, even if that implied the mounting of surgical strikes against a China, an India, or a South Africa. While the possibility of a condominium has sometimes been discussed — it was said to have been proposed by Brezhnev to Nixon in 1972[2] — it constitutes a perennial fear for conservatives in Western Europe and understandably seems to have preoccupied Mao Ze Dong. In any event, the negotiation and management of a condominium would pose formidable problems. The Pope can hardly be expected to draw another line dividing the two realms.

Local revolutionary situations would be unlikely to disappear even if a line were drawn, and one would have to imagine complete indifference on the part of the superpowers if intervention were to be avoided. Nuclear proliferation has gone so far as to necessitate a number of massive surgical strikes to make it fade away; it is unlikely that the strikes would be delegated to the Israeli air force even in a condominium arrangement. We had better exclude this strategy from our repertory of options.

The other five strategies remain as possibilities. Should any of them be chosen by us? I do not believe so. Rollback and containment assume that the Soviet Union is inherently expansive; détente and entente are based on the supposition that the Soviets seek to live in peace and equality with us. Yet, as I shall show, we do not know what motivates Soviet policy. Hence it is not safe to choose on the basis of these assumptions and suppositions. All five strategies focus on the Soviet Union as the centerpiece of world politics, as the lodestar of all American concerns. A better strategy cannot confine itself to counting the countries in the democratic and the totalitarian columns and fashioning military policies to protect the democracies. It must integrate all values that we profess, whether they serve democracy and deterrence or not. The fragmented approaches in our past policies fail to meet this criterion because they confound the Soviet threat with Communism in general. The articulation of a new strategy of *selective engagement* demands that we think clearly about Soviet motivations, state and rank our own values, and become conscious about our limitations in realizing them. Having done so, we must hedge our bets.

What Do the Soviets Want?

We knew what Hitler wanted, at least after a period of puzzlement and thrashing around; but after Lenin, Stalin, Khruschev, and Brezhnev we still cannot be sure what the Soviets want. It seems unlikely that Andropov will enlighten us. The perennially most popular school of thought in the United States argues that Soviet conduct is due to an ideological commitment to establish Communism as a global system by way of the outward expansion of the Soviet state. I answer that even though there is evidence that some Soviet leaders do believe in such an ideology, Soviet conduct has never conformed to the theory sufficiently to establish it as a valid explanation of policy.

If the argument that the Soviets have an inherent drive toward aggression were valid, it would be very difficult to account for their failure to do a number of things. In the following instances the Soviets had the capability but failed to:

- reassert full control over Romania and Albania;

- insist on domestic and foreign economic policies in Hungary and Poland patterned on their own;

- remove Chinese nuclear installations in the 1960s, or escalate Sino-Soviet fighting in 1969–70;

- provide fuller support for Vietnam in its war with China;

- prolong American involvement in Vietnam, rather than encouraging negotiations after 1969;

- provide energetic support for Kurdish and/or Azeri secession in Iran;

- provide energetic support for socialist governments in Chile and Central America;

- provide much more consistent and plentiful nonmilitary support for Kwame Nkrumah in Ghana in the 1960s and for Sékou Touré in Guinea in the 1970s;

- provide more efficient military support for African groups likely to interrupt Western access to key minerals (in Zaire, Niger, Zambia, and especially in South Africa);

- take a more flexible negotiating stance toward allies of the United States who might be wooed away (Japan especially); and

- take a more flexible negotiating stance in arms control discussions, promising to cut back and then cheating instead of taking the ceilings seriously.

The Soviet realm has not expanded territorially since 1948, with the exception of the Afghan adventure. Its hegemony in Eastern Europe is weaker today than it was in the aftermath of the Second World War. Soviet influence waxed and waned outside Europe in mirror-image fashion to American influence. But Communism as a mode of government has spread to Africa, Asia, and Latin America, though not necessarily as an expression of a Soviet imperial drive.

There is a more subtle way of making the argument for the inherent aggressiveness of the Soviets.[3] We may safely assume that Soviet pronouncements contain a heavy dose of ex post facto justification and some plain propaganda to legitimate the leadership of the moment. Even after we allow for this, there remains an impressive residue of Soviet concepts that seems to serve as a consistent bedrock of discussion and analysis, such as "the world correlation of forces," "two camps," and "proletarian internationalism." Consistent use of these concepts suggests that the Soviets do have a view of permanent struggle. But since the exact nature of the moment's "world correlation of forces" must always be a subject of debate and judgment, the Soviets can think in terms of gradations, of increments, of advance-and-retreat.

We, on the other hand, are at a disadvantage because we tend to fall back on all-or-nothing categories: conflict or cooperation, peace or war, détente or confrontation. Our reliance on the concept of the "balance of power" is static as contrasted to the Soviets' "world correlation of forces"; our "defense of the free world" is a weak and reactive counterpoise to the dynamic notion of the "two camps," in no small measure because the members of our "camp" are a far more mixed lot than those of the Soviet Union's.

Given this difference between Soviet and American modes of analysis, the subtle version of the aggressiveness thesis argues that the Soviet Union cautiously and prudently expands by skillfully manipulating policy measures that stress both cooperation *and* conflict. In this perspective, détente with rapprochement is a tactic for avoiding confrontations while at the same time facilitating the eventual victory of the Communist camp; détente can never be an end in itself for the Soviets. This explanation cannot easily be proved wrong or right. It may hold for a segment of the Soviet leadership, or for all of it at certain times. The history of détente and its failure is an ambiguous story; it does not dispose of the issue. But even if the subtle explanation were correct, we should not draw the inference that the only proper response is a strategy of containment, total or selective.

The major rival to the argument that the Soviets are motivated to expand holds that the Soviet Union is and wishes to be a super-power, concerned essentially with its own security and survival in a world dominated by the classical security dilemma. Ideology here is not seen as an important determinant of policy. The United States (and China) are considered by the Soviets as threatening, as a serious danger to be warded off. If we were to adopt this view of Soviet conduct, we would expect that policies of rolling back or containing Soviet power would be seen by the Soviets as confirm-ing their fears. Policies of détente and entente, however, would provide reassurance that those fears are wrong. This explanation is popular among those who see the wellsprings of Soviet conduct in internal forces and problems, who believe that by influencing the shape of Soviet economic and social policy we can also mold Soviet foreign behavior.

There are two objections to this view. One is empirical. If the Soviets merely wished to be assured that we recognize them as a superpower with legitimate security interests that entitle them to help manage the world's trouble spots, they would not have to devote great energy to asserting the primacy of the Communist Party of the Soviet Union over other Communist and Marxist movements. They would not have to revile Yugoslavia and China as ideological deviants. Nor would they have to train and arm the Palestine Liberation Organization, the Southwest African People's Organization, Joshua Nkomo, Sékou Touré, or Angola's MPLA. There would be no incentive to ship, via Cuba and Nicaragua, arms and supplies to El Salvador, arm first Somalia and then Ethiopia, and continue to give vociferous verbal support to every self-proclaimed national liberation movement from Puerto Rico to the Philippines. This behavior has been consistent since 1945. It cannot be squared with the notion that Soviet mili-tary security dominates policymaking.

The second objection to this explanation is rooted in our ten-dency to analyze Soviet decision-making as the mirror image of our own. We know how our decisions are made and how our leaders calculate. Hence we think Soviet processes are equally un-problematic. We do not allow for the force of divergent concepts, for belief in strong historical processes, and for the possibility that at some level the idea of historical materialism informs behavior.

It is also true that we do not know whether all or only some decisions are so influenced, and whether the concepts are self-correcting at the level of strategic choice as well as for more mundane tactical steps. Our commentators disagree volubly and at length on how such things ought to be interpreted and understood, and how the Soviets reconcile contradictions among their own concepts. Nevertheless, those who believe that "the Soviets are just another superpower" tend not to worry about these conundrums. Their analysis conforms to the following description of the American attitude toward foreign affairs:

You Americans easily forget the price of peace. When you do think up ways by which wars may be prevented, you think you can easily convert your adversaries to the logic which led you to your conclusions. Because you hate arms races you think you can persuade your adversaries to accept projects to bring them to a halt. You "mirror-image" them in your conviction that down deep they harbor the same humanitarian instincts and goals that you do.[4]

These explanations, though popular, represent only the extremes of the possible. There are various mixed explanations that insist that the two extreme theses may be compatible if we consider how the Soviets see the world, instead of being transfixed by our ways of interpreting it.[5] Such mixed perspectives suggest that Soviet policy is both reactive *and* initiatory, alternatively defensive *and* aggressive. They also suggest that, at least under Brezhnev, relations with the United States were to be both cooperative *and* competitive, not one or the other. Everything depends on whether we are talking about arms control, technology transfers, grain sales, emigration, defense budgets, armed assistance to liberation movements, or the situation in the Middle East, Southeast Asia, East Africa, and Central America. Linkages among issues and areas may be explicit in the minds of American leaders; but we should not make the mistake of assuming the acceptance of the same connections in Soviet thinking.

Thus it is possible that Soviet policy in the Middle East is reactive to uncontrollable Arab and Israeli moves, and to the American response to such moves. Yet Soviet policy in Africa and Central America can be initiatory at the same time. The motives of the moment may call for compensating for the failures of Soviet economic planning—implying collaborative moves—while also suggesting that Moscow take advantage of a target of opportunity in Ethiopia or Angola—thus implying conflict. There is no need for the Soviets to opt exclusively for collaboration or conflict as long as the Western response remains open to both. Prudence and restraint can be abandoned when a target of opportunity arises; they can be restored when the American response is overtly and dangerously hostile. Linkage imposed by Washington can be accepted by Moscow when the Soviets reexamine their priorities, at least as long as the structure of economic and technological interdependence remains tenuous. We know that the Soviet leadership is sometimes faction-ridden; we know that there are sharply differing internal priorities. Hence, these commentators say, why assume a uniform and linear form of behavior, or a single mode of thought?

Persuasive as this line of argument undoubtedly is, it does not take us very far in accounting for Soviet behavior. I find it wholly credible that succession crises in the Soviet Union would influence foreign policy, as would shifting domestic priorities and the associated factional struggles. Yet it is a fact that Soviet policy over the long run has been consistently true to its ideology, even if the USSR has been no more militarily aggressive than other major powers in their heydays. These mixed explanations correct overly simple analyses of the mystery without giving us a satisfactory clarification of the mystery itself. They may explain single episodes, but not the historical trajectory of policy. And they are too multifaceted to provide unambiguous explanations of one diagnostically crucial episode: détente in the 1970s.

Détente, and its failure, illustrates our continuing uncertainty about Soviet motivations because it provides ammunition for all the explanations while failing to establish the superiority of any one of them. Did Soviet bad faith cause failure? If so, those who argue that the Soviets merely used détente as a way of catching up and surpassing America may be right. Did American bad faith cause it? If so, then those who argue that bad relations were due to American misunderstanding of Soviet aspirations to secure superpower status have a point. Did mutual misunderstandings about the degree of competition and the extent of collaboration undermine the process? If so, mixed explanations must be brought to bear on the problem.

Unfortunately, we cannot be sure. The two powers did indeed disagree with each other from the start of détente about the issues and areas in which there would be collaboration as opposed to continuing competition — especially with respect to postcolonial struggles in the Third World. Détente, to Western Europe and to Japan, meant permanent collaboration in trade, investment, and arms control; these notions were never equally acceptable to the United States. Linkage of issues aroused expectations in America that were obviously not shared in the Soviet Union. Washington thought that interdependence due to economic ties would increase the Soviet appetite for more butter and fewer guns, thus limiting foreign military activity; the Soviets had quite different plans. They apparently thought that linkage would work toward the loosening of the Western Alliance, and events tended to bear them out. We thought linkage would weaken the Soviet hold on Eastern Europe, but our puny sanctions against Poland and NATO's lackluster response eventually demonstrated the error of our ways. Détente was understood differently in Washington, Moscow, Tokyo, Bonn, and Paris. That much is clear. But what did the Soviets really want: a breathing space for resuming their expansion of influence, or steps toward eventual entente with mutual appeasement?

Soviet policy in the Middle East since 1967 can be read as confirmation of either argument. There were episodes that led American negotiators to conclude that Moscow had no interest in any peaceful settlement; there were many others that support the notion that Moscow sought a *modus vivendi* with Washington to permit a settlement, provided that the coequal role of the Soviet Union were publicly acknowledged. A close reading of the events in Angola and the Horn of Africa suggests that it was not a foregone conclusion that Moscow would manipulate situations so as to favor its clients, because Moscow had good reason to suspect Washington of doing precisely the same thing. The Soviets, after our toleration of repression in Eastern Europe, were entitled to believe that we would not react to the Afghan intervention as we did, since that intervention sought merely to prop up a shaky client. Again, in the repeated crises over the Soviet military presence in Cuba it was not clear whether the United States was attempting a rollback or whether the Soviets were cautiously testing the limits of acceptable penetration into the Caribbean. We still cannot be certain whether the SALT process and the talks for limiting the transfer of conventional arms were aborted because of Soviet or of American second thoughts. And most importantly, it is not yet possible to link decisions in these episodes to specific perceptions and events in the Soviet Union. We have no explanations that can be generally accepted. All we can affirm with certainty is that the Soviets understood détente to mean something other than what we hoped for.

Does Our Ignorance of Soviet Motives Matter?

It seems obvious that we cannot choose a strategy for our foreign policy if we cannot fathom the motives of our main adversary. But is this really so? Some commentators argue that our ignorance need not foreclose choice because many of the things the Soviet Union could accomplish should not really matter to us. The importance of this argument cannot be denied. Even though I do not accept the argument that "it doesn't really matter what they want," I concede that a full knowledge of Soviet motives is not necessary because not all aggressive moves must be a matter of concern. Hence, I wish to present the case for a permissible American indifference to Soviet motives.

What follows is a worst-case scenario. I assume the Soviets have concluded that the global correlation of forces gives them the capability safely to embark on a number of enterprises now perceived by Washington as harmful to American interests. After setting forth these enterprises, I ask how their accomplishment would harm the American national interest.

Take war-making capability. Suppose the Soviets develop a workable antiballistic missile (ABM) system and the capability to eliminate American surveillance and communications satellites, thus making even our submarine-based deterrent forces ineffective. Having neutralized our deterrent, they could attack or threaten Western Europe with conventional forces, leading to the dissolution of NATO. The European Common Market would then be integrated with COMECON, though the Western European countries would remain formally sovereign. Having accomplished this, the Soviets then would offer us a nonaggression pact, promising to maintain correct and normal commercial relations and to respect American private property in Europe. Western Europe would become nonaligned and retain a limited capacity for self-defense. NATO would disappear, but in other respects things would remain much the same as before.

What might then happen in other parts of the world? China now would have to make its peace with the Soviet Union, recognizing the finality of its borders in Asia and the moral authority of the CPSU, but domestically it could continue much as before. We assume further that China would not oppose the consolidation of the world socialist system. Japan would now have to choose between maintaining its alliance with the United States and continuing to rely on trade within the Northern Hemisphere in general, or embarking on an independent policy of massive rearmament and penetration in Southeast Asia, or opting for a close partnership with China. Members of the Association of Southeast Asian Nations (ASEAN) would face the same unpleasant choices as Japan, made worse for them by the fact that a united Greater Vietnam would now be fully integrated into a Soviet-led Communist bloc. Eventually, India and Pakistan would also have to bend their policies of official nonalignment; either they would pursue a nuclear arms strategy immediately and seek to distance themselves from the Soviets, or they would be forced to join them.

In Africa, the Soviets would simply continue to support left-leaning governments and movements, especially if they confronted their more conservative neighbors. There would be no need to interfere with European and American purchases of minerals, though the increased Soviet leverage for influencing this trade is obvious. In the Caribbean and Central America the Soviets could then safely continue their current policy of permitting Cuba to support insurgent movements and leftist governments and of seeking closer economic and diplomatic ties with any regime willing to reciprocate. That Mexico, Venezuela, and a number of the Caribbean islands might then seek such ties at the expense of relations with the United States seems obvious. There would almost certainly be an increasing Soviet military presence. And in South America the Soviets might merely exploit such targets of opportunity as presented themselves by virtue of normal domestic unrest without having to go out of their way to establish bases or special access. The Western Hemisphere would gradually cease to be the preserve of the United States.

More dramatic changes would seem to be in store for the Middle East. Lacking a credible nuclear deterrent, the United States would have much more difficulty extending its protective umbrella over Israel than at present, and Israel would seek nuclear capabilities — if the Soviets can be imagined to permit this. More likely, energetic Soviet support for the Arabs would force the kind of settlement on Israel (assuming the Soviets wished to avoid a war) that all Israeli governments have desperately sought to avoid. Arab governments now leaning toward the United States would then face the same unpleasant choices as the countries of Southeast Asia.

Would such developments threaten the United States? While the might of the Soviet Union would eclipse ours, we would not simply disappear from the scene. While Communism would surely expand as a principle of social and economic organization, it would not suddenly engulf all other forms of organized existence. Soviet hegemony would certainly change the world for the worse and trigger changes in our lives we could not easily square with our values. Yet many would prefer such an outcome to a nuclear exchange. Our worst-case scenario is unacceptable only to people who would unequivocally prefer "freedom"—political life as we lead it now—to "peace"—the subordination of that life to the avoidance of massive violence and destruction.

My reasoning here takes for granted that the global political and economic system is tightly coupled—that events in one part of the world have inevitable consequences everywhere else, and that diplomatic and military success or failure engenders a proportionate gain or loss in economic well-being. A major expansion of Soviet influence anywhere is thought to engender a decline in American influence everywhere. Past and present American policies have been predicated on the validity of this assumption. What happens if we take the world to be weakly coupled and the course of action less obviously determined? Scenarios are mindstretchers, not certified descriptions of the future. The strategy of selective engagement I propose rejects several of the assumptions built into the scenario.

I do not believe that the motives imputed to the Soviets are incontrovertibly correct. Nor do I believe that all aspects of international relations are as tightly linked to the preservation of American technological superiority as I have suggested. A fallacious belief in overly tight coupling proved to be one of the reasons for the failure of détente. Trade, investment, human rights, the use of the oceans, and the political future of many parts of the world are far more autonomous from the Soviet-American military balance than was suggested.

For these reasons, tolerating ambiguity about Soviet motives — for which I am arguing — need *not* imply surrender on the installment plan. Our choice need *not* be "freedom" or "peace." In the short run, there is no alternative to maintaining a credible nuclear deterrent. This does require that we guard against Soviet technological breakthroughs of the kind imagined in our scenario and prevent the one-sided obsolescence of our deterrent capability. We also must maintain the present deterrent value of NATO and encourage Japan to upgrade its defenses. On the other hand, a strategy of selective engagement can dispense with the continuous upgrading of our defenses, with the search for ever more expensive technological fixes — provided the Soviet Union can be persuaded to follow the same course. Hence such arms control measures as bilateral freezes are quite consistent with selective engagement.

For the long run, I am persuaded that a stable Soviet-American security relationship cannot be achieved by means of two invulnerable nuclear deterrents in *perpetual* confrontation.[6] But I do believe in maintaining a minimal perimeter of joint defense planning, under which we continue to underwrite the security of the part of the world that matters most to us; this perimeter includes Western Europe, Japan, South Korea, and the Pacific. But why commit ourselves also to maintaining American influence in the Third World, as argued for by devotees of rollback, containment, and even détente? Soviet power in Africa may, or may not, endanger access to natural resources; but it will not pose a military threat to the United States. The same may be said of Vietnamese power in Southeast Asia. The circumstances under which Cuban influence in the Caribbean poses a military threat to us require careful analysis; Marxist victories in Surinam, Grenada, and Nicaragua do not necessarily threaten our way of life. Crudely put, my argument says: who cares what happens in Ethiopia, Laos, or El Salvador? Selective engagement is committed to restraining Soviet power, not Communism everywhere in the Third World.

Why the United States Can No Longer Dominate

When American values and preferences are contrasted with the long list of demands made by other countries, America is properly described as a conservative power, a defender of the status quo. Because we are stronger and richer than other countries, and because the existing world order was shaped in large measure by us, it can come as no surprise that American policy is essentially reactive and defensive. It has much to defend and it must therefore react to challengers, to states that prefer a different or- der — about 125 of them.

The defense of our values is becoming more costly and more risky. Hence we must define our values modestly, and limit our- selves to what is essential for protecting our own and our allies' freedom while also maintaining peace. And we must do this in full recognition that the world is not going our way.

I am pessimistic about democracy and capitalism as enduring institutions. I want to protect democracy where it has roots; I despair of finding new converts. I fear that free-market economies have served their purposes and will find a hospitable soil neither in the First World nor in the Third. The dominant role of the state in certain Third World nations is a fact. Few people are committed to its demise. In Africa and parts of Asia where the state remains more fiction than fact, the trend is toward building states, not self- reliant voluntary groups and entrepreneurs. Economies free from state regulation have long been a tonic for nostalgia rather than a fact of life in the First World. I find it difficult to believe that the strains of industrial adjustment, of more integrated welfare policies, and of inflation and unemployment will leave more than faint traces of an idealized capitalism in the years ahead. If we wish to serve individual human welfare we must make our peace with these trends. If we wish to create a safer world in which we can coexist with the Soviet Union in relative peace we must so con- struct our overall foreign policy as to serve these values safely. This task requires the decoupling of the major economic and human rights issues from the Cold War setting. Considering the realities now confronting policies designed to enforce old-fashioned containment, retrenchment is inevitable.

One reality is domestic. The political culture of America is inhospitable to the implementation of any long-range international strategy. General Marshall knew his countrymen when he urged that we wage World War II as rapidly as possible, with overwhelming force, and toward the goal of the enemy's unconditional surrender, because he feared that the country did not have the stomach for a long and indecisive war that might have to end with protracted negotiations. American world order values are conservative as compared with those of the Third World and the Soviets, but that does not mean that American institutions and public opinion are willing to bear the burden of their ideology.

We have become increasingly reluctant to earmark enormous sums for weapons that may never be used and that will not come on line for a decade, though during the height of the Cold War we bore this burden willingly. America, like the rest of the West, is increasingly a culture of economic and social entitlements. Financing entitlements while also rearming poses the classical "guns versus butter" problem. We accepted mass conscription in 1941 without complaining about the infringement of personal freedom, but only after considerable travail—and we disbanded our huge forces rapidly in 1945. Today, even the mild requirement that young men register for a possible draft resulted in 500,000 cases of defiance of the law. The cultural bias favoring individual growth, personal self-realization, and the autonomy of small groups militates against the notion of the acceptance of personal sacrifices in the service of national values. A sybaritic and self-indulgent culture is not likely to provide the support for a foreign policy of armed assertion. How can one justify the fine-tuning of the fiscal and manpower policies implied by containment to a public more concerned with private gratification than public welfare?

One solution for this conundrum is professionalization of the military. What cannot be achieved with human beings might be attainable with technology. The design and use of more and more automated weapons systems call for a military profession that is highly technicized and an industrial infrastructure organized to cater to it. Such a change implies the abandonment of citizen armies. It suggests industrial development along the lines of the aerospace industry rather than the "dual use" organizations familiar from the automotive and steel industries. President Eisenhower warned against this situation in 1960. It seemed undesirable then, and it is unlikely to be more palatable now. The substitution of technology and technique for people poses awkward questions for democracy.

A still more difficult domestic constraint on the realization of American values is the oft-described swing in the moods of the American public, the condition so feared by Marshall. Our ritualistic and highly personalized presidential election campaigns tend to force these swings into a regular four-year cycle. Consistency and flexibility, as George Kennan complained in 1950 (following David Hume's doubts about the viability of balance-of-power diplomacy), are not to be had in a country whose citizens think in moralistic terms of "either/or." There is no hope for any long-term strategy if the Soviet Union is seen either as a hotbed of Communist conspiracies aiming at world conquest, or as just an insecure newly modernized country eager for reassurance, and if the American public shifts rapidly from one extreme perception to the other. It makes little difference whether the public mood says "get the U.S. out of the UN and the UN out of the U.S." or whether it announces "enlist in the Army, meet exotic people, and kill them." Both sentiments express moralistic extremes common to American culture.

The government that has to cater to both is burdened with some difficult trade-offs. During the 1950s the mood favored harsh confrontational measures against the Soviets. In the 1970s the legacy of the failure of such measures in Vietnam pushed sentiments in the opposite direction. Today, the mood oscillates between the advocacy of nuclear disarmament and the commitment to a new generation of more deadly and more accurate nuclear weapons, between "getting the U.S. out of El Salvador" and mounting an intensified global resistance to Communism.

These are some of the domestic constraints on policy. The picture abroad offers little reassurance for a consistent long-range strategy. To repeat the obvious, there are now two superpowers quite capable of destroying each other in a short war, and much of the world with them. The Soviet Union insists on being recognized as a world power, with all this might imply. And the Third World has grown in power and heterogeneity so as to defy any single and simple policy of catering to it.

Our allies are no longer our clients. They are willing and able to assert their individual (and collective) national interests on dé-tente in Europe, nuclear weapons, arms control, the Middle East, Central America, and the sale of high-technology items to the Soviet bloc. Their views of the difficult trade-offs diverge more and more from ours. During the 1970s the mood favored their preferences on détente and even entente. It is far from clear that our allies will continue to reject Soviet demands for full super-power status.

The independence of our allies is caused in no small measure by the fact that the societies of all industrialized countries show the same signs of declining national unity as does ours. Wealth engen-ders self-indulgence, the unwillingness to make personal sacri-fices. In Europe this mood has led to the extremes of the contem-porary unilateral disarmament movement, a movement that prefers faith in the benign motives of the Soviet Union to a willingness to accept the logic of nuclear deterrence. The move-ment sees us, not Moscow, as the enemies of peace. It seems to prefer life under the shadow of Soviet hegemony to the continua-tion of an armed confrontation along the Elbe River. Given all of this, a return to containment cannot count on consistent Euro-pean and Japanese support. Since going it alone also would imply the growth of a garrison-state mentality in America, retrench-ment is inevitable.

Aspects of Selective Engagement

Selective engagement as an alternative to past strategies must answer certain perennial questions: When and where should the expansion of Soviet influence be opposed with military aid and, if necessary, with counterinsurgency and conventional military operations? When and where should we intervene militarily in the Third World to prevent the spread of Communism?

I now discuss each of these questions in detail.

Where should we be ready to fight? We should continue our commitment to the military defense of all democratic countries against Soviet threats, provided these countries wish to be defended. This commitment also covers threats by allies of the Soviet Union against Third World countries with a democratic tradition. Military action is justified to defend democracy in Western Europe and Japan but also in such countries as Costa Rica, Venezuela, India, Sri Lanka, Israel, and Colombia.

Moreover, military action may also be justified if the Soviet bloc expands into an area containing key commodities that are essential for the economic welfare of the democratic countries. This rule is subject to great abuse. We must be certain that the commodities lost to Soviet control cannot be obtained elsewhere. Soviet penetration of the Middle East oil fields would be a very serious threat to Europe and Japan, though not to us. Soviet control over African copper, chrome, or uranium might or might not be serious, depending on alternative sources of supply. We can reduce the temptation to invoke this justification for war by a timely policy of stockpiling and by the development of alternative materials and sources. Unless these measures are taken the rule can too easily justify an unthinking policy of supporting South Africa, Mobutu's Zaire, or Saudi Arabia's subsidies of the PLO.

In short, the United States need *not* be committed to the military defense of all countries not currently part of the Communist camp. But there is a third contingency that justifies fighting: Soviet penetration of regions so close to the United States as to afford the adversary an opportunity for offensive action. We cannot tolerate the establishment of strong Soviet influence in Canada and Mexico; we must be careful at all times that Soviet power in Cuba remains confined to nonoffensive levels.

How can we prevent the use of this rule from leading to repetitions of the Vietnam tragedy? We must distinguish between spurious and genuine "domino" effects. A genuine domino situation exists when the Soviet Union is able to profit from an indigenous insurgency to assume control over the victorious Marxist government that emerges, then uses this new ally/client as a base for additional subversion in neighboring countries, and finally establishes itself in the area as a military power able to threaten the United States. This did *not* happen in Vietnam. The military hegemony of Hanoi in Indochina does not threaten the military security of the United States, Japan, or Europe. Nor does the expansion of Soviet power in East Africa have such an effect. Normally we should not rely on multilateral agreements for controlling Communist expansion in the Third World on the grounds that such expansion threatens American security. However, we might well encourage multilateral agreements to persuade Third World countries to insure each other and to distance themselves from the Soviets and from us.

The obvious instance of a genuine domino situation is the Caribbean. We may not be threatened by Cubans in Angola and Ethiopia, but Cubans in Nicaragua and Grenada are potentially a different matter. I repeat: the issue here is not the spread of Communism and the replacement of a repressive authoritarian government with a more repressive totalitarian one. The issue is the potential military threat to the United States. There is no domino effect as long as, *but only as long as,* Cuban and Soviet-supported indigenous insurgencies do not lead to the creation of a Soviet-controlled offensive military capability. The Caribbean, then, poses a problem because the success of Marxist insurgencies may endanger the stability of such democracies as Costa Rica, Jamaica, Barbados, and Trinidad, and also lead to the creation of a Soviet military threat.

My reasoning thus leads to these specific rules for selective engagement:

- Do not expect the Soviet Union to abide by spheres-of-interest agreements in the Third World; be prepared to enforce the ones that matter most to American security (as in the Caribbean), and refrain from negotiating others likely to be violated and of secondary concern to us (as in Africa).

- Do not raise symbolic issues critical of the Soviet Union if there is no chance of strong action; do not intervene by deeds in Eastern Europe; and do not make a big issue over Soviet aggression when it does not really hurt American security.

- Do not deny the Soviet Union public recognition as a great power when such recognition entails no substantive cost to us.

- Use conventional forces to oppose Soviet or proxy aggression against the states considered genuinely vital by us.

- Rearm so as to have adequately equipped and sufficiently mobile forces for these missions. This calls for re-equipping conventional forces, *not* equipping our strategic forces with a new generation of missiles or hardening them beyond the needs of MAD-type deterrence.

- Continue arms control negotiations designed to stabilize strategic forces for deterrence and do not seek qualitative improvements not needed for this purpose.

- Continue policies designed to slow down horizontal nuclear proliferation, recognizing that the process cannot be stopped completely.

- Sharply control scientific exchanges with the Soviet Union and the sale of technology and intensify efforts to persuade other NATO members to do the same, until a decline in Soviet defense spending becomes apparent.

- Declare the Caribbean to be a "zone of peace and self-determination." Encourage a consortium led by Mexico, Venezuela, and Colombia to guarantee the confining of insurgencies to the countries of origin by stopping arms transfer and asylum practices for insurgents and by interposing military forces in case of border violations. Support such efforts by adjusting current U.S. military and economic aid practices.

- Approach Cuba and the Soviet Union to spell out the limits of permissible intervention on their part. Intensify pressure on Cuba; reward it for loosening ties with the Soviet Union and for not encouraging insurgencies. Failing such an agreement, intensify naval and air activity to stop Cuban assistance to Marxist regimes and insurgencies.

Should we act to prevent the spread of Communism? Should we support authoritarian governments with diplomacy, military hardware, training, and advisers because they are preferable to totalitarian ones? My way of putting the question assumes that while Communism will spread in the face of our inaction, the power of the Soviet Union need not. I assume that Soviet control over other Marxist states is tenuous, that there are many kinds of Marxism, and that the Soviet model of governance will not necessarily determine the evolution of political life elsewhere even though all successful Marxist regimes begin their programs under totalitarian auspices.

This question leaves us with the most controversial aspect of American policy: what to do in the seventy largely Third World countries whose annual per capita income is less than $1000. Do we protect them from foreign invasion, urge them to respect human rights, make them into democracies, merely cater to their most basic human needs, or give them military and diplomatic aid to defeat indigenous insurgencies? Or do we overthrow their governments when they turn anti-American? Unless we scale down our values, we are committed to encouraging human betterment, to the diffusion of democratic values, to representative democracy and popular participation. Yet of these countries, twelve have Communist regimes, nine are democracies, four are too unstable to permit a classification, and forty-five have single-party authoritarian institutions—some military and some civilian—that are intermittently and haphazardly repressive. We know that these regimes are in no sense committed to our notions of human rights. We know that they rule by coup and countercoup. Despite our efforts to use foreign aid and military assistance for "state-building" and "nation-building," we cannot be optimistic that many of the seventy will soon develop into well-integrated national communities.

Given this situation, American policy has drifted between two poles: aid and intervention designed to strengthen human rights and economic development (under the Kennedy, Johnson, and Carter administrations), or support for local regimes, however repressive they may be, provided they oppose Marxism and are aligned with American positions vis-à-vis the Soviet Union (as under the Nixon, Ford, and Reagan administrations). Either way, there was and is a marked bias in American policy for less toleration of violations of human rights (and a greater tendency to intervene) when the offenses are committed by left-leaning regimes. Either way, our policies were justified by the alleged need to contain Communist and Soviet influence.

I accept the argument that, in principle, authoritarian governments are preferable to totalitarian ones. Both practice repression; neither respects human rights; neither serves democracy.

Why then favor one over the other? Authoritarian governments pose less danger to democracy because of their sloppiness, their corruption, and their lack of principled ideology. They are easier to overthrow than totalitarian regimes; they can be and have been transformed into democracies, as illustrated by the modern history of Venezuela, Colombia, and Greece. We have no instance of the transformation of a totalitarian state into something more humane. Totalitarianism—being thorough, ruthless, and imbued with ideological fervor—is not easily displaced. The harm it does to human freedom far exceeds the clumsy repressions of most dictatorships, even though ruthlessness and fanaticism also make possible social and economic improvements often shunned by authoritarian regimes. Authoritarianism, in short, is reversible, but totalitarianism may not be. Hence, if we have to choose, we hedge our bets by supporting authoritarian dictatorships. But why do we have to choose?

We need not support every authoritarian regime that claims to be defending freedom. Support them we must when and if they control countries considered vital for our and our allies' defense or economic welfare. Whether this condition is met can be decided only on a case-by-case basis. Whether a specific insurgency is a response to purely indigenous discontent or whether it is part of a Soviet plan cannot be determined ahead of time. In general, there is no need to take sides and extend any support to an authoritarian government engaged in fighting an insurgency unless it is clear that the defeat of the government will inevitably lead to a military or economic threat to the United States.

Soviet political and military penetration of the Third World is as real as is ours. But how deep and how lasting is it? Egypt, Somalia, Ethiopia, Iraq, and Indonesia have switched sides. Argentina, Angola, Zambia, India, and Iran hedge their bets, sometimes catering to one camp and sometimes to the other. At the moment, Morocco, Zaire, Chile, Colombia, Nigeria, and Saudi Arabia are aligned with Washington, an alignment buttressed with military understandings, arms sales, commodity purchases, and the willingness to mount an American (or French) military operation when requested. At the moment, Mozambique, Nicaragua, South Yemen, and Ethiopia are tied to Moscow (or Havana, or East Berlin) in much the same ways. So what? Each camp's penetration of these Third World countries remains superficial. Neither camp can prevent defections. Neither Moscow nor Washington can fashion links that cannot be undone. Neither camp dispenses methods of control and penetration that can fundamentally transform Third World societies and cultures without the energetic and active cooperation of the local leadership.

If the Soviets are no better placed than we in asserting effective control over the Third World, we should worry less about "losing" countries. We should recognize that the Third World is diverse and diffuse, subject to nobody's control, and increasingly populated by countries and leaders who are able and willing to follow courses of national development amenable to nobody's tutelage. And we should be willing to decouple our policies toward the Third World from our fixation with Moscow's unfathomable plans. The global system is not as tightly coupled as many leaders believe it to be, but our safety demands that it be loosened even further. Tightly coupled systems — whether in reality or only in the perceptions of decision-makers — are inherently dangerous because the failure of a single part implies the collapse of the whole.

My reasoning leads to the general prescription that we seek to disengage militarily from the Third World. By decoupling from the South in terms of military activity and militarily justified foreign aid, we need to worry less about occasional Soviet forays. We strengthen our position vis-à-vis the Soviets by being able to disregard some of their moves. Moreover, by engaging to deal with the legitimate economic demands of the South, we disengage from confrontation with Moscow because we can then stop thinking in terms of an undifferentiated and seamless Third World about to be preyed upon.

Disengagement of this kind calls for reducing Northern dependence on imports of raw materials essential for military and economic well-being. Bringing about the relative autonomy of the North from Third World commodities implies the need for compensating the South for its loss of export revenues. My specific suggestions are as follows:

- Make another effort to achieve agreement among NATO and Warsaw Pact countries to eliminate or limit the transfer of arms to Third World states. Failing such an agreement, transfer arms only in situations resembling the circumstances under which it would be legitimate for the United States to fight.

- Do not take sides in wars among Third World countries unless one of the parties occupies a truly crucial position with respect to American strategic needs. There was, for example, no need to support Pakistan in its 1971 war with India. There is good reason to support Egypt and Sudan against Libya in 1983.

- Avoid the formal declarations that proclaim certain areas to be of special military and political concern to the United States (except the Caribbean), such as was done in the Eisenhower, Nixon, and Carter "doctrines."

- Initiate a NATO/OECD (Organization of Economic Cooperation and Development) program of systematic research and development (R&D) aimed at decreasing Western dependence on vital primary commodities from the Third World—notably oil, minerals required for specialty steels, and bauxite.

- As a consequence of the policies of substitution, develop a new approach to Third World exporting countries to compensate them for loss of markets, involving acceptance of those items in the New International Economic Order (NIEO) that deal with technology transfer, multinational corporations, and aid to industrialization.

- Pending success of the R&D program, continue the NATO/ OECD program of energetic stockpiling of militarily and industrially vital commodities. Third World opposition to this program should be moderated by generous concessions to a version of the UN's Integrated Program for Commodities.

Selective engagement is a strategy of moderate moods, of not expecting too much, of accepting graciously what cannot be changed without a crusade so bloody as to defy historical experience. It is also a strategy to assure the survival of institutions unique in history, found in few places, and destined to suffer some rude shocks. Hedging one's bets is never as satisfying as indulging one's true desires. But in the face of intractable uncertainty it is certainly safer than gambling with the lives of hundreds of millions.

7

AARON WILDAVSKY

Containment plus
Pluralization

Imagine that citizens in both the USSR and the U.S.A. fell asleep in 1957 and awoke today. How surprised would they be? After (following Khrushchev's 1956 revelations about Stalin) the Communist elite decided not to decimate themselves over disagreements, they remained unchanged; the Soviet is the most static political culture of modern times. American citizens, by contrast, would find that nearly everything has been in flux: the media, sex roles, race relations, the scope and legitimacy of government — all have undergone more or less radical change.

In the Soviet Union, changelessness at home goes hand-in-hand with change abroad; Marxism, like revolution, is solely for export. One finds Marxist theorists in Europe and America but not in the Soviet Union. The charisma of the Communist party — whatever is left of its élan and daring — is reserved for foreign affairs. And whatever is left of early Communism, of striving for equality and of anti-establishment views, can be found only in other countries.

In foreign affairs, by contrast, the United States is a status quo power. It wants and needs nothing from anyone, except normal trade relations. America's frontiers remain internal. Americans care about the relationship (or lack thereof) between black and white, man and woman, the individual and the state, man and God, technology and the natural environments—not about foreigners or foreign conquests.

The United States does not want trouble abroad because it cannot sustain the conflict foreign policy produces at home. The defensive character of American foreign policy did not begin or end with President Carter; it is inherent in the situation of a superpower that is satisfied to hold on and unwilling to act except when provoked. Were the United States to do the opposite, it would become offensive not only to its opponents but to itself. The U.S. does not really want what belongs to others, and it cannot sustain the domestic support to make sacrifices for what seem to be surplus possessions. The truth must out: the United States acts like a defensive power because that is precisely what it is.

The peoples of the Soviet Union are not so different from this. They are not yet finished with Western civilization. Having struggled so long to achieve it, they are perhaps more passionate devotees of its culture than those further west. Russia remains an important reservoir of Western values — values that are better appreciated because they have been abused, that have become cherished through suffering. The critique of materialism retains a moral meaning where urban-rural difference remains so large and where the economic standard of different peoples varies so substantially. Such a congeries of peoples has something in common with the most diverse, restless, and experimental people of the West—the Americans. Why, then, do we seem to be at each other's throats?

The Theory: Change Abroad to Prevent Change at Home

Because Leninism cannot live with diversity, it must try to destroy all challenges by eliminating all challengers. This fear of differences is the source of the paranoia that brands Bolshevism with its mark of Cain. And it is this fear that must be ameliorated if the world is to avoid a nuclear war among the superpowers.

I will explain. Overwhelming evidence suggests that the Soviet Union is an unsuccessful society.[1] The regime can do well at only one thing: armament. In the running of a command economy, only the first command—arm!—gets obeyed. The shortages are attributable—as everyone, including the Soviets, knows—to socialist economics. They know they could be much more productive if they allowed sway to market principles. But that would mean giving up control; a whole new leadership cadre would emerge, rather than being chosen by the current rulers. Everyone in the regime got where he is (it is male supremicist) by being chosen by someone else in it; so if the system lets go, they all go with it. Even if they individually think it vile, which they may, no one wants to be first.

Without an empire, the Communist party would be bereft of rationale. Turning its attention to improving the domestic standard of living would leave it open to an evident riposte; if this were the goal, there would be modes of political and social organization better suited to the task. Broadening the *nomenklatura,* the privileges that go with rank in the USSR, would signify the subordination of political to economic goals, i.e., in Communist parlance, "right-wing deviationism." Besides, a dismantling of armaments in Eastern Europe would suggest that the same policy might also be appropriate for the big sister socialist state. What then, since there are other governmental bodies to do all it does, would maintain the legitimacy of the Communist party as the ruling body of the Soviet Union?

Demands that the Soviet Union cease activity adverse to American interests in different parts of the world are likely to prove counterproductive. For one thing, the Soviets will always claim Eastern Europe as their sphere of influence. Failure to concede this sphere to them dooms the idea of reciprocity — "you stay out of my sphere, I'll stay out of yours" — from the start. Conceding to the Soviet Union this "socialist" sphere of influence, however, immediately removes any incentive on its part to extend the arrangement to other parts of the world. What matters most to the Soviets are threats to their internal order. Pluralization in Eastern Europe might undermine that order. Once that potential is removed, the Communist party can concentrate on shoring up its system by showing that its foreign (unlike its domestic) policy is successful. To say that Communism cannot operate abroad (to those who know it does not operate at home) is to conclude that it should not operate at all. The Soviet Union will not agree to stop stirring up trouble abroad because that would mean starting to stir up trouble at home.

If the hypothesis outlined here is correct—that the Soviet Union sponsors change abroad in order to preserve changelessness at home, a dynamic foreign policy supporting a static domestic policy—what can the United States do about it? Obviously, the United States cannot invade the Soviet Union, thus starting the nuclear war it has set out to prevent. Obviously, also, the objective of the United States cannot be to convert the Soviet Union to democracy, if only because there is no way to do that. Though "condominium" would gain a temporary peace in exchange for rendering its allies impotent, America would then become not only the main but essentially the only target of the Soviet Union.

Yet there is a lesser goal that will suit America's foreign policy—namely, political pluralization: the larger the number of independent centers of power within the USSR, the more the Soviets will be constrained to secure domestic consent for their foreign policy, and the more they will have to "pay off" their partners by providing domestic largesse. When the domestic constraints on foreign policy in the two countries tend to be more equal, so will their incentives for accommodation at lower levels of violence.

My main point is far broader than the economics of turning the Soviet leadership inward so it will wish to spend less on defense. The Soviet Union cannot live at peace with nations that are different and independent because it cannot tolerate those selfsame qualities within its own regime. Unless there is pluralization within the Soviet Union, it is only a matter of time and opportunity before it seeks to subjugate the only force in the world capable of resisting it.

If foreign policy is the continuation of domestic policy by other means, to play on Clausewitz's remark about war, then the secret (the motive or intention) of Soviet foreign policy is found in its domestic political organization. The leaders of the Soviet Communist party seek to maintain their form of rule. So does the United States. The difference is that America plays pluralist politics; it tolerates, even welcomes, a diversity of political regimes. The Soviet way of life cannot tolerate sources of power independent of itself. Just as it does not abide diversity at home, it cannot be indifferent to it abroad. For one thing, the independence of diverse life forms abroad gives hope to those who would pursue them at home. Without hope of external support, tomorrow's potential dissenters would become fatalists, inured to a future in which decisions affecting them are made by others. For another, Soviet leaders are keenly aware of the intrinsic shortcomings of a regime that is less efficient than capitalism, less egalitarian than social democracy, and less popular than almost any other system. All the Soviets seek, as they often say, is a world order conducive to their safety. Unfortunately for us, they deem their safety and our survival to be incompatible.

For its own people, the Communist party created the Gulag; what, I ask, can we in the West, who have no ties or affinity or affection, expect from a party devoted to the eradication of political differences? Containment called for blocking Soviet aggression until its internal organization altered; unless the Soviet Union pluralizes its political structure, I argue, it will continue to be aggressive, employing means up to and including the threat and use of nuclear weapons.

We in the United States wish to be prudent. We also know we may be wrong. We could be persuaded by events—a withdrawal from Afghanistan, independent trade unions in Poland, a reduction of military forces as opposed to the increases of the past decade. If the Soviet Union does not undertake or support new aggression, a policy of encouraging Soviet pluralization would be less justifiable. But if past trends continue, the United States may be well advised, without using physical force, to attack the source of the enmity against it and all independent regimes—rule from a single center over a whole society.

It is this structure that generates Soviet intentions to permit no rivals and that creates the dilemmas of American foreign policy for which a policy of containment can be only a partial response. Containment should be supplemented by a policy of pluralization to weaken the structure.

I think it is possible to devise a doctrine for American foreign policy toward the Soviet Union that will give it a cutting edge, a doctrine that will give the Communist party leadership reason not to undertake so many offensive actions. Like most successful policies, a policy of pluralization would work by anticipating reactions, rather than by repairing damage that already has been done. Effective policies do not require continuous compliance; they operate to deter wrongdoing before it occurs. Instead of focusing its policy on the peripheries of the world, the new doctrine would focus on the heartland, the Soviet Union itself. Debate would be not only about whether it should stop doing something it should not have done in the first place, but about its very form of political organization.

Instead of being endlessly on the defensive, the United States would take the offensive in encouraging a more pluralist regime within the Soviet Union. Instead of merely reacting to Soviet moves, in the mode of containment, the United States would make waves on its own. And instead of being bereft of a rationale for foreign policy, other than containment, the American government could ask itself how the various resources at its disposal, and the situations with which it contends, could effect the pluralization of its adversary.

Though pluralization is apparently more pacific than a military line, it is aimed at the jugular — the Communist-Leninist form of political organization — and therefore should be approached with care. Having, in effect, declared political warfare on the Soviet Union (never mind that it does this against the United States as a matter of course), what gain is there to compensate for the increase in enmity? Without using military means, there is no way the United States can directly alter events in Poland, Afghanistan, or any other place within or just outside the borders of the USSR. Would a political approach, then, merely demonstrate American impotence — "speak loudly but carry no stick at all"? Worse still, the Soviet Union might be encouraged to engage in greater aggression without the United States' being able to bring greater force to bear for countering these efforts. Why rile the beast, as the folk saying goes, if one cannot cope with the consequences.

The answer is that a change in focus would enable the United States to take a broader view of containment. Instead of being viewed strictly as a problem of resistance — attack against and defense of a given country—containment can also be viewed as offensive, aimed at the internal position of the Soviet Union from which the danger emanates. By adopting containment plus political action, the United States would also have a foreign policy that would make it easier for itself and more difficult for its adversary to gain domestic support.

What would containment plus pluralization do to alter the situation? On the Soviet side, its leaders would learn that they face increasing internal upset in return for their foreign interventions. If the purpose of Soviet foreign policy is to maintain its domestic form of rule, counteractions aimed at that rule may give them pause. As for the United States, its options would have expanded. In addition to deciding whether to use force, the United States could consider offsetting actions aimed at the Soviets. Where military action would be politically infeasible, political action may be sufficiently threatening to persuade the Soviets to loosen their grip.

The Practice: Pluralizing the Soviet Union

Are there things the United States can do, and can get support at home for doing, that would enhance the prospects of pluralization in the USSR? Or would the American government be putting itself in the position of the person who kicks a television set in order to make it work, and who is as likely to electrocute himself as to fix it? No doubt there is much to learn, but I will offer illustrative examples. I also wish to suggest how political action aimed at pluralization might help order priorities within American foreign policy toward the Soviet Union.

At the outset, it would be wise to keep in mind the dual purpose of a policy of pluralization: to take advantage of both American internal strengths and Soviet internal weaknesses. As things stand, America's strengths—its spontaneity, variety, insistence on internal consent—become its weaknesses in foreign policy, whereas what should be Soviet weaknesses—its coercion, uniformity, bureaucracy—become its strengths. A policy of pluralization is designed to take advantage of what America can do and the Soviet Union cannot, whereas containment alone does the reverse. Thus compatibility with American values is as important as incompatibility with Soviet internal structure.

Americans, for instance, do not believe in politicizing most aspects of life; the Soviet Communist party does. While Americans are aware that international sport, for example, has been politicized, they wish to limit, not to extend, this process. Thus it was not desirable for the United States to respond to the Soviet invasion of Afghanistan by withdrawing (and seeking to persuade others to withdraw) from the 1980 Olympic Games. In addition to its inefficacy, this action violated an American principle while affirming a Soviet standard. To make pluralization feasible requires self-limiting ordinances lest the United States be tempted to seek changes beyond its capabilities. I begin, therefore, with what the United States should not do—its "don'ts"—before coming to its positive principles of action.

Evolution, not revolution. Soviet citizens should not be urged to oppose their regime. That is their business, not ours. Rather, people at each point of identifiable cleavage are to be provided with information so that they may form preferences of their own and, as circumstances permit, organize to make those preferences known.

What about the Leninist form of organization? It is to be opposed; no person has a right to decide for others or to kill or imprison on the grounds that people who organize to express their differences of opinion with the regime deserve death. Human rights requires political pluralism. So does national defense; to show that this is true, Stalin's sacrifice of his people's defense against Nazism (through his purges, his enmity against entire ethnic groups, etc.) should be emphasized. Beyond that there is no need to go.

Pluralization does not demand democratization. Elections are not our fetish.[2] There must be separate centers of power and some process, deemed suitable by the people involved, for invoking consent and maintaining responsibility.

Don't take sides! Emigré battles, domestic differences between dissidents, are not our business. It would be wrong (that is, contrary to American principles) to think we know more about what is good for other people than they do. Our interest is that they, not we, should have a chance to pursue their vision of the good life.

Comparisons are odious. This "don't" (wholly in accord with American skepticism—a consequence, it might be said, of the pluralization of perspectives) asserts that comparisons to the United States are inappropriate and self-defeating. They are inappropriate because we wish to concentrate attention on the Soviet experience. They are self-defeating not only because the United States is no exemplar, but also because the evident riposte is that the Soviet Union should not and could not imitate America. Slogans like "catching up and surpassing the United States" can safely be left to the Stalinists who originated them.

Don't dissemble. This last bit of negative advice warns decision-makers that pluralization is what the Soviets fear most, not some flaccid recital of truths Americans hold self-evident. The attitude revealed in President Carter's diary—"It's important that he [Brezhnev] understand the commitment I have to human rights first of all, and that it is not an antagonistic attitude of mine toward the Soviet Union"[3]—is bound to drive Soviet leaders wild, as well as to hide from ourselves the profundity of the challenge the human rights movement offers to Communist institutions.[4] Pluralization is the policy about which Leninist leaders have fantasized in the past, as if it existed so as, according to a member of the Politburo, to result in "undermining socialism [read 'Leninism' or 'rule from a single Party center'] from within."[5]

The positive principles of pluralization are the following:

Act in accord with American values, as already indicated. If the United States government does not consider its actions moral, why should its people?[6] Continuing political support, moreover, depends, in a democracy, on acting in congruence with underlying values. To illustrate, I shall present a number of issues, such as economic sanctions and cultural exchange, that create conflicts between the desire to retaliate against aggressive Soviet actions and incompatibility with American values.

America is a capitalist country. It is also a trading country. Restricting trade runs up against the American belief in enterprise and competition. On a practical level, American efforts to exert pressure against the Soviets through grain embargoes and denial of "most favored nation" treatment have proved ineffective abroad and divisive at home. America's reputation as a reliable agricultural supplier has suffered. Food embargoes, in addition, make the United States seem inhumane, while at the same time we do not control enough of the world's food to prevent resupply to the Soviets from other sources. And once sanctions are applied or concessions granted, the economic policy instrument is used up.[7] What principle, then, applies?

Normalize trade, unless there are compelling reasons to the contrary. Acting out our own beliefs would have avoided the American inconsistency and inefficacy of the last decade.

So long as a policy of containment is necessary, of course, *there should be no trade in strategic goods. Nor,* following good capitalist doctrine, *should there be subsidy of Soviet trade.* Rewarding the Soviets for aggressive behavior is the last thing the United States (or its allies) should do. Indeed, it is questionable as to whether the Western Alliance can last if its members continue to subsidize Soviet economic activity (viz., the Siberian gas pipeline), thus allowing it to expend greater resources on military force. A businesslike approach to trade, as the Soviets say, neither conferring advantages nor imposing sanctions, always excepting strategic items, is best calculated to maintain support for American foreign policy. However, when the Eastern bloc asks for concessions, that is, for "unbusinesslike behavior," the United States should insist on further pluralization. The price for not foreclosing on Polish loans should have been the survival of Solidarity.

Facilitate free flow of information. American values stand in favor of the utmost cultural and scientific exchange. Insofar as exchange is not free, our government and the private agencies involved in these exchanges are encouraged to *demand reciprocity.* This is fine as far as it goes, but it does not confront the critical question of balancing pluralization versus Party privilege.

Foreign travel is used as a reward for behavior acceptable to the Communist party. To the extent that cultural and scientific exchange reinforces a system that crushes creativity, therefore, it contradicts the moral foundations of exchange as well as running counter to the prospects for pluralization. Were we to conclude that cultural exchange increases Party control, we would be duty-bound (by virtue of our respect for human rights, reinforced by a policy of pluralization) to stop giving a lofty name to low practices.

The other side of the coin is that cultural exchange can (and sometimes does) enhance pluralization. By increasing the number of Westerners in the Soviet Union, especially those doing research about it, listening posts are increased. This is, as the Soviets would be the first to say, a form of intelligence, even though no contact whatsoever is made with Western governments. And by increasing the number of Soviet specialists on the United States, though many may be Party "aparatchiks," the range of ideas to which Soviet citizens are subject is increased. These specialists may learn to value their American contacts. They may also facilitate return visits by their American hosts. In short, the presentation of American life within the Soviet Union may improve. Maybe.[8]

The question remains of whether cultural contact promotes pluralization. *When in doubt,* the government of the United States should, in accord with its principles, *continue contacts.* Reasonably *persuaded to the contrary,* depending on evidence that may vary from time to time, *the United States should cut off contact so exchange can no longer be used to reward people for participating in and/or benefiting from repression.*

Should the United States encourage Soviet citizens to emigrate? Not if that reduces dissidence and hence the prospects for pluralism. *Emigration should be supported only if it enhances pluralization.* (Jews may be a special case, if their emigration aids Israel, but then they would have to go there instead of America.) The foreign policy of the United States, though it should be morally sensitive, should not be used primarily to improve the position of selected Soviet citizens but to protect its own people. Pluralization, I should add, would do more for the Soviet population than any emigration policy. I shall, therefore, move on to principles for promoting pluralization.

Expose privilege. Special stores for foreigners may be justified on the grounds of acquiring foreign exchange. Special stores for members of the *nomenklatura* may be justified by the superior contribution they make to society. Eating foods otherwise unavailable to the average person is not so easy to justify, even when inequality is accepted. Weaken these privileges and you erode the organizational glue that keeps the Party together. By what Marxists call "unmasking," by making the Party face up to the full extent of the privileges it confers, it may be induced to retract or to justify them in public, either of which would be painful.

How is this to be done? By publicity. It should not be too difficult to discover what food or luxury, otherwise unobtainable, can be had at which special store. Daily "specials" may be announced. This exposé might be combined with an information service aimed at helping the hapless shopper in the Soviet Union discover which goods in short supply are on sale, when, and at what place. A reputation for reliability would help. So would a reputation for service. A consumer catalogue testing ordinary Soviet products for defects, from vodka to violins, much in the manner of our consumer magazines, would gain credibility for whoever produced it.

How would this information be produced and disseminated? By unorthodox but by no means unavailable methods. The United States has barely begun radio reporting; its transmitters could be more numerous, more powerful, and more diverse, so as to escape or overcome Soviet jamming. Consumer information could be broadcast; it could also be put on tapes, mailed to random addresses, dropped over borders. American ingenuity can do much more to penetrate the Iron Curtain than has been considered possible.

Amplify dissent. The best clue as to what material would interest and motivate the Soviet people is that being produced by dissenters. Rejecting those that preach violence, a policy of pluralization would amplify every other one of these voices, making their thought more widely available. Small, lightweight printers now exist for home computers that could be made available to lessen the Communist party's monopoly of publication. *Samizdat,* self-publication, would be aided by mechanical methods, enabling many more copies to be produced from the original typescript. (Unauthorized use of printers is illegal in the USSR, but we will follow the rule that if an activity is legal in all Western nations, it will be morally proper to carry out in the Soviet Union.) The American government would add nothing to these home-based products, no commentary or compliments, except formal publication as books, pamphlets, tapes, microfiche, or any other form in which they can pass through the boundaries of the Soviet Union.

Supporting dissidents entails some effort at understanding them. What makes a dissident?

Demands for reform raised outside of official channels, and demands that call for systemic reform rather than correction of a particular abuse, are consistently treated by the regime as revolutionary, because they threaten the regime's monopoly power of defining the political agenda. No Soviet dissident can act entirely legally, since writing unapproved literature for circulation or just meeting to discuss actions are regarded by the Party as illegal acts.

The Soviet dissidents' basic activity is challenging the state's monopoly on information and interpretation of events. They produce historical studies, educate their readers, conduct philosophical discussions, and report on current events of interest to their movement. Dissident study groups and seminars provide ways for people to interact and discuss problems of common interest, and to maintain and develop professional skills that the regime will not permit them to utilize. The dissidents expose abuses and act as a kind of grievance committee, providing expertise in how to deal with the regime.

There is no standard dissident ideology. Most dissidents agree that liberal freedoms, such as the right to free speech, are desirable, and most are willing to defend people of various political persuasions against the regime. Beyond this general consensus, there is a wide variety of beliefs. I note only that the growth of nationalism as a powerful ideological trend among the dissidents parallels the growth of Jewish religious and Israeli national feeling among Jewish activists. In both cases, the discovery, or recovery, of a belief system provides the dissident with the moral resources to stand up against the regime.[9] Stress should be laid, therefore, on works about religion,[10] democracy, and other moral systems of thought and practice. There should also be practical advice.

Just as political prisoners in the Soviet Union are denied "internal communication" among their cells,[11] thus mimicking the Party ideology of separating citizens, a policy of pluralization should be aimed at overcoming isolation. People with independent ideas in the Soviet Union are likely to wind up in prison. They need to know about each other. The society at large needs to know about them. It should be possible to disseminate lore about prison life to help those who are there and to make others aware.

Be redundant. To whom should this material be directed? We should try all sorts of categories of people—environmentalists, feminists, nationalists, skilled workers, unskilled workers, managers, farmers. From the outcries of the regime and from the responses of the populace, the American government, after the fact, should learn a good deal about how to be effective with what sorts of people. There is no need to know everything in advance. In current jargon, policy evaluation should be retrospective, not prospective. The United States is rich enough, the problem important enough, the cost, compared to weapons, low enough, to rely on trial and error. Long before the United States learns how to target its actions with pinpoint accuracy, the Soviet Union will be initiating discussions of ways to achieve mutual forebearance. Its apparatus won't know how well pluralization is proceeding, but it will certainly be worried.

Be open. The usual tactic of Soviet leaders is to link dissent with the machinations of imperialists. Thus, Yuri Andropov, former chairman of the KGB (the Committee for State Security), now the successor to Leonid Brezhnev, accused dissidents of trying to shake "the Communist convictions of Soviet people" by spreading "views foreign to socialism"; these dissidents, he alleged, were engaged in the "special services of imperialism" for which they were paid "generously." Now, shaking Communist convictions and spreading views foreign to the Soviet system, to the extent that has not already occurred, is exactly what pluralization, or free speech for that matter, is about. It could be dangerous, therefore, to have the views of dissidents linked surreptitiously to covert American support. That is why I advocate an aboveboard, overt, official, congressionally authorized, and presidentially approved policy of pluralization.

How is a policy of political action to be presented in public? For what it is: a war of ideas to counter a war of violence.

By this time it should be clear that there are as yet unsuspected possibilities in Jimmy Carter's much-abused human rights policy.

As a general stance it does not unambiguously point to particular decisions in difficult cases. As a major vehicle of political action against the Soviet Union, it has considerable value. Human rights can be made to speak directly to the issue of political pluralism, on which all other rights depend. Hence, programs now considered subsidiary would take on primary importance. Instead of being a place where the United States is usually stigmatized, for instance, the United Nations could become a forum for pushing pluralism.

Counterarguments

A policy of pluralization is aggressive by design and by deed. It is not a military policy of aggression; it does not threaten change by force. Pluralization does not advocate a change in regime or argue for elections or preach for democracy. It does not favor nationality, religious, ethnic, labor, farm, or underprivileged groups. What it does do is provide information that breaks down the Communist party's monopoly, information that is potentially useful for the self-realization of any individual or group so motivated. If it falls on deaf ears, nothing happens. Yet information can be threatening to those who seek to withhold it. Ideas can be threatening if their targets are threatened by ideas. If the major motive of the Soviet system is to maintain the privileges of its members by monopolizing power, then pluralization, the growth of independent centers of power, is a mortal threat.

The Soviet Union will charge the Union States with interfering in its internal affairs. This accusation will be correct. In return, the United States can respond by saying not only that the Soviet Union does this all the time all around the world but also that its numerous interventions create internal strain in America by requiring containment. If they stop doing what discomforts us, we will stop doing what discomforts them.

If the structure of their system makes it easy for the Soviets to support drastic change abroad but requires them to suppress modest change at home, whereas the United States encourages substantial change within its borders but finds it difficult to cope with Soviet-aided change in other countries, agreement not to challenge each other's domestic rule but to carry out their competition in foreign lands is adverse to American interests. That is why containment alone is unsatisfactory.

We can take it for granted that the Party leadership will be extremely, perhaps excessively, worried. What can it do?

Suppose the Soviet Union, stung by political attack, were to take a larger number of aggressive actions in a shorter time. Obviously, this would raise the temperature of world politics. This is dangerous, but so is being nibbled to death. More blatant aggression has political advantages for the U.S. and disadvantages for the USSR. Under such a circumstance, the United States gains substantial domestic support for rearmament in support of containment. Since America is richer, it can do more. The Soviet Union, meanwhile, would undergo two types of strain with which the United States is familiar—the complexity of coping simultaneously with many diverse situations, and the inability to explain to its own people why it is imposing heavier sacrifices on behalf of strange and distant peoples. The covert antagonism of the Soviet Union makes it difficult for the United States government to respond directly. Overt competition is better for us and worse for our opponent.

Suppose the Soviets react by cutting off or severely curtailing contacts with the United States or the West as a whole. The most drastic measures, such as the recent abandonment of direct telephone dialing, have to apply uniformly to the external world. Such a move would punish the Party elite that could no longer be rewarded (or reward others) with travel. It would damage Soviet technological development. And it would strain relations with Western Europe and Japan. A Soviet policy of isolation, moreover, would severely harm efforts to drive a wedge between the United States and its allies. By outwardly manifesting its monolithic, implacable, unyielding characteristics, the Soviet Union would make it easier to mobilize opposition.

A policy of pluralization, it might be said, would lead the Soviet Union to take aggressive action in order to preserve its regime. Maybe. The reverse more nearly represents my position: if the Soviet do not change their form of rule, which is the source of their evil intent, they will continue to be aggressive.

Would the Soviets, so angered, invade Western Europe or, perhaps, Iran? Hardly. Military aggression would be extremely disadvantageous. If directed toward the Middle East, Western Europe and the United States would unite not only on all-out conventional but also on greatly enhanced nuclear rearmament.

Directed toward Western Europe, without being able to be certain of Eastern Europe's support, such a thrust might be unsuccessful. At the least, all of America's military capacities would be energized. Domestic opinion would be unified. In any event, these "worst-case" behaviors are inappropriate reactions to an American information campaign and are bound to seem so to the Soviets as well as to us.

Far better for the Soviets to respond in kind. They can step up information efforts of their own here. Good. Let them. Indeed, the United States should offer reciprocal arrangements. After all, everything they can say (and probably worse) is already being said here.

A policy of political action undoubtedly opens up the United States to charges that it is less than perfect. True as charged. If this leads the United States to improve its domestic policies, so much the better.

Unanticipated consequences are a staple of social life, and a policy of political action may not be an exception. It could be, as some say, that political action would strengthen hard-liners within the upper echelons of the Soviet Communist party. Of course, the United States does not really know whether such hard-liners exist or whether supposed "soft-liners" would be any better from its point of view. In such circumstances, the American government is better off understanding the Soviet regime as determined by its organization rather than as by the quality of the individuals who people it.

One reason a policy of pluralization has not been seriously considered is the sense of fatalism surrounding the subject. If nothing can be done, why think about doing it? A second reason is the mutual restraint that follows from the unwritten rule that neither side should directly threaten the political regime of the other. Yet the Soviet pattern of opportunistic aggression does in fact work indirectly to weaken the ability of a democratic nation, operating under the separation of powers, to maintain a coherent policy supported by its people. Given the variety of circumstances surrounding each episode, policy is bound to become inconsistent over time. And given the uncertainties involved, some actions are bound to be unsuccessful. Mobilizing support to act here, there, and elsewhere overburdens the delicate but essential art of coalition-building. Whether the United States appears to some of its citizens in danger of becoming a "garrison state" or to others to be weak and vacillating, respect for its political institutions suffers. By concentrating its energies on the Soviet system of rule itself, therefore, the United States restores symmetry to its relations with the Soviet Union. The threat is equalized. And the ratio between America's actions and its capabilities, including sustained domestic support, is more favorable. Now it takes low-cost action that does not strain its pocketbook or its resolve—action that its opponent, given its lack of domestic consent, is not well-suited to counter.

The third (and most powerful) reason inhibiting the United States from focusing on Leninist political organization is the understandable but debilitating desire not to confront the fundamental problem of American-Soviet relationships: the incompatibility of regimes. For if regimes so constituted as the United States and the Soviet Union cannot forever live together, this opens up the prospect that peaceful resolution of differences may not be possible. Failure to face up to this prospect explains the oscillation between being too soft (continued conflict being too awful to contemplate) and too hard (continued losses being too awful to tolerate). For behind the challenge to this peaceful premise will be seen to lurk the specter of nuclear war.

Do we suppose that our efforts to disseminate information inside the Soviet Union will provoke nuclear war? Were the Soviets able to count on the success of a preemptive strike, they would be better off acting sooner rather than later, for the very existence of the United States poses a possible future threat. In my view, this specter justifies the maintenance of three separate and viable nuclear deterrents (water, land, and air) as the indispensable foundation of American defense.

Even the horror of a nuclear war (I think of those who quietly contemplate surrender but know that the Soviets, if aware of this fact, would exploit their advantage) cannot be avoided but only postponed by giving in. For the Communist confederation would be bound to split apart, leaving the earth with irreconcilable forces who would know well what the other would try to do. Is 2024 so much better an Orwellian future than 1984?

Supplementing containment with peaceful but provocative

efforts to alter Soviet internal structure has received a thorough-going critique by Seweryn Bialer and Joan Afferica. According to their argument:

While the roots of Soviet foreign policy are to be found in the Soviet domestic system, the extent to which Soviet foreign policy is able to be expansionist depends very largely upon international factors: on the temptations and opportunities which the international environment offers, on the risks and costs of exploiting those opportunities. Here the potential ability of the West to increase the risks and costs of Soviet expansion has a significant influence on Soviet behavior. It is not within the West's power to effect a significant change in the Soviet system or to redirect the Soviet leadership's preoccupations from international to domestic concerns. It *is* within the West's power to frustrate those Soviet global ambitions which are most threatening to the West.[12]

Right before the reader's eyes the fundamental rationale for a policy of containment emerges: the Soviet regime is structured to provide endless challenges; yet nothing can be done to counter that structure, so attention must instead be focused on trying to beat the Soviets back when they go on the offensive. I do not disparage the policy of containment or its rationale. It has put us where we are today. But where we are is not good enough.

Because it presents the rationale for existing policy so well, it is worth listening to Bialer and Afferica take the position exactly contrary to the one developed here:

By making clear that the direct objective of American policies is not to work for the radical change of the Soviet system or its collapse, the Reagan Administration could be much more effective in mobilizing the West, influencing the course of specific Soviet policies, and diminishing the aggressiveness of Soviet international behavior. Those objectives fall far short of what any team of American policymakers may wish, but it describes what is realistic and attainable in dealing with the Soviet Union. The Soviets can hardly be expected to respond to policy overtures of an Administration whose avowed goals are the destruction of the Soviet system or at best the renunciation by Soviet leaders of their aspirations for international influence.[13]

Yet since no American administration has actually tried to alter the Soviet system, one wonders why its conduct has not thus far improved. Acceptance of the legitimacy of the Soviet system in its homeland and in Europe has in fact been American policy, con-tinuously reaffirmed by inaction (beginning with East Berlin in 1953 and Hungary in 1956). What we are offered is the same old policy. There is no reason to believe it will prove any more efficacious in containing Soviet aggression now than it has in the past. It is possible, no doubt, that while containment is inadequate, pluralization could only make things worse. But claiming this is not the same as arguing against a policy of political action on the grounds that containment would produce results not yet achieved in over thirty years.

One should not speak of the Soviet system as evil, it is often said, because the United States needs to make agreements with it and no one wants to be in league with the devil. I disagree. I would be glad to make treaties with the devil, provided it was in our mutual interest. But I would not, while doing so, wish to persuade my people that the devil had suddenly become their guardian angel.

It cannot be done, and it should not be done: these are the objections to a policy of containment plus pluralization. There is no way for the United States to reach inside the Soviet Union, it is said, and if there were, it would be undesirable. Democracies, especially the American version, are said to be unsuited for carrying out a variegated and consistent policy. Either the policy will appear ludicrous, enhancing charges of ineptitude at home, or it will appear threatening, worrying allies more than enemies. What alternative is offered? Containment plus patience. There is nothing America can do, in this view, except to contain where it can while hoping for change inside the Soviet Union. However, if foreign policy is used to stabilize domestic organization within the USSR, as I claim, such a containment policy will only encourage it to do more of the same, leaving the United States to counter increasingly serious challenges abroad without an effective rationale for bearing the burden at home.

Containment must be part of American policy. The question is whether it will remain the only part or will be joined by other elements to make up a broader strategy. What is required is a strategy that will resolve the dilemmas posed by the containment policy as it has operated since World War II without creating new, even worse dilemmas.

In an insightful collection on *Managing U.S.–Soviet Rivalry*, Alexander L. George reminds us that

"crisis prevention," as it was called, was one of the important objectives of the détente process that Nixon and Brezhnev set into motion in 1972.

This objective, however, was not clearly defined. Soviet leaders were interested primarily in avoiding crises that raised the danger of war between the two superpowers. Nixon and Kissinger shared this hope, but increasingly over time, they emphasized that crisis prevention should include the avoidance of crises in third areas resulting from or exacerbated by assertive Soviet behavior that damaged Western interests *even though* these crises did not create the danger of a U.S.–Soviet military clash. The conception of détente held by U.S. leaders and, indeed, by many congressional leaders and much of the interested public, therefore, included a belief that Soviet adherence to the goal of "crisis prevention" implied a willingness on Moscow's part generally to moderate its foreign policy behavior in third areas.[14]

The Basic Principles Agreement Nixon and Brezhnev signed in 1972 glossed over, rather than resolved, this difference. Efforts to redefine the scope of containment so as to reduce the prospect of clashes with the Soviet Union failed, in my view, because the rationale for the Soviet system is bound up in its foreign adventures. By giving the Soviet Union good reasons to reduce aggression, a policy of pluralization is designed to remedy the imbalance of incentives that makes one power perennially offensive and the other largely reactive.

8

CHARLES WOLF, JR.

Extended Containment

Disputes about U.S. policies toward the Soviet Union usually focus on such specific issues as the Strategic Arms Reduction Talks (START); Intermediate-Range Nuclear Forces (INF); "two-tracks," and zero or other options in Europe; human rights and Helsinki's "basket 9"; East-West trade, credit, and technology transactions; the Yamal pipeline. Whatever the specific content of these disputes, at their heart lie two fundamentally opposing beliefs concerning the nature of the Soviet system—how it behaves and responds, and the objectives and motivations of its leaders. The opposition between these outlooks explains the contrasting positions on specific issues, as well as the general foreign policy stances, adopted by such antagonists as Walter Mondale and Ronald Reagan; Cyrus Vance and Zbigniew Brzezinski; George Kennan and Paul Nitze; Marshall Shulman and Richard Pipes; Tom Wicker and William Safire; or *The New York Times* and *The Wall Street Journal*.

These differing beliefs are typically so strongly held as to have the properties of "cognitive dissonance": any fact that is apparently inconsistent with them is either (a) dismissed as deception and falsehood, or (b) interpreted in such a sophistical manner as to be construed as proof rather than disproof of the maintained belief.

Because these fundamental beliefs are usually unacknowledged, or even subconscious, the specific disputes that spring from them are like the images seen by Socrates' cave dwellers: reflections of a distant reality, rather than the reality itself. Similarly, because these beliefs are highly resistant to evidence that is inconsistent with them, they rarely change. To the extent that they are deeply held yet difficult to explicate, they appear to be similar to what Michael Polanyi has referred to as "tacit knowledge."[1] Yet to the extent that those who hold the assumptions avoid or dismiss evidence that is inconsistent with them, they represent dogma rather than knowledge, tacit or otherwise.

Nevertheless, it would be refreshing to see the underlying beliefs plainly identified at the outset of a discussion of policies and policy alternatives, rather than hidden from it. At least this would help those whose minds are not already made up. It might also help those whose minds *are* made up to arrive at "second-order agreement": namely, a mutual understanding of what precisely they disagree about, and what evidence would be required by each party to alter its position.

Toward this end, I will begin by stating what seem to me to be the two main conflicting views about the nature of the Soviet system and the motivations and objectives of its leaders, views that underlie many of the disputes that arise about specific issues and policies. I will also indicate where my own predispositions lie, because this affects the new measures I shall propose later to extend U.S. containment policies. I do not mean to imply, of course, that the two sets of beliefs are the only possible ones; combinations and nuances occur. Not everybody subscribes exactly to one of the two views. Yet the two contrasting positions capture something fundamental about what separates many of the people, institutions, and organizations active in the U.S. policy community, and account to a considerable degree for the alignments that emerge on specific issues.

Mirror-Imaging vs. *Power-Maximizing*

For convenient, if not entirely accurate, reference, I will label the two views as *mirror-imaging* and *power-maximizing*.

The mirror-imaging view of the Soviet system and its leadership holds that Soviet preoccupation with defense grows out of Russian history and culture. Admittedly, this preoccupation may border on paranoia, and consequently may take quite aggressive forms. Such manifestations, however, are considered understandable in the light of Soviet history, including the experience of Western efforts from 1917 to 1920 to abort the Bolshevik Revolution, the twenty million casualties suffered by the Soviet Union in World War II, and the virulently anti-Communist rhetoric that sometimes emanates from right-wing circles in the West. Soviet preoccupation with military strength, and the resulting priority accorded to allocating resources and technology to the military, are, in the mirror-imaging view, explained mainly by this history. But in this vision, the long-term aims of the Soviet system are much like our own: human betterment and well-being, combined with peace, prosperity, and justice. Hence, a more forthcoming U.S. foreign policy, one that combines firmness with concessions, is likely to produce over time a symmetrical rather than an exploitative response from the Soviet leadership, as well as an irenic evolution of the Soviet system.

The power-maximizing view holds that, whatever the bitter and tragic experiences of Soviet history, and whatever the philosophical and ideological antecedents of Soviet Communism, the overriding objective of the system is to maximize the political and military power of the Soviet state at home and to expand it abroad. According to the power-maximizing view, concessions made to the Soviet Union by the United States or the West, and agreements and transactions with it, are fair game for exploitation and deception by the Soviets in the interests of expanding and maximizing their power. This view denies, or at least seriously doubts, that economic and social betterment are basic goals of the Soviet system. Instead, the power-maximizing view suggests that the sacrifice of such goals will be accepted and even obscurely welcomed by Soviet leaders as a way of justifying to the Russian people the enhancement of Soviet vigilance and power in response to ubiquitous external and internal "threats."

These two views dictate contrasting dispositions toward the Soviet Union. Adherents to mirror-imaging tend to favor a policy of accommodation or, at most, of limited containment. They will be relaxed, compared with power-maximizing adherents, about the consequences of Soviet "gains" if containment does not work. After all, such gains may entail some gains for us, too. For those who view Soviet values as mirroring our own, Soviet gains may be seen as providing reassurances to the Soviets, thus easing their defensive paranoia. This in turn will enable us to live more amicably with them.

By contrast, those adhering to the power-maximizing view regard Soviet realization of gains as much closer to a "zero-sum" process: gains realized by the Soviet Union contribute to its power and thereby to its further expansion. The result works increasingly to the detriment of the United States, which is why resistance and reversal of Soviet expansion are important in this outlook.

Those who see the Soviets as power-maximizing tend to endorse the disestablishment of the Soviet empire by all prudent means. Several of the ideas I will present later reflect this disposition. By contrast, adherents of mirror-imaging tend to disagree with these ideas and the purpose to which they are addressed. For, say the mirror-imagers, Soviet gains are not really too significant. After all, these apparent gains are beset by costs and uncertainties (e.g., Poland and Afghanistan). And, if such gains do contribute to Soviet self-confidence, that may be good for us, too (i.e., mirror-imaging is a *non*-zero-sum process).

Another striking contrast between the two views lies in their divergent positions concerning nuclear deterrence.

Holders of the mirror-imaging view gravitate toward "mutual assured destruction" and "minimum deterrence" in nuclear strategy. Threatening Soviet leadership with a second-strike capability, one that can inflict huge casualties on *population and civil industry,* will, according to adherents of mirror-imaging, suffice to deter Soviet attack on the United States and (less assuredly) on our NATO allies. Why? Because these targets are held to represent the fundamental *values* that are, through mirror-imaging, attributed to Soviet leadership by reason of the fact that we ourselves adhere to them. *Countervalue* then is the name of the deterrence game, and the values implied are precisely the ones we ourselves cherish.

The opposing view suggests that power, rather than human life and well-being, is the preeminent value motivating the Soviet party and state. Hence, nuclear deterrence should rely more heavily on "counterforce" capability, or an ability to strike the military forces, bases, and command-and-control centers on which Soviet power depends. Because, according to this view, the instruments of Soviet power are the leadership's quintessential "values," *counterforce* targeting is likely to be a more effective deterrent than targeting people and civil industry. According to this position, counterforce *is* countervalue!

As I have indicated, my own position is close to the latter; this will be evident in some of the proposals I advance below for "extended containment." It is, nevertheless, important to recognize that many, and perhaps most, putative "experts" on the Soviet Union subscribe to the mirror-imaging view, as does each of the first-named members of the six paired adversaries mentioned at the outset of this essay, as well as most of our European allies.

Two brief quotations convey, rather cogently I believe, the essentials of the power-maximizing position. The first passage comes from a former professor and chairman of the Department of Civil Law at Leningrad University, Olympiad Ioffe; the second comes from Milovan Djilas, whose intimate experience with Soviet as well as Yugoslav Communism extends over four or five decades. According to Professor Ioffe:

> The consistent policy of the Soviet State is to subordinate purely economic goals to the aim of building unlimited political power . . . and the legal regulation of the Soviet economy is carefully designed to implement that policy. . . . The leadership has made the economy work splendidly as the source of its dictatorship. In this regard, Soviet economic policy has never suffered a single real failure. . . . The Soviet economy is inefficient only as a source of material wellbeing, [but] material welfare there is simply incompatible with the aims of the Soviet system. . . . What could be done . . . to improve fundamentally the Soviet economy as a source of material welfare, without simultaneously undercutting the might of the state? Given the existing political system, only one answer is possible—nothing.[2]

According to Mr. Djilas:

Soviet communism . . . is a military empire. It was transformed into a
military empire in Stalin's time. Internally, such structures usually rot . . .
but to avoid internal problems, they may go for expansion. The West
must be strong if it wants to save peace and stop Soviet expansionism. If
it is stopped, the process of rotting will go faster.[3]

As I have implied above, the power-maximizing view underlies
some of the specific directions for U.S. policy that I will propose
later in this essay. Of course, I cannot prove or test, in any
meaningful sense, the hypothesis embodied in this perspective. A
few salient considerations, however, seem to me to provide support
for this view of the Soviet Union in contrast to mirror-imaging:

- While Marxist-Leninist ideology proclaims economic and social
  well-being for the masses as the ultimate aim of the system, the
  system's performance is very different. In reality, there have
  been much more limited rates of improvement in civilian consumption, nutrition, housing, and health than have been experienced in Western economic systems. The Soviet Union is
  the only industrialized country in the world in which life expectancy has decreased and infant mortality has increased in the
  past decade—at the same time that Soviet military power has
  grown enormously and expensively.

- The declared political aim of the Soviet system is to move
  toward a "dictatorship of the proletariat," with the working
  class playing a "leading role" in the process. Again, the reality
  is quite different: namely, dictatorship *to* the proletariat, as was
  blatantly illustrated by the military suppression of Poland's
  trade union movement beginning in December 1981.

- The social aim of Marxism-Leninism is a classless society. In
  reality, the system is a rigid hierarchy within each of the three
  dominant bureaucracies: party, government, and military.
  Sharp differences of power, privilege, and perquisites exist even
  among the controlling elites.

- In terms of economic performance (as contrasted with power
  maximization), the Communist system has been relatively unsuccessful. In the Soviet Union over the past decade (and pro-
  spectively over the next decade), the economy has shown

declining rates of growth in real GNP, increasing capital/ output ratios, declining labor productivity and total factor productivity, and only very limited improvements in personal consumption, as noted above.

- Only in one field has the system been strikingly successful: the development of military and political power. In the Soviet Union, there has been an extraordinary buildup of nuclear and conventional power, of ground forces, naval forces, and air forces. Growth of real defense spending has been sustained over the last decade at a rate slightly above that of the growth of the Soviet economy as a whole. Growth of Soviet military investment—that is, procurement of military equipment—has been substantially larger than that of the United States. In most other Communist systems, too—e.g., Cuba, Nicaragua, Vietnam, North Korea— the most dramatic evidence of sustained growth is found in military forces and military production rather than in civilian economic development and betterment.

With this as background, let me turn to two ideas for extending containment in new directions. One direction is concerned with countering and reversing the expansion of the Soviet empire; the other is concerned with realistic rules for the conduct of economic relations with the Soviet Union in an environment of "extended containment." I intend these as extensions, rather than as a fundamental revamping, of containment. "Extended containment," like "extended deterrence," is not without its limits. The reasons for advocating these extensions lie in the unsatisfactory outcomes that have resulted from "limited" containment—that is, from U.S. policies that have, at their best, faced the Soviet Union with uncertainty concerning the *rate* of its expansion, not the *sign*. Extended containment, in the proposals described below, would change this by providing *competition* for gains that the Soviets have already enjoyed, as well as containment of further gains. Thus the Soviet Union would face uncertainty regarding the sign as well as the rate of expansion of its empire.

Reversing Expansion of the Soviet Empire

The years since World War II have seen either the demise or the severe diminution of the colonial empires of the past—British,

French, Japanese, and Dutch. The less formal reflections of U.S. "hegemony" in various parts of the world have also waned sharply after their transitory appearance in the 1950s and 1960s. Only the Soviet empire, despite occasional setbacks, has expanded in a sustained and substantial manner.

Is it appropriate to use the term *empire* to describe the Soviet Union's expansion?

There are, of course, three different Soviet empires: the empire "at home" (i.e., the empire that lies within the geographic boundaries of the Soviet state); the geographically contiguous part of the empire (i.e., Eastern Europe and, more recently, Afghanistan); and the empire "abroad."

The empire "at home" is the subject of Hélène Carrère d'Encausse's recent study.[4] The Soviet Union is a multinational state, consisting of fifteen distinct national republics and over sixty nationalities, twenty-three of which have populations larger than a million. The internal empire is the product of the eastward expansion of Czarist Russia during the century before the Leninist revolution. But it is the two other Soviet empires that interest us here.

In the past dozen years or so, the Soviet imperium has come to include Angola, Ethiopia, South Yemen, Vietnam, Laos, Cambodia, Benin, Mozambique, Afghanistan, Nicaragua, Syria, and Libya, in addition to its prior and continuing satellites, allies, and associates in Eastern Europe, Cuba, and, more ambiguously, North Korea. Of course, the pattern and degree of Soviet influence or control vary considerably across these countries.

The degree of Soviet control varies: it is strongest in Eastern Europe and weakest in North Korea. Nevertheless, all these nations lie within the "sliding scale" of possibilities classified by J. A. Hobson under the term *empire* in his classic study of the nineteenth-century British version.[5]

Although there have been some Soviet setbacks (e.g., Somalia, Egypt, and Indonesia), the gains and extensions of the Soviet empire have vastly exceeded its losses and retrenchments. This is not to deny that the Soviet Union is beset by serious problems in Eastern Europe and on its eastern border with China, to say nothing of its increasingly serious economic, social, and ethnic problems at home. Nor does it deny that the acquisition and ex-

pansion of the empire impose significant costs on the Soviet economy. However, the benefits to the Soviet Union resulting from the
empire—the political advantages, both at home and abroad, as
well as the tangible military advantages of bases and base rights
in various parts of the empire—are likely to appear to the Soviet
leadership quite substantial in relation to these costs. Consequently, we probably should expect continued efforts by the Soviet
Union to expand its empire.

Current U.S. containment policy lacks any appropriate means
to counter or reverse this trend. To reduce the Soviet empire requires a basic policy resolution, as well as the development of pru-
dential means for implementation. This is the reason why an extension of containment that is explicitly "anti-imperialist" as well
as supportive of pluralism and self-determination is needed in U.S.
foreign policy. To formulate this extension requires a brief consideration of how the Soviet Union has expanded its empire in the
past decade.

The dramatic expansion of the Soviet empire has been accomplished through a skillful combination of military power, political
adroitness, covert operations, economic and financial support, and
organizational inventiveness. It has been carried out under two
broad doctrinal positions that allow ample room for adaptation to
specific opportunities and circumstances: first, the doctrine of
support for "wars of national liberation" from Western colonial-
ism and imperialism; and, second, the Brezhnev doctrine of Soviet
support for "fraternal states" in which Communism is threatened
by efforts to undermine it.

Under these doctrines the Soviet Union has successfully
developed a wide range of policy instruments to expand its do-
main: providing trade subsidies and export credits; extending economic assistance; providing military equipment and training; fur-
nishing airlift, sealift, logistic support, and command, control,
communications and intelligence (C³I) services in support of
foreign operations; and developing and managing Cuban and East
German allied or proxy forces for combat, internal security, and
police roles abroad. In these operations Soviet combat forces have
rarely been used directly, except as a last resort in such excep-
tional circumstances as Afghanistan.

Current U.S. containment policy is conceptually, materially, and organizationally ill-suited to contest and reverse the operational techniques—political, military, and economic—by which the Soviet Union has expanded its empire. Indeed, Soviet efforts to expand the empire have been considerably more subtle, flexible, and adroit than U.S. efforts to contain it. Use of the Rapid Deployment Force (RDF)—to look ahead—may be valuable in certain extreme contingencies, such as seizing and protecting oil production centers on the eastern or western side of the Persian Gulf, as well as ports along the Gulf. But such uses are likely to be rare. If attempts were made to use the RDF in the more likely and recurring appearances of Cuban or East German proxy forces in such ambivalent and localized contingencies as Angola, South Yemen, and Ethiopia, the result would probably be hostility abroad and the loss of political support at home. These are precisely the kinds of contingencies that have arisen in the past decade in the Caribbean and Latin America, as well as in Africa and the Middle East, and that have provided opportunities for the Soviet Union to expand its empire. Such contingencies are likely to provide similar opportunities in the next decade as well.

Extending Containment

To extend existing U.S. containment policy, so that it confronts more realistically and effectively the realities of Soviet imperial expansion, requires a combination of new declaratory policies, reallocation of U.S. resources, organizational changes within the executive branch, altered policies for guiding the programming of military and economic assistance, and changes in the conduct of U.S. diplomacy.[6] These changes would focus principally on U.S. policies in that amorphous and heterogeneous group of countries loosely referred to as the Third World.

Declaratory policies. Extended containment requires two innovations in U.S. declaratory policies. The first is a declaration of explicit and overt—yet selective, limited, and measured—support for genuine and legitimate movements within the Third World that seek to achieve liberation from Communist imperialism and totalitarianism, and that also seek to advance more pluralistic, open, and at least incipiently democratic forms of government. Achieving support both at home and abroad for such a declaratory policy requires emphasis on both the positive elements, indicating what the policy seeks to achieve, and the negative elements, plainly labeling what the policy opposes.

The anti-Communist liberation movements that we may wish to support are not likely to be ideal democracies, either in operation or in aspiration. Instead, they will usually be characterized by elements of demagogy, elitism, repression, and even brutality. These characteristics, where they occur, should be recognized and labeled for what they are. At the same time, we should emphasize the elements of openness and pluralism that differentiate the movements we might support from the Communist totalitarianism they seek to supplant. We should emphasize the positive differences in favor of these movements, while acknowledging the shortcomings that remain.[7] Like the Soviet doctrine of support for "wars of national liberation," the doctrine of support for Movements of National Liberation from Communist Imperialism (MNLCI) should be overt and explicit, and not directed principally toward covert assistance. Equally important, such support should be limited in scope and magnitude. It should be confined to selected contingencies in which the legitimacy and demonstrated capabilities of a candidate movement augur well for effective and successful utilization of the limited support to be provided. Yet the real uncertainties involved in providing such support should be explicitly recognized as part of the declaratory policy. It should be understood that implementation will entail losses as well as gains; "calculated" losses are to be anticipated. Recognition that the outcome is uncertain is essential to avoid escalation of the intentionally limited support.*

Where might such movements arise? Prospects are modest at best. The principal reason is that Communist systems accord such high priority to strengthening their surveillance and security apparatus that aborning movements seeking "national liberation"

---

*Anticipation of losses creates an obvious temptation to proceed covertly and thereby avoid damage to U.S. prestige, a temptation that should be resisted for several reasons. One reason is that to acquire and sustain support within the United States for the policy redirection I am proposing, prior debate, including recognition of costs as well as benefits, is necessary. Without the former, the credibility of the latter will be diminished. Another reason is simply the difficulty of assuring covertness, and the high likelihood in the U.S. context that efforts to do so will backfire.

tend to be spotted early and coopted or ruthlessly crushed. The Shah's heralded and hated security system, Savak, was much less extensive and thorough, for example, than Castro's "normal" state security apparatus. Under the circumstances, fledgling movements will face an uphill struggle to get started. But the start-up is a problem they must solve themselves if their prospects for survival, growth, and legitimacy are to be helped by limited and measured U.S. support. Among countries in the Soviet empire where such possibilities exist are Nicaragua, South Yemen, Mozambique, Angola, Benin, and Cuba. Genuine and legitimate movements in two or three Communist states would turn what has been a one-sided Communist-led "national liberation" arena into a more genuinely competitive one.

The Western media and the American Congress have often gone out of their way to uncover elements of legitimacy (e.g., land reform, or the reduction of exploitation and inequality) in Communist-led guerrilla movements. The Sandinista movement in Nicaragua was one example; El Salvador is another. One sign of success for the policy redirection I am proposing would be registered when the media and Congress could discern some degree of legitimacy in the anti-Communist guerrilla movements seeking national liberation from Communist imperialism.

A second innovation in American declaratory policies would affirm a U.S. intention to collaborate with, and provide support for, certain *associated countries* whose interests converge with those of the United States in opposing the use of Communist proxy forces in the Third World, and in advancing more pluralistic and open societies in these areas. The countries that might participate in such a loose association with the United States need be no closer geographically to the areas in which their forces might operate than those areas are to the Cuban and East German forces associated with the Soviet Union.

By focusing on such associated countries, this doctrine would not exclude the possibility of collaboration with our traditional NATO allies in activities outside the NATO area as well. The aim would merely be to give greater attention to such Third World countries as South Korea, Pakistan, Turkey, Egypt, Venezuela, and Taiwan as more promising candidates for these collaborative roles than our traditional European allies.

Reallocation of resources. To implement these new declaratory policies, modest reallocations of defense resources would be necessary. It would obviously be easiest if these incremental needs could be met by budget increases, but it is possible that they will need to be met within existing or planned budget levels. Underlying these suggestions is an important assumption: that the balance of forces in the strategic area (especially if a suitable basing mode for the MX can be formulated) and in the NATO theater (assuming that some INF deployment goes forward, together with suitable modernization of conventional NATO forces) is more stable and secure than is the balance in the Third World areas where the Soviet empire continues to expand. Hence, the development of a more realistic extension of containment policy requires actions that focus on these latter areas.

To implement the proposed extension and redirection of containment policy, U.S. airlift and sealift forces should be specifically earmarked to provide mobility for forces from the associated countries. If this policy is to be taken seriously, specific U.S. units should also be designated and exercised to provide resupply and logistics support, as well as C^3I. These earmarked forces should be configured to operate in conjunction with the Associated Country Forces (ACF), rather than with wholly American units such as the proposed Rapid Deployment Force. While these forces would presumably have joint capabilities to provide support for U.S. forces and for the ACF, specific training (including language training), as well as suitable equipment, would be needed if the operations in conjunction with the ACF were to proceed smoothly.

For implementing the declaratory policy of providing support for indigenous movements, special organizational and intelligence capabilities would be needed within the U.S. government (see below). In addition, there would be a need for light weapons designed for easy and speedy delivery by air and sea, as well as for easy maintenance and decentralized delivery and use by appropriate "liberation" movements. Provision of individually operated anti-tank and anti-aircraft weapons for Afghan freedom fighters would be an example.

None of this would obviate the need for a Rapid Deployment Force. Notwithstanding its limited utility for meeting challenges posed by expansion of the Soviet empire, the RDF retains an es-

sential function in these contingencies: to provide a backup to
deter Soviet intervention. Such forces would be deployed only in
the event that Soviet forces were directly committed, or seemed
likely to be. Yet even unused, the RDF would perform an invalu-
able role as a reassuring guarantor for the ACF; indeed, without
such reassurance, the likelihood of ACF participation would be
severely diminished.

Organizational changes. To implement the declaratory policies and the types of operations described above would require organizational changes within the U.S. government. There is need
for an organizational entity with authority to span the military
services and to mobilize the multiple instruments of foreign and
defense policy for the purpose of providing support for the ACF
and for MNLCI.

To conduct these operations, organizational innovation is
needed to provide planning and C³I; to call up airlift, sealift, and
logistic support; to provide military and economic aid; and, in some
cases, to supply direct financial assistance. No such centralized
organizational entity now exists. Instead, the required functions
are spread loosely among the Departments of Defense and State
and the intelligence community.

**Planning and programming economic and security assis-
tance.** Forms of U.S. economic and security assistance have
typically been considered, planned, and administered separately
from one another. Although there have been divergent views on
this issue in the recurring debates on foreign assistance, separation between the two has been favored on various grounds. Principal among them is the view that security assistance is a direct or
indirect aspect of U.S. defense preparedness, whereas economic
and technical aid have a longer-term and broader relationship to
U.S. foreign policy, to a brighter and more progressive image of
the United States in the world, and so on.

To implement the objectives and declaratory policies advocated
here—both for supporting indigenous movements and for developing an ACF—a tighter link is needed between the planning and
operational responsibility for economic aid and that for security
assistance. Both forms of assistance are instruments of U.S.

foreign policy; they are not ends in themselves. These programs should be planned and conducted together, permitting them to be more sharply focused toward the achievement of U.S. objectives.[8]

Diplomacy and "linkage." The Soviet Union has repeatedly asserted that its support for wars of national liberation, and for Cuban and East German allied or proxy forces in the Third World, is entirely compatible with arms limitation negotiations and with agreements in both the strategic area and the NATO area, as well as with continued economic relations between East and West.[9]

The United States should adopt a similar stance in public and in the conduct of private diplomacy. U.S. support for indigenous movements and for the ACF should not be viewed as incompatible with the pursuit of opportunities for mutual benefit between East and West in the domains of arms limitation and of economic, financial, and technological exchanges. For the United States to conduct diplomacy in support of the extended containment policies advocated here, while at the same time maintaining a receptive stance toward other dimensions of relationships with the Soviet Union, is as difficult a task to bring off domestically as it is worthwhile internationally, especially in relations with our European allies.

F. Scott Fitzgerald once observed that the test of a first-rate intelligence is the ability to hold two opposed ideas at the same time and still retain the capacity for effective action. To create and sustain political support for a two-track policy in the domestic political environment of the United States requires first-rate leadership no less than first-rate intelligence. In principle, and in the abstract, the opportunity exists to link the two: if both tracks are cogently articulated and prudently implemented, they can provide the makings of a reasonable coalition between the Right and the Left, between conservatives and liberals. Translating the abstract into the concrete is what requires first-rate political leadership.

Extending Containment in the Economic Realm

It is useful to distinguish three different directions for United States and Western economic policies toward the Soviet Union, although various combinations among them are also possible:

- Government subsidies to encourage East-West transactions.

- Embargoes or sanctions to cut off such transactions.

- Removing subsidies and avoiding embargoes, letting the market function to facilitate or foreclose particular transactions.

Subsidization was pursued in the 1970s by the West in the spirit of détente. This effort was notably unsuccessful in influencing Soviet behavior along the congenial lines that were hoped for by its advocates. Instead, throughout the decade the Soviets pursued an unprecedented buildup of military power, continued to expand their external empire in Angola, Nicaragua, Mozambique, Ethiopia, and South Yemen, invaded Afghanistan, and managed the suppression of Solidarity in Poland.

Both embargoes and a strict market regime would represent a restriction of East-West trade and West-East credits compared with subsidization.

Clearly, the side effects of the latter two policies are likely to differ sharply: opposition within the Western alliance to a strict market regime would be much more limited than opposition to a policy of embargoes, as was indicated by the overreaction of our European allies to the relatively short-lived embargo by the president on compressors for the Yamal pipeline.

The market regime probably comes closest to what might be termed *economic realism*. Such a policy would, on the one hand, avoid the discredited optimism of the 1970s subsidization policy, while on the other hand limiting the intra-Alliance damage and the serious difficulty of implementation that would ensue if embargoes or sanctions were adopted instead.

This position may seem rather bland: advocacy of a strict market regime is like support for balanced budgets and motherhood. General support is expressed for the principle, but sharp differences emerge over specific issues. For example, the Germans argue that the loan guarantees extended to the Soviet Union by their Hermes organization do not represent inappropriate subsidies, but simply constitute a normal means of carrying on international trade. In fact, it can be shown that such guarantees really do constitute a subsidy, and the amount of the subsidy is substantial.[10] Similarly, the French say that charging the Russians an interest rate of 9.5 percent on loans connected with the Yamal pipeline did not represent a subsidy, and in any event was a higher rate than the Germans were charging!

To effect the removal of subsidies requires that certain rules of the game be established for conducting East-West economic relations. Although it is important to seek agreement on these rules with the Alliance, I will argue later that if such agreement is not forthcoming, the United States should pursue and apply the rules unilaterally. The following are examples of rules I would propose:

- No loan or investment guarantee should be available to Western lenders or investors engaged in transactions with the East unless these guarantees are extended *without* direct or indirect government underwriting.

- No concessionary interest terms should be made available to either government or commercial borrowers in the Soviet Union or in Eastern Europe. The minimum criterion for implementation of this rule should be that interest rates applying to loans to the Soviet Union and Eastern Europe should not be less than the *highest* rates charged to domestic or other foreign borrowers on loans of equivalent duration.*

- No preferential tax treatment should be accorded to either individual or corporate income derived from transactions with the Soviet Union or Eastern Europe. (The preferential tax treatment extended under the Domestic International Sales Corporation Program in the United States would have to be modified to comply with this rule.)

The purpose of such rules would be to reduce and remove the extensive network of subsidies that has undergirded economic transactions with the Soviet Union and the other countries of the Council for Mutual Economic Assistance (CMEA) over the past decade. These subsidies have contributed to the huge expansion of net West-East resource flows, totaling more than $80 billion during the 1970s. The intended result is to restrict such flows in the

---

*This rule assumes that the additional political, as well as economic, risk involved in loans to the Council for Mutual Economic Assistance (CMEA) countries inevitably makes such loans at least as risky as any other domestic or international loans of equivalent duration. In light of the record of delinquency, due to political and economic circumstances, in these loans in recent years, this assumption seems quite justifiable.

future to no more than what an unsubsidized market would allow. Such restrictions can help, albeit only modestly, to constrain Soviet allocation decisions, to impede the management and expansion of the Soviet empire, and possibly to bring resource pressures to bear in the longer run that will tend to reduce the Soviet military buildup.[11]

Two arguments are usually raised against such attempts to put teeth into the rules governing East-West commerce. One is that these measures would amount to economic warfare and would therefore be politically undesirable, especially from the viewpoint of our European allies. The second argument is that while such rules might have some effect if applied collectively by the West and Japan, collective action is really unlikely, and unilateral application would have only negligible effects. I will consider these arguments in turn.

The term *economic warfare* does not have a precise technical meaning, and the loose and diverse ways in which it has been used in the media and elsewhere have not contributed to resolving this imprecision. The official *Dictionary of Military and Associated Terms* defines it as "aggressive use of economic means to achieve national objectives."[12] Elsevier's *Economics Dictionary* defines it as "non-violent activities aimed at making one nation's economy dominant over that of another nation."[13]

A better and more comprehensive definition of economic warfare is presented in the *Encyclopedia of the Social Sciences:* "state interference in international economic relations for the purpose of improving the relative economic, military or political position of a country." *Interference* is further described as having two components: *coercion,* through denial of trade or resources, or the threat of such denial; and *persuasion,* through the conferral of economic "favors . . . [by which] a country may expect in return reciprocal favors in the form of political support, or alliance, or perhaps neutrality."[14]

According to the last definition, economic warfare includes the conferral of economic "favors." Hence, it would seem that the subsidies provided during the past decade to encourage East-West trade have already constituted a form of economic warfare. Consequently, removing these subsidies can hardly be said to constitute economic warfare![15]

It may be worth recalling Lenin's maxim: "When we are ready, the West will sell us the rope with which to hang them." While refusing to *sell* the rope may be economic warfare, refusing to give it away or to subsidize its sale is certainly not!

The second argument against my proposed rules of commerce is that they cannot be adopted multilaterally, and will be ineffectual if adopted unilaterally. Clearly, action taken in concert with our European allies and Japan is far preferable to action by the U.S. alone. This is partly because the United States has been a minority lender in the West-East capital flows of the past decade—about 15 percent of the total CMEA debt is held by U.S. banks and agencies. Including the "majority" lenders would make the rules more effective. Also, multilateral action would promote rather than strain the cohesion of the Alliance. Nonetheless, I believe that announcing and observing these rules unilaterally, if necessary, would be worthwhile, provided that the action were preceded by a serious but non-hectoring effort to convince our allies to join us.

The United States has tremendous influence in the international financial community. If U.S. banks and exporters were to follow these rules, several important consequences would follow:

- Other members of the international financial community would simply feel less confident about going it alone, without U.S. financial participation in the usual consortium arrangements.

- While European exporters might realize some one-sided gains, these would probably be short-lived.

- American banks would probably extend more credit domestically and in other parts of the world than in Eastern Europe and the Soviet Union. Thus, U.S. credit would be redirected, probably with beneficial consequences.

- Even if the European banks were to continue to extend credits facilitated by government subsidies, their asset portfolios, I suggest, would be damaged by the accumulation of questionable loans to the CMEA countries. Consequently, these institutions would become less attractive to depositors and investors than would their American counterparts. Anticipation of this outcome would probably lead the European institutions to follow a more prudent course of action.

Although it is conventional to observe in banking circles that, after all, the Soviet Union itself is a good credit risk, this is a more dubious proposition than most bankers realize. It is true that the financial ratios that bankers typically look at in assessing credit risks are relatively favorable for the Soviet Union. But this is only a small part of the true story. Several adverse contingencies (by no means adding up to a "worst case") could sharply reverse Soviet financial prospects. Such contingencies would include, for example, reductions in Soviet oil exports and persistent soft world oil prices, continued poor Soviet agricultural performance together with large Soviet grain imports at high world prices, and a diminution in the international market for weapons (which has been a major hard currency earner for the Soviet Union in recent years). Thus, the Soviet Union's hard currency position is especially vulnerable to adverse changes in just a small set of product and commodity markets. In fact, the creditworthiness of the Soviet Union is more precarious than is usually recognized.

I conclude these remarks concerning economic realism with one slightly whimsical observation. Even if the rules advocated here are not adopted multilaterally, and even if they are applied less rigorously by the United States acting alone than I would like to see, the "invisible hand" of international financial markets may accomplish much of what the visible hand of government does not. In the 1980s, capital is likely to be less readily available in international markets than was the case in the 1970s. The petrodollar recycling phenomenon of that earlier decade is not likely to recur. Hence the Soviet Union and Eastern Europe will find their access to foreign borrowing much more restricted than before, even apart from the policies I have suggested.

How would Soviet behavior be affected by the policy of economic realism I have proposed? There are three logical possibilities. First, what is economic realism to us may be so provocative to the Soviet Union that it might actually devote more rather than less effort to military spending, external mischief-making, or internal repressiveness, notwithstanding diminution of the aggregate resources on which it could draw.

Second, once the Soviets become convinced of the firmness and credibility of U.S. and Western intentions they might instead adopt a more accommodating and conciliatory stance.

Finally, Soviet behavior may not be discernibly affected by this policy at all. It is possible that Soviet actions are impelled almost exclusively by internal pressures, forces, and factions, and will fail to be either provoked or restrained by Western economic policy, at least in the short run.

I have heard plausible arguments in support of the first two possibilities. Nonetheless, until much stronger evidence is offered, my own inclination is to say that the third outcome is most likely. In the short run, Soviet priorities and behavior are likely to be governed by factors inherent in the Soviet system rather than by changes in Western economic policy, and these factors differ very little under Andropov from what they were under Brezhnev.

Nonetheless, a policy of restricting resource flows, by removing the subsidies that have lubricated such flows in the past, would place greater pressure on the Soviet economy in the middle and longer run. Such a policy would thereby tend to expose the inherent economic, political, and social contradictions within the Communist system. It is important to remember that what is being suggested here is simply a policy of economic realism; it is *not* a policy for bringing the Soviet Union to its knees, or bringing about the "collapse of the Soviet system," as some of the media critics of the policy have occasionally portrayed it. Instead, the effects on Soviet behavior of such a policy would be modest and gradual, and would be felt only over the longer run. This argues for moving our policy in an economically realistic direction now rather than later.

Pluralism and Extended Containment

None of the proposals described here is incompatible with the strategy of "containment plus political action" advocated by Aaron Wildavsky—the effort to sow the seeds of pluralism in Soviet soil by means of broadcasts, cassettes, leaflets, and books composed and transmitted through private American groups. I endorse this approach. The attempt proposed here to develop Associated Country Forces to counter the use of Cuban and East German proxies by the Soviet Union is similarly pluralistic in aim because it extends containment in the direction of competition.

Nevertheless, while I applaud efforts to develop pluralism within the Soviet Union, I am skeptical about their effectiveness. I share the view expressed by the principal figure in Saul Bellow's *The Dean's December:*

It was one of the greatest achievements of communism to seal off so many millions of people. You wouldn't have thought it possible in this day and age that the techniques of censorship should equal the techniques of transmission.[16]

In short, promoting pluralism in a system as tightly shackled as that of the Soviet Union is a formidable task. One should not expect too much from a Western informational barrage, although the effort is surely worth undertaking.

9

MAX SINGER

Dynamic Containment

The danger of nuclear war is well known. Although most human life would survive, an unlimited nuclear war with current weapons systems could end the history of the United States and kill as many as a billion human beings in only a month or so. This means that close to a quarter of all the people alive in the world today could die within a relatively small number of days. Such a war would also have secondary and tertiary effects that would be detectable for centuries, although it is very unlikely that all such effects together would be as harmful or horrible as the short-term death and destruction. Since the biggest wars in this century killed on the order of thirty million people during four or five years (1 or 2 percent of the world population), it is clear that nuclear war threatens a new level of destruction; and future technology could make it worse.

The other stakes in our conflict with the Soviet Union are less well understood, and rarely felt by most Americans, but they are equally real. During this century a number of countries have come under totalitarian rule—including Russia and Germany before World War II, and Eastern Europe, China, Cuba, Vietnam, Cambodia, etc., since 1945. It could happen to the United States, too. If it did we would not necessarily suffer as much as the Cambodians have, but there would be horrors and they would not be theoretical.

Like adolescents who rarely understand that accidents do not happen only to other people, Americans rarely understand that political disaster—violent and polarized politics, civil war, conquest, or tyranny—does not happen only to other countries. Most Americans talk, think, and act as if the strong and righteous could not be conquered, as if power always reflected the popular will, and as if safety were assured by the fundamental "health" or legitimacy of a society. Furthermore, some Americans behave as though stress on our system could only improve it because it could not be worse. Unfortunately all of these ideas are demonstrably false.

There are four possibilities for the United States:

• We will be safe because the Soviets will stumble.

• We will be able to protect ourselves with our present leadership community, even without a Soviet stumble.

• We will suffer a shock great enough to change our leadership community in time to protect ourselves.

• We will come under Soviet power, whether on the model of Finland, Cuba, Poland, or Cambodia.

My own view is that each of these possibilities is as likely as any other, give or take a factor of two.

The Soviet Problem

The basic theme for understanding the Soviet Union is the interplay of contradictory truths: on the one hand great power, insatiable defensive interests, and therefore grave threat; on the other hand caution, fundamental weakness, failure, decadence, disillusion, and eventual collapse. They do not want war but they are dangerous.

The Communist party has succeeded in organizing what seems to be a stable apparatus for governing as well as protecting itself. It is also able to generate reasonably competent military, diplomatic, and political warfare programs. (Although even here its performance is by no means outstanding, given the resources used.) The Party seems to have developed techniques for succession and high-level competition for power that are less sudden and deadly than those used during the first forty years after the revolution, although it would be a mistake to assume that these techniques have achieved the reliability of stable institutions.

From the point of view of genuine believers in Communism as well as of the people of the Soviet Union, the Party is a dreadful disease. It is unimaginably corrupt, cynical, and in large part incompetent, except at personal aggrandizement and the maintenance of power. This selfish, vicious, immensely conservative, and uncreative mass of millions of men and women dominates the Soviet Union and exploits its peoples.

Control of the instruments of force provides the Party with its direct power, but Communist ideology is the basis of whatever legitimacy it has. In the long run both elements — coercion and authority — are needed. Communist ideology is also important as a motivating and socializing mechanism within the Party and to a lesser extent in the government.

Unfortunately for the Soviets, the central features of their ideology have proved to be largely a failure. Very few people who have experience with or substantial knowledge about Communist governments believe in Communism. It is widely recognized, especially inside the Soviet Union, that the ideological prescriptions, as the Soviets have been able to apply them, have failed to produce either a happy people (a "classless society") or economic success relative to other countries — although the substantial growth in Soviet wealth since 1917 has limited the sense of failure because people notice that living conditions have improved a great deal, even though many also notice how much better other countries are doing.

Nevertheless it seems likely that a few of the top Party leaders still believe in some form of their ideology in a way that is important for them — i.e., not only as a useful organizing charade. And sad as the ideology is, for the Party it is their own and all they have, and they need it; so they will go to great lengths to preserve and protect it. It must be added, however, that the ideological points they will insist on are not necessarily those that believers would care about, nor those that logical analysis would consider important. The Party's ideological sticking points will be deter-mined instead by symbolic significance, fashion, politics, and sometimes even chance.

In any case, failures notwithstanding, for purposes of foreign consumption their ideology retains a good deal of potency.

Some analysts, in discussion of which forms of government are the worst, make much of the "authoritarian-totalitarian" distinc-tion. Others create rating systems in terms of degree of allowed debate, numbers of political prisoners or executions, and so forth. But it is better to try to understand countries in terms of overall "personality" or type, rather than merely rating them on one or two objective scales.

Totalitarianism is a kind of governmental system that claims the right—often exercised—to control any aspect of its citizens' lives, including what they think, or at least what they say. Such systems require extensive ideologies in order to control religion, culture, etc., or to compete with family.

To maintain themselves in power, totalitarian governments can torture and kill opponents, or they can "just" harass them bureaucratically, threaten them indirectly, have "toughs" beat them up on the street, confine them to be treated with drugs for mental illness, or send them to forced labor camps. All these methods serve the same ends: maintaining the required power and depriving the people—and not just those immediately af-fected—of freedom.

Now the Soviets use less direct torture and murder than they used to, and less than "more primitive" oppressors; but less tor-ture and murder does not necessarily mean more freedom. The Soviet Communists have developed indirect and relatively non-bloody techniques of control to a very advanced state. As a result, practically none of the more than a million people who are cur-rently in Soviet forced labor camps and prisons for "political" reasons was part of any "political opposition." Some say that Andropov is an especially effective devotee of indirect techniques.

It is difficult to comprehend how large and pervasive is the Soviet internal security apparatus for maintaining Party control. It employs well over a million people full time, and has first call on Soviet resources.

No thinking person can believe in a monolithic Communist threat. There is no doubt that there is rivalry, enmity, and even war among Communist countries and groups. Andropov does not control Castro. But neither does Reagan control Schultz or Weinberger. In politics no one gets much use from a person who has so little power that he is "controlled" in the sense that all his acts are the wish of the controller. People who are like Edgar Bergen's Charlie McCarthy play almost no part in government or politics or international affairs; everybody else, however dominated, has some room for following his own wishes in preference to those of whomever he is dominated by.

The straw man of monolithic Communism (or of "control" defined in the Charlie McCarthy sense) is put forward in order to argue that since Communism is not monolithic, one Communist victory doesn't necessarily strengthen the other Communist countries, and that "Communist strength" or "Communist victories" are not meaningful ideas (i.e., there are only Soviet, Chinese, or Cuban strength or victories). This view, that the power of various Communist countries and groups should not be added together in any way in order to assess a "Communist threat," is at least as erroneous as the "monolithic Communism" view.

[The straw man of the domino theory should be cast aside with the related straw man of the monolithic Communist threat. If the domino theory means that the fall of one country will automatically cause the fall of other countries like dominoes, then clearly it is silly.] But that version of the theory is not believed by anyone; it only diverts attention from the political reality that often the fall of one country to Communist control increases the danger to other countries that are related to the "first domino" in significant ways.

The fact that at any moment the Communist world is mixed, divided, differentiated, and partly fighting among itself clearly weakens it and sometimes can be used. Nevertheless, as a general rule, any increase in Communist power anywhere adds to the total long-term threat from Communism and usually from the Soviet Union; and no people anywhere have had their lot improved by coming under Communist control, although some individuals have done nicely.

Soviet Prospects and Dangers

Despite its power, the future of the Communist empire is bleak. Its best prospect for being "saved" is through foreign victories — although I do not believe that this perception drives the Soviet leadership.

A significant indicator of the economic and social prospects of the Soviet Union is its life expectancy trend, which is the only one in the world that is going down. It is quite likely that Soviet economic performance will be more a liability than an asset to the regime during the next twenty years. The same can be said for what might be called social issues.

Internal political prospects in the Soviet empire are more erratic but probably even bleaker. For example, the Polish Communist party has by no means solved its problems with Solidarity and the Polish people. It is not likely to be able to make enough of a deal with Solidarity to persuade the Poles to really start working, because Solidarity's minimum requirement is some form of independent existence as an organization, which is what the Communist party cannot afford. Therefore, living conditions in Poland are likely to get poorer and poorer as it declines toward Albanian standards. This is not a disaster for the Soviet Union, but it is likely to be a negative factor.

Other nationality groups besides the Poles still do not see things as the Soviets think they should, and there are also other potential sources of political conflict.

There is a possibility that a new kind of internal threat to the Communist party may have been presaged in Poland: a tendency for professional military/security elites to gain power at the expense of the Party apparatus. There is some evidence that the people Jaruzelski is bringing to power in Poland are not the officers who staked their careers on Party work and politics (that is, the military sector of the Party), but rather the professional leaders of the army. It is possible that if the Party — in the Soviet Union and other Communist countries — becomes more decadent and incompetent, and some of the military and security services prove to be much more vital and competent professional organizations, these organizational elites will be able gradually to build power at the Party's expense. Industrial or other elites constitute much less of a threat because the Party will always be ready to sacrifice efficiency to maintain its own control, because there is less "professional tradition" outside the military/security services, and because the services have physical power and a special claim to national legitimacy.

A growth of professional military/security elite power relative to the Communist party is a conceivable long-term escape from the trap of Communism for the Soviet Union and its empire. But that escape would take many years, could be derailed in many ways, and is not without its own dangers.

To sum up, there are at least four sources of internal political problems that could influence the nature or strength of the Soviet empire: (1) more national revolts like past examples; (2) substantial and systematic conflict between military/security elites and the Party *nomenklatura;* (3) conflict growing out of efforts to reform from the top; and, (4) least likely, some kind of effective internal pressures for freedom or national justice.

The Soviet system has fundamental internal contradictions and no process for adjusting to them. Sooner or later this means a problem that will get out of hand, although the Soviets may be able to use their highly developed techniques of totalitarian control to contain the problem for generations. The impact on foreign policy of these potential political conflicts is impossible to predict but is likely to be of critical importance.

◁Since the Soviets face bad news on the internal economic, social, and political fronts, their best prospect for maintaining or improving their position is to achieve foreign triumphs, in a much less dramatic and clear-cut version of Hitler's rescue from military overthrow by his early external successes. Unfortunately for us, foreign successes are not unlikely.▷

In brief, one reasonable way to look at the Soviet prospects is as a race between internal collapse and external victory. Either one can happen and the one that comes first may prevent the other.

Fundamentals of Soviet Foreign Policy

The fundamental objective of Soviet foreign policy has to be to preserve their double empire—the Russian empire embodied in the Soviet Union and the Soviet empire embodied in the Warsaw

Pact, to which Afghanistan will probably be added. The requirements of Soviet empire maintenance produce permanent enmity to the United States.

Since an empire always faces centrifugal forces, its safety cannot be assured so long as there is another country in the world with comparable power, because in case of internal crisis the existence of an equal power in the world might prove fatally inhibiting. No matter how sure it is that the other power would never directly intervene, the empire must still be concerned about the possibility that the existence of a countervailing force might make its task of restoring dominance harder.

Therefore American power, however great our good will and peaceful our policy becomes, will always constitute a potential threat to the Soviet empire, and the Soviets must and do see the United States as a potentially deadly enemy. (Also, however benign our policy at any moment, prudence requires that the Soviets protect against the possibility that it might change.)

I believe that although this is Andropov's long-term perspective, he does not fear us in the short term. He has seen how little we have done to counter Soviet efforts in recent years. He knows that the United States knows about most of the activities of the Soviet Union, even if most of the world does not want to hear about them and the truth is not accepted in the Western press and political discussions. I believe he has confidence in his ideas about the reasons that have kept us from responding in the past, and therefore is sure that unless our leadership community changes the United States poses no threat. It is most likely that the conclusion he draws from this is that he has the opportunity and the obligation to use current American weakness to change the correlation of forces so greatly that if a different community ever comes to power in the United States it will be too late, and his successors will never have to worry about the United States, no matter how serious an internal crisis the Soviet empire may be facing.

To gain a clear view of the situation Americans need to understand that profound feelings of hatred and enmity may be non-pathological emotions. Appreciation of the meaning of enmity is necessary to understand the Soviet attitude toward the United States, although it by no means implies that we must hate the Soviets.

The Soviet Union is best understood as *insatiably* defensive. There are those who argue, with substantial basis, that the Soviets are committed to an offensive policy — although probably an extremely cautious and patient one — because of ideology or the desire for imperial aggrandizement. However, since their policy, and the danger to us, may be essentially the same regardless of whether their motivation is defensive or offensive, I see no point in insisting on the assertion that their motivation is offensive. Perhaps it is, but we are no better off if it is not.

The insatiability of their self-perceived defensive requirements takes all the relief out of seeing the Soviet Union as a defensive power. This insatiability follows from the fact that they cannot make their fundamental objective — preservation of the empire — truly secure so long as our strength lasts. Therefore they cannot be satisfied as long as we are capable of resisting their demands. (In addition, as students of the Communist culture such as Nathan Leites pointed out many years ago, the whole operational style and drive of those who succeed in the Soviet system is continuously to push for exclusive power and not to be comfortable with "checks and balances.")

The term *insatiable* implies that no concession we make, no victory they achieve, no guarantees or promises we give them, nor any policies that we might adopt, could allow them to conclude a satisfactory and stable peace — the kind of peace that so many Americans assume is natural, desirable, or even essential (Communist culture does not produce any such assumption).

Nor would any weakening of United States capabilities satisfy them, because we might become stronger again. If we were weakened internally or by a division in our alliances, prudence would require that they move cautiously to weaken us further in order to eliminate any possibility that we change our policies and restore the former level of threat to them. If we had already weakened ourselves, the reduced urgency to weaken us would be more than balanced by the fact that it would now be safer to do so.

We cannot make the Soviet Communist party safe by our policy, however favorable to them it may become, because if Party safety is based on policy in Washington it follows that a change in policy there would endanger them. They profoundly and correctly understand that their ultimate safety cannot be achieved without ending either the independence or the potential power of the United States.

I should quickly add that saying that the Soviet Union has an insatiable need to weaken us, and eventually to eliminate all power that might match theirs, certainly does not imply — and I do not believe — that it is impossible to construct a political-military reality that induces the Soviets to accept the status quo. If there is no offensive action they can prudently take, they will probably be patient and wait, however insatiable they are at bottom.

While I find this argument compelling, and probably better than any alternative understanding, I have only limited faith in any analysis of such questions. People and history find paths that analysis conceals — an unpredictability that is consoling when the conclusions of analysis are unpleasant.

Much of the apparent disagreement about judgments of Soviet intentions comes from the posing of unrealistic alternatives. On the one hand people justly deride the idea that there is a Soviet master plan and timetable to conquer the world, coordinating offensive efforts in all spheres — missile procurement, ideological and propaganda campaigns, diplomatic maneuvers, covert support of terrorists, etc. — and all geographic regions. But equally foolish is the idea that the Soviets do no more than sit back and wait for opportunities to gain political advantage to come along.

I believe the more realistic view is that the Soviets support many programs in all spheres and many regions designed to gain a variety of military or political advantages. Some of these offensive efforts may be contradictory. Frequently they create or help groups or political forces they cannot control or with which they end up disagreeing.

In some cases the Soviets may have mutually supporting actions in mind, but more often I believe they try approaches that seem to have a reasonable prospect of leading to some advantages on balance, although exactly what or how may initially be unclear. And they see virtually anything bad for the United States and the West as good for them (with important exceptions).

They have a long view. This means both great patience and a willingness to support programs with very long-term goals, as well as a willingness to work with enemies. They have no great commitment to any particular effort. How much support they will give an effort depends on what seems to be working, what opportunities arise, how the general world political situation develops, and internal political and personal factors.

In brief, the Soviets are cautiously and opportunistically offensively minded. They do not have a grand master plan, but they are also not passive. They support with large resources a broad range of efforts of all kinds to weaken the West in a variety of ways. And they have an integrated view of the conflict, so that on occasion they can combine different kinds of efforts to good effect, even though each part of the combination may originally have been conceived independently.

The Nature of the Threat

Most Soviet efforts to weaken their enemies have been indirect. From the very beginning the Soviets exploited the distinction between party and government, pursuing a "two-track" policy in many foreign countries. In addition to using foreign Communist parties, they have learned to work through other governments. They can operate through Bulgaria or East Germany, Cuba or Grenada, any of several of the components of the Palestine Liberation Organization (PLO) or the PLO itself, or a number of other governments. And now some of the countries they use as proxies even use proxies of their own (a country does not have to be completely controlled to serve on particular occasions as a proxy).

In addition to the sizable number of states to which they have very useful access, there is a large collection of terrorist organizations, nationalist groups, guerrilla armies, and "peace" or "hunger" or "justice" organizations that they can often induce to do things for them—or that do things useful to the Soviets for their own reasons. Of course the Soviets do not control these organizations. They are not, in most cases, "Soviet creations." Some of them are anti-Communist, even fascist. But usually, even without control, the Soviets are able to find an appropriate organization that is willing to do what they have decided they want done.

Overall these hundreds of organizations, on which the Soviet Union has spent billions of dollars, weaken the West and give the USSR a flexible set of instruments (albeit balky ones that require skill to play). Because of these instruments, the Soviets have great flexibility in choosing among political or low-level military options to pursue some immediate objective. One or more of their "connections" are likely to be just what they need. And they have been highly successful in keeping most such operations politically secret. (*Politically secret* means that even if the CIA and the State Department, and similar groups in other countries, know about the secret, the information is not in public circulation and therefore does not have political consequences.)

This array of instruments for indirect political and military conflict at all levels puts the Soviet Union in a very good position to use classic totalitarian tactics of aggression, developed to a high art by Hitler and refined by Communists in a dozen countries since Hitler was defeated. These tactics combine just claims, false claims, propaganda and political organization, local schisms and conflicts, local subversive organizations, diplomatic maneuver, and low-level military force and/or the threat of military force, to weaken and isolate their target so that large-scale military force is not necessary or can be used with little chance of significant opposition.

It is important to stress that this by no means implies that all or even most opposition groups, guerrilla armies, nationalist movements, revolutionary parties, or peace or justice organizations are Soviet creations or Soviet controlled. The only point is that the Soviet Union has spent thousands of man-years and billions of dollars helping such organizations and building relations with them, with extremely useful results.

In short, the American problem with the Soviet Union comes from the fact that the current regime there is a totalitarian empire that knows it cannot be safe as long as the United States is powerful.

The situation is profoundly asymmetrical. Our economic and social prospects are good unless foreign events ruin things. Their domestic prospects are bleak unless foreign events save them. Also, American concern about the Soviet Union is based primarily on the nature of the Soviet regime, in that we would not be troubled by Soviet power if they were not a totalitarian empire. But for the Soviets the situation is just the opposite. They do not care at all about our regime; they care about our power and independence. While we are strong and independent they feel threatened by us regardless of our regime. Thus while our safety does not depend on Soviet weakness, their safety does depend on ours—because of the nature of their regime, not because of the nature of ours.

Despite the Soviet "defensive" need to expand its relative power, competent and persistent efforts by the West probably could contain the danger without a major war. However, the threat presented by the Soviet Union is both direct and indirect, and prudence requires that we be prepared to meet it at all levels, from ideas through political action to strategic nuclear weapons.

Dynamic Containment

There are a number of points on which there should be a fairly broad consensus:

- There is a Soviet threat. If we do nothing the Soviets will move gradually to increase their power and their control over larger parts of the world.

- The threat cannot be eliminated. We cannot stop the Soviet pressure in the short run. Neither positive action to modify the Soviet regime or to reduce its power, nor any form of conciliatory policy, nor any weakening of the West would reduce the Soviet pressure—and the latter would be more likely to increase it.

- We cannot allow the Soviets to operate unopposed. If not countered, Soviet pressure to increase its safety by increasing its power will endanger the United States and cause great social injustice and physical harm to hundreds of millions of people.

- Therefore we must contain the threat. If there is a threat, and we are unable to remove it yet cannot allow it to be carried out, some form of containment is the only alternative and the logical conclusion.

- Restraint must be a central feature of such containment. Because of the horrors of war and the potentially immense destruction of a nuclear war, because we must assume that this conflict may continue for generations, and because of the great pressures and temptations for each side to overreach and to fail to see the point of view of the other side, we must conduct our containment policy with great respect for the danger that the conflict might get out of hand, particularly when armies are used.

The "dynamic containment" policy proposed here would also include the following somewhat more controversial elements:

- Containment should not be a static defense of a line. A policy limited to the defense of a single fixed line, either forward at the borders of the Soviet double empire, or backward at the borders of the United States in a "Fortress America" policy, or anywhere in between around a set of "vital" assets, will not work. While defense of a line has the virtue of simplicity, and the virtue of satisfying those citizens who want to make sure that our policy is only defensive, such a rigid concept of defense increases the chances both of war and of defeat.

- Thus we need some form of dynamic containment policy. The dynamic approach sees the effort to contain Soviet pressure as an overall struggle in which we have to be ready to deal with everything from ideas and political action through various forms of submilitary violence to military force, potentially at any level. Dynamic containment recognizes that if we are to have any real chance of success in the overall struggle to contain the Soviet Union more or less within its existing double empire, sometimes we may have to move backward and at other times we must try to move forward. This means that dynamic containment includes efforts to reduce the "third" Soviet empire—the collection of protectorates, dependencies, and satrapies outside the contiguous double empire (e.g., Cuba, Angola, Ethiopia, and Nicaragua).

- While limited efforts to change the Soviet system should be included in our dynamic containment policy, they should not be allowed to become a commitment or requirement. Since an essential component of dynamic containment is active competition in the war of ideas, and since the virtues of freedom and pluralism and the failures and injustices of the Communist systems are central to the debate, it is natural, and perhaps even essential, to make at least intellectual efforts to change the empire within its borders. We cannot let our safety depend on the success of such efforts. But neither can our self-respect and the need to demonstrate our values permit us easily to avoid some sort of challenge to perpetual totalitarian control of the Soviet double empire. Because of Soviet strength and the horrors of war — nuclear or conventional — and in light of our own fallibility, we should *not* countenance any sort of national commitment to the ending of Communist control of the Soviet Union. We should be prepared to live at peace with them for centuries, despite the fact that their insatiable defensive efforts to expand their power are likely to continue to require constant vigilance. Although we should not commit ourselves to replacing the Communist regime in the Soviet Union, we should be clear and unswerving (but not strident or undiplomatic) in our identification of it as evil and dangerous.

- Arms control must be a central feature of dynamic containment. It must be a high priority to further policies designed to recognize and act on our common interests with the Soviet Union and to reduce the chance of war and the damage if war occurs. Also, our policy should always be ready to recognize the need to build a better peace in the future.

- A dynamic containment policy can have almost any "tone" desired. The decision about the tone or atmospherics of the United States–Soviet Union relationship is virtually independent of its substance. The approach to the Soviet Union described here is consistent with a wide variety of tones. It is consistent with détente. It does *not* require or imply that the United States be bellicose or contentious (although it is inevitable that we will be called even worse epithets if we follow the policy). The question of the appropriate tone and style of relations with the Soviet Union is a tactical issue that depends mostly on political and diplomatic considerations concerning third countries. But whatever the tone, whether détente or Cold War, our moral position must be clear. Sometimes one must do business with evil people, and in doing so usually it is appropriate to be civil and sometimes even cordial; but it is wrong to try to make it easier by fooling oneself.

To implement a dynamic containment policy we need to think of the United States as in a single overall integrated conflict with the Soviet Union. The phrase *overall integrated conflict* will bring to some minds the straw man specter of a "Soviet master plan for world domination." This straw man is put forward by those who do not want to recognize that our national security requires that we have an integrated overall view of our relationship with the Soviet Union that includes: (1) military and other force balances at all levels; (2) the changing economic, political, and idea terrain; (3) the current policies and fundamental characteristics of the Soviet Union; and (4) both long- and short-term dangers, and both conflicting and common interests.

Current history is an immensely rich, multidimensional tapestry of events and ideas and patterns, each with its own time scale and shaping dynamics. Because the conflict with the Soviet Union is interwoven with other patterns of events, we need to emphasize the concept of an essentially integrated world conflict (although one that is ever so diffuse and chaotic) in order to see the distinctive nature of this conflict and to understand its characteristics, dynamics, and potential results. (Of course, we must also recognize and deal with other patterns that are shapping the overall tapestry at the same time.)

The War of Ideas

Everybody knows that in a conventional military battle the terrain is important. The pattern of roads, heights, woods, swamps, rivers, railroads, etc., powerfully influences the choice of tactics and strategies available to battalions and to armies. In the current world conflict, the ideas held by various groups at any particular time are a significant feature of the terrain that shapes tactics and strategy and the course of the conflict.

The meanings of the word *ideas* when applied, for example, to the American public or the Congress, the West European leadership community, the Socialist International, the Catholic Church, and various intellectual or academic communities, are each very different. The structure and dynamics of the ways in which each of these groups interacts with ideas, and the ways in which their ideas in turn interact with the world conflict, are all unique.

The complex terrain of ideas in which the world conflict between the United States and Soviet Union is conducted includes the facts accepted as "true" in different political environments, the political agendas that limit the positions nonfanatics can take in public, the definitions of *moderate,* and other effective—albeit unnoticed—limits on debate.

Like the physical terrain in which military battles are fought, the idea terrain is changed by "natural forces" as well as by deliberate efforts to change it; not all influences on it are purposeful. Thus I am not at all suggesting that adverse changes in the terrain of ideas are primarily the result of some great plot. Nor am I saying that those who advance ideas that make our situation more dangerous are necessarily, or even usually, badly motivated.

Ideas, of course, have important dimensions of validity and controversy, but these dimensions are by no means all that determine their success and significance. We must also ask, with great intensity, "How will the sets of ideas held by relevant groups at home and in the world influence the course of the conflict in the situations that may become important?"

While sometimes, of course, truth is used against us, mostly we are endangered by falsehoods and distortions. Apart from normal diplomatic and political imperatives, we do not need lies or shoddy thinking. At the most fundamental level our principles have tremendously broad (although not universal) appeal, and there is no doubt about the achievements of our system for the mass of people, particularly compared to the immense failures and unpopularity of the systems we are competing against. Beyond this fundamental level the situation is perhaps somewhat more mixed; but there are many more cases where we would gain by wider public understanding of the real facts than there are cases where wider knowledge would hurt us.

It is clear that the Soviets are very concerned about the effects of ideas, and that they devote very substantial efforts and resources to trying to shape the idea terrain in ways that will improve their position in the conflict—efforts that are often, but not always, futile or self-defeating. Soviet efforts have been at least part of the forces responsible for adverse changes in the idea terrain in the last twenty years.

We too need to look strategically at the conflict of ideas and the ways in which it is changing. I believe that if we pay attention to this process, and begin to work to try to bring about changes that are favorable to us, we can be effective. If not, we may well find the terrain so adverse that we will not have enough maneuvering room to conduct a successful defense of our freedom.

The frightening fact is that the American discussion does not even have a vocabulary for the conflict of ideas. We are not even considering the significance of existing patterns, much less thinking about the forces that are working to change them. We have not noticed how drastically the terrain of ideas has changed to our disadvantage in the last dozen or so years (even though there have also been important favorable changes). We certainly are not working seriously to influence public ideology and perceptions. And even most conservatives, or "hawks" or "realists," do not recognize the importance of devoting great efforts to the war of ideas, which at present is almost totally one-sided.

Yet the immediate power of ideas is immense. For example, it is entirely fair to say that if the Communists win in El Salvador it will probably be mostly because they were able to sell a false picture of the nature of the war.[1]

On one point I want to be very careful that there is no misunderstanding. I am not saying that all or most of the people who believe the false picture and therefore help to propagate it are agents of Marxism, or even sympathetic to the Soviet Union. In fact my point is almost the opposite. When the Communists began organizing international support for the new FMLN guerrilla army in 1980, the idea terrain was so favorable to their task that it was easy for them to sell a completely false picture. Also, even though there is very little support for the USSR or for any variety of Communism in the United States, adverse features of the idea terrain, to which now have been added the false picture of the nature of the war in El Salvador, may very well make it impossible for the administration to give consistent enough support to the moderate democratic regime in El Salvador to enable that regime to protect itself against its unpopular, totalitarian-dominated attackers.

If such extreme manipulation of public opinion can effectively conquer El Salvador, we should not doubt that it can hurt us in many other ways, and there is even a possibility that a similar manipulation could deliver a small but fatal stroke against us at some critical point.

Communism and the War of Ideas

One of the reasons we are not engaged in the war of ideas is that we have no name for the idea system we need to fight against. Many people don't notice how badly we are doing in the war of ideas because Communism is in such obviously poor shape as an ideological opponent. Today it is hard to take Communism seriously as an opponent in a world-class intellectual debate. But people who are doing practical political work around the world understand that even though Communism is no longer intellectually respectable, it still has political potency for some special and often significant audiences—mostly among young or less politically sophisticated people. Much of the action that shapes events in the world is taken by people who are not politically sophisticated and who are largely unaware of the world's experience with various forms of Communism.

Each year a new cohort of young people comes of age and different countries and groups become more significant as politics shift. This is only the least of the reasons for what George Will recently referred to as "the remarkable and dangerous recuperative power of innocence." Patient and creative work is essential to teach each new cohort and group the painful lessons that victims and serious observers of Communist operations have learned. If we fail to do this unpleasant task, too large a share of that new group will make the same mistakes that have been made so often and that contribute to Communist victories. (Doan Van Toai, a Vietnamese supporter of the Viet Cong who escaped after learning what the Communist government of Vietnam meant, has been particularly eloquent about the importance of this task.)[2] Even though the information has been available for a very long time, we need to make sure that people know about what it is like to live in a Communist totalitarian country—in terms of the lack of political rights, of economic inefficiency, and of social injustice. And we need to help people remember how Communist and other totalitarian aggression has succeeded in the past by successfully fooling idealistic people.[3]

Whereas one group of people fails to take the war of ideas seriously because it sees Communism as having so little intellectual appeal, there is another group that does just as much to prevent us from engaging in the real war of ideas by seeing that war as *only* a debate against Communism, thereby making it harder to recognize and combat the more subtle ideological and informational challenges.

Of course there is a tradition—which I share—that says that we cannot be genuinely threatened by ideas, that we can rely on the power of truth eventually to prevail. While the values underlying that tradition are still valid, recent history shows that it must be modified to take new facts into account.

The idea system that serves the Communist purpose and multiplies the danger of Communist power does not consist of only Communism or Communist ideas. It is this unnamed idea system that is shaping the debate in ways we must resist. While the ideology of Communism, per se, has largely lost its appeal outside as well as inside the Soviet Union, Communists have done much better at selling a number of other parts of their ideology, or ideas derivative from it, that serve their political purposes. (In many cases these ideas are developed and propagated for them by people who are anti-Communist.) They have found it easier to undermine the idea systems that support the West than to gain support for the Communism they no longer believe in themselves—partly because there are so many others to carry out the former project.

Unfortunately I cannot give a good name to or a deep summary of the system of ideas that endangers us. The nature of this system is not easily encapsulated, and it may be only a collection rather than a system. An important task that needs to be done is to define the following elements of the war of ideas:

- the main lines of thought;

- the relationships among people and organizations on the other side (which is a complex network, with KGB ideological and political planners at one corner, patriotic and idealistic Americans at another corner, and various connections between them through different types of intermediaries); and

- the points of political impact of ideas on events and relative strength.

One of the difficulties in carrying out this task is that we need to contest several different idea systems before several different kinds of audiences. The misunderstandings and falsehoods that cause us trouble are different in underdeveloped countries, in Europe, and among ourselves. Different issues are emphasized in Latin America, the Middle East, and other regions. In fact, one good rhetorical technique is to display in the United States the lies used by the Communists' allies in places like El Salvador that are so preposterous that they would backfire if exposed here (e.g., that hundreds of Israeli soldiers were fighting in El Salvador).

Some of the pieces of the idea system we need to deal with are the following:

- Rich (capitalist) countries are responsible for poor countries' poverty (and vice versa; their poverty—a result of exploitation—is responsible for our wealth).

- For selfish reasons, the United States was against the mass of ordinary people in Vietnam, El Salvador, Nicaragua, etc.

- The United States is allied to the least democratic forces in the world because of its fight with the Soviet Union and "Communism."

- Multinational corporations are bad for poor countries and good for the United States.

- Defenders of the United States, especially businessmen, are selfish, and therefore their arguments are to be rejected as self-serving. On the other hand, socialists and other "do-gooders" are well-motivated and therefore the best source of information and leadership.

- Blind, selfish anti-Communism dominates American foreign policy.

- The Left ought to be given credit and tolerance because at least they are trying to help the people.

- American anti-Communism, desire for military superiority, openness to influence by the military-industrial complex, and indifference to the dangers of the arms race are the main cause—or at least half of the cause—of the arms race, the danger to peace, and the lack of arms control or disarmament.

- While the United States is not as bad as the Soviet Union, their behavioral similarities are so great that usually they should be considered in parallel.

- Disputes must be settled by negotiation and compromise.

- Paranoid responses to alleged totalitarian tactics are a threat to peace and justice.

- A critical problem facing the world is the growing scarcity of raw materials, and the United States uses much more than its fair share.

- We should work against evil wherever we see it, without worrying about making comparisons.

- Too much attention is paid in the United States to the bad things about Communist governments; they are probably exaggerated and in any case they are not our problem and there is not much we can do about it.

Because of the venality and complexity of politics, people's political acts rarely turn on intellectual judgments about points of ideological controversy; nevertheless, wide acceptance of such an idea system can have enormous practical political impact. This impact is felt in a wide variety of arenas — weapons procurement and peacetime operation of military forces, arms control and other negotiations, Third World disputes such as El Salvador or Vietnam, anti-terrorist efforts, intelligence operations, etc.

No single piece of the antagonistic system of ideas is decisive. Many truths are incorporated and used as part of the opposing arguments, which often, as a result, have substantial merit individually. None of the arguments is used primarily by enemies.

America needs a sophisticated apparatus for recognizing the importance of the war of ideas, organizing United States participation, and devoting substantial resources to it. (The most important resource needed is the right kind of commitment at the top.) Such an apparatus does not now exist in the U.S. government — not even in primitive form.

A successful program for the war of ideas could improve our national security by as much as could a twenty or thirty billion dollar increase in our defense budget, and should be given comparably serious attention. This is not to say that we should emphasize ideas instead of arms; we need both.

Political Action

The war of ideas is largely fought through political action; only rarely do people change their minds as the result of argument. Ideas change as the result of producing and delivering information, of organizational action that leads to two-sided discussion where only one side had been heard before, and of changing political contexts.

The kind of political action program that is needed includes the following two elements.

First, we need to support reformist, moderate, pro-Western political forces, especially when they are in danger from groups receiving outside help and are likely to join the enemies of freedom. We have to find ways to provide support to friendly groups such as political parties, labor unions, civic associations, the media, and religious groups — discreetly, but normally without covert action.

Second, we need to initiate offensive action against terrorist groups and their transnational supporting networks (Cuba, Bulgaria, the PLO, etc.).

There are many connections between the war of ideas and political action. For example, current terrorist organizations survive because of ideas and political understandings built up over the last dozen or so years. If more reasonable and traditional attitudes and practices were restored, a heavy blow would be dealt to the terrorist system, which has not yet demonstrated its full power to influence political directions. However, terrorists will always be one step ahead if we continue to make basic conceptual errors, such as judging the political responsibility for terrorism according to evidentiary canons that are appropriate for criminal trials but not for detecting deliberate threats to our safety.

Strategic Nuclear Forces

United States strategic nuclear forces should be designed primarily to deter Soviet use of nuclear weapons. The best way to deter a Soviet attack is to give them good reason to believe they would lose the war.

⌊ Deterrence is more likely to fail because of a Soviet belief in American political weakness (at a time when they are in a desperate situation) than because of their confidence in some kind of technical superiority — although, of course, it would be extremely imprudent to allow them to get major technical advantages. Therefore the easiest useful change in U.S. policy would be to stop talking about nuclear war in apocalyptic terms. To help avoid war we should be as relatively matter-of-fact in discussing nuclear war as the Soviet Union is in its internal documents.

We should greatly increase our ability to limit damage if war does occur both by increasing active and passive defenses and by planning and equipping ourselves to fight a controlled[4] nuclear war as long as possible if necessary. Our current condition in both of these areas is extraordinarily bad.

Since we are now spending much less than is needed, and will probably continue to do so, the most difficult questions concern priorities. However, since these questions do not particularly turn on our relations with the Soviet Union, they need not be addressed here.

The problem of the inadequate level of our defense expenditures is made worse by the lack of seriousness of the American defense planning effort and the low priority given to battle concerns in the U.S. officer corps. Despite recent improvements in the army, any betterment of our posture depends on changing attitudes and organizational behavior drastically within the Department of Defense (DOD). This would be possible with good political leadership. If DOD performance were improved it would also be possible to improve the political situation for defense in the Congress and elsewhere. (And we should note that the situation at the DOD is no worse than that at the State Department and the CIA.)

People often avoid mature recognition of the stakes in our relations with the Soviets — the danger of nuclear destruction and the danger of subjugation — and of the connection between these dangers by relying on two comforting ideas: first, they believe that there can be no winner in a nuclear war; and second, they are convinced that nuclear weapons increase our danger without contributing in any way to our safety. Both ideas are false.

To consider the potential political significance of nuclear weapons, it is useful to think for a minute about a hypothetical situation in which we had no nuclear weapons and the Soviets had, say, 100. In this case the Soviets might feel compelled to try to gain enough control over the United States to make sure that a nuclear arms race could never get started.

Since preventing United States nuclear armament is a cause that would naturally appeal to many Americans, the Soviets might be able to use indirect control through chosen "peace" groups and other organizations. They could use such groups, even without "controlling" them, to define, secure, and enforce a disarmament agreement that would keep the nuclear balance from changing.

Preventing clandestine nuclear weapons production by the United States—a country with private enterprise and with a CIA that spends billions of dollars a year secretly—could require a substantial set of "special police powers" for the groups implementing the arms limitation agreement. Many people would accept the necessity of such special powers to preserve the peace. The importance of maintaining an agreement that eliminated the threat of nuclear destruction of the world would be so great that people would recognize that it was only a small price to pay if these powers were misused somewhat from time to time (even if some paranoids saw the alleged abuses as systematic power-seeking).

But it is not inconceivable that the process of exerting power in the United States to ensure that we did not build nuclear weapons would become increasingly attractive to the Soviet Union. They might try to use that process first to extend the scope of the peace and to enforce other requirements related to arms control, and then to control matters that were less and less directly related to any agreement.

While such a scenario is difficult to imagine, I do not believe it is impossible. Always the beginnings of such a process are possible only because so many people are convinced that the end is completely impossible and need not be feared.

The ultimate support for the groups the Soviets might use to achieve their purposes would be the fact that the Soviets could back up their demands with nuclear weapons, and there would be nothing we could do to stop them. It is not clear how overt such a

threat would have to be to be effective. Nor is it clear whether—
or how often—they would have to demonstrate willingness to
carry out the threat. This scenario is horrible to think about. Unfortunately, that does not make it impossible.

One of the social mechanisms that makes this kind of scenario
possible is that when compelled to do something, many people
develop reasons for believing that they want to do it and even that
it is their own idea. Therefore in this kind of situation there could
be many well-organized Americans who sincerely believed that
the U.S. should do what the Soviet Union was "requesting" and
who would exert political pressure on the government to do it
not because of Soviet threats—which they might deny—but
"because it is right." Others would add their political voice out of
fear of the Soviets' weapons and the feeling that "it doesn't really
matter." And we all know how, in many relationships, giving way
on one thing that "doesn't really matter" after another can gradually lead to practical subjugation. Those who believed that what
was being "requested" was wrong, that it did matter, that we
should risk Soviet use of nuclear weapons against us, and that
doing so would do any lasting good, would have a difficult task of
persuasion.

But if a weapons balance of 100 to 0 might lead to Soviet control,
perhaps through a process of expanded enforcement of a disarmament agreement and support for the political groups necessary to
implement it, what about a balance of 50 to 1? or 200 to 2? or 100
to 10? It is not clear how unbalanced the forces must be for this
process to work.

I believe that arms control is not only a potential foundation for
peace and security, but also a potential mechanism for turning
marginal disadvantage into absolute defeat. Despite the great
positive value of arms control we need to understand how it could
be a part of a new mechanism for what might be called "sneaky
absolute defeat." This possibility has gone largely unrecognized
because the idea of defeat, i.e., of America's being conquered or
coming under the effective control of another nation, seems so
preposterous.

In the past, great powers have rarely been absolutely defeated
by a single event. But if we enter a disarmament agreement that
is one-sided in effect, the result could be a situation comparable to

the unfortunate hypothetical considered above. Thus the combination of nuclear weapons, political war, and some kinds of arms control agreements could provide a new potential mechanism to produce absolute defeat, almost all of a sudden, while we seem to be still powerful and independent.

Such disastrous agreements need not be one-sided on their face. There would never have to be an overt decision to give the Soviets a decisive advantage or to disarm unilaterally. An agreement could, for example, be phrased in terms of equal obligations, but provide that binding arbitration of any dispute would be made by a committee of three nations acting by majority rule—such as the United Kingdom, Rumania, and the former head of the group of nonaligned nations (Cuba).

It is easy to parody this concern. This sort of scenario could really happen only if the outline presented here were covered by a wealth of subtleties, confusing rhetoric, special understandings developed over time, etc. I cannot hope to capture the feeling of such a potential future history, although these subtleties would be necessary to make it possible. (In *Animal Farm* and *1984,* Orwell's genius gives a feel for how the seemingly absurd can be made frighteningly believable.) But it is clear that events with a structure something like these scenarios may not be as impossible as they seem today.

Now let us consider the truism that "no one can win a nuclear war." Unfortunately it is wrong, not only trivially (as shown in 1945) but also in a profound and dangerous way.

Of course it is entirely reasonable to say that even the supposed "winner" of a two-sided nuclear war is almost certain to suffer so many deaths that the result cannot be called a victory. It is also reasonable to say that no political gains justify the loss of tens of millions of lives (much less hundreds of millions), so "victory" is an absurd notion. After any such war both sides would have been better off if the war had not started. How can you call it "victory" if you were better off before? And if victory is absurd, there can be no winner.

But we need to consider another definition of victory that is based on a comparison between the positions of the two parties as a result of the war. There could well be a situation in which neither side is a winner compared with their condition before having started, but one side is indeed a winner compared with the other. (And I am not talking about any nonsense like "two Americans and one Russian left, we win," or "if we kill more than they do we win.")

This is by no means to say that any nuclear war has to have, or is even likely to have, a winner—but it might have one. And it is certainly not to say that it was a good idea for the winner to have started the war (if it did).

Realistically defined victory occurs when only one side can compel (or induce) the other side to make concessions. (A slight victory gives the power to compel minor concessions.) However, the possibility of camouflaged absolute defeat through the aggressive use of a disarmament agreement raises the frightening question: suppose the "minor concession" consisted of merely a few "details" in a disarmament agreement that both sides were eager to reach?

The scenario of a perverted arms control agreement is much more likely in the aftermath of a limited—or even aborted—nuclear war. At such a time the political power and appeal of a disarmament agreement might be unstoppable, and quibbling over details to make sure that it was strictly fair would seem like dastardly inhumanity.

If one side can compel the other side to accept an apparently balanced but actually one-sided agreement, it may turn what seemed to be essentially a stalemate into a complete victory. (For example: if the Soviet Union agreed to destroy 10,000 nuclear weapons in exchange for 5,000 American ones, the advantage would seem to be for the United States—unless the result were that the Soviets ended up with 100 and we ended up with 2. Or, to mention a more immediately plausible scenario, suppose we both agreed to destroy all nuclear weapons, but they had better ability to supervise compliance?)

In short, because of the technical fact that a few details of a peace treaty/arms control agreement can turn a stalemate into an absolute victory, the question of victory in a nuclear war—a question the United States has virtually ignored—requires great attention, although it is truly distressing to think about.

Unfortunately there is a second distressing technical fact about nuclear war that also tends to make the question of winning more realistic and demanding. After a nuclear war it is quite possible that the recovery of both major participants will depend on how quickly they receive outside help. But the "winning" side is likely to be able to compel undamaged countries to give aid only to itself. It could say, for example, that the "loser" was the aggressor and that the aggressor should not be helped until after the victim of aggression. The loser would not be in a position to argue about history. That would be one of the consequences of losing.

If the winning country still had a few nuclear weapons and could communicate, no country would be likely to feel that it was safe to disagree with it, even if it were grievously hurt and weakened and needed help. Every day we see bigger lies being perpetrated with far less coercion than there would be in such a postwar situation.

Advantages in the war of ideas that have proved helpful to Soviet objectives in peacetime might also be useful for selling their view of who was the aggressor in a nuclear war, and to influence decisions in Europe, Japan, Canada, and Mexico about whether to grant the requests of the surviving "victim of aggression" (the Soviet Union) rather than those of the defeated "aggressor" (the United States).

Thus our policy with regard to strategic nuclear war should be: (1) not to start one; (2) to try to prevent the Soviets from starting one by maximizing the chance that they would be defeated; (3) if the Soviets do start a war, to be prepared to fight as well as possible, particularly with the use of defensive strategies and arms; and (4) in case of war to use the following elements of strategy in appropriate combination: stop the war, protect civilians, attack Soviet military forces wherever the "dynamic exchange ratio" is substantially positive, attempt to disrupt their command-and-control and communication system by using the Electromagnetic Pulse (EMP) effect, hold out no hope of arms control concessions, "play poker," and do not waste many weapons on trying to destroy the Communist party leadership.

A Different Direction for Arms Control

Arms control considerations, defined as recognition and pursuit of our common interests with the Soviet Union, should be one of the central features of a dynamic containment policy. The goals of arms control are to reduce the likelihood of war and to limit damage if war occurs. Since these are also goals of strategy, one must define arms control not only by its goals but also by its distinction from the rest of strategy: that distinction is the focus on common interests with the enemy.

But if our arms control policy is to succeed in moving toward its objectives, its direction must differ from previous so-called arms control programs, which have on balance made war more likely and probably more destructive if it were to come.

The simple goal of trying to reduce the numbers of weapons is sterile: as few as 100 nuclear weapons can kill fifty million or more people. That goal is also dangerous because a nuclear balance at low numbers of weapons on each side would make it easier for small changes to decide the outcome — which is a good definition of *instability*.

The goal of arms control should not be to reduce or limit the number of nuclear weapons. It should rather be to move the posture and plans of both sides gradually in two directions: first, to increase the chance that any nuclear war that begins will be a "military" war, at least as long as possible (a military war is one, like most wars of history, in which the object of military forces is to destroy or defeat other military forces, not to kill civilians or destroy property); secondly, to increase the percentage of strategic expenditures used for active and passive defense rather than for offensive forces — at least to 50 percent and then to as high a percent as possible.

If this arms control approach were adopted, after some years nobody would have the faintest hope of predicting the military outcome of a war because there would be several levels of offense-defense interaction, none of which could ever be tested. Even if such a war occurred, it is likely that the number of people killed would be a fraction of the number of people who could be killed today by only 100 missiles.

Both countries would be well-protected against all but clandestinely delivered weapons from small powers. Thus a small nuclear power would constitute much less potential threat (and there would be less temptation to become a small nuclear power). The military balance in this situation would be very difficult to change. It is hard to imagine technological developments that could quickly make a big difference; it would be a long time before even a 50 percent increase in the budget of one side would be able to buy enough equipment to mean anything. So there would be little vulnerability to technical change, to surprise, to sudden changes in policy or force procurement, or to clandestine weapon programs.[5]

Thus the primary arms control agreements with the Soviets worth pursuing would emphasize defense or limit total strategic offensive force expenditures. These agreements need not be explicit or formal. The United States should move sharply in the direction of defensive emphasis without waiting for an agreement with the Soviet Union.

An additional major arms control policy that I would recommend is for the United States to move away from all political uses of nuclear weapons (such as their use in the official theory of European security). The avoidance of all positive benefits from nuclear weapons may be the key to constructing an effective policy against their general spread.[6]

The policy proposed here, or any generally sensible policy of any kind, will be extremely difficult to implement until there is a profound change in the thinking, or the personnel, of the community of people who normally determine and influence public policy. (There would be no great problem with the general public.) Nevertheless, a president who understood and cared about pursuing this kind of policy would be able to make major strides toward implementation and would be likely to find the political difficulties, while considerable, no worse than with any other reasonable course of action.

10

JAMES L. PAYNE

Foreign Policy for an Impulsive People

The logical starting point for a discussion of U.S. policy toward the Soviet Union is the issue of major war. Doing our best to avoid this catastrophe must certainly be a central aim. Indeed, a policy that does not succeed in this objective could not, almost by definition, succeed in any other. Whether one wants to encourage the cause of liberty in Poland or boost grain sales at the Port of Houston, one assumes, almost automatically, that World War III is not taking place at the time.

One difficulty in devising a policy directed at the danger of major war lies in realizing that this danger is irrevocable. There is, practically speaking, nothing we can do to *end* the danger of a cataclysmic nuclear war. That danger is now with us forever, a consequence of man's moral and intellectual imperfections. Our available options offer only different ways to limit the risk.

Limiting the Danger of War

Many approaches to peace are seriously weakened by the failure to confront this dismal reality. Disarmament proposals, for example, at first glance promise to make war impossible by eliminating its implements. But since they do not treat the disposition of men to rebuild these implements, such proposals are typically nugatory. World government suggestions are another try at "solving" the problem of war. A single authority is presumed capable of wielding a worldwide monopoly of force, thereby abolishing war. Again, proponents overlook the more fundamental problem: namely, the absence of the worldwide consensus necessary to energize such an authority.

Some would note as a theoretical (but unacceptable) possibility that we could end the danger of nuclear war by outright capitulation to the Soviets. Even this apparently simple point cannot be conceded. Capitulation in peacetime is an awesomely complicated task. It would require, in our system, the prolonged concurrence of many institutions from the Supreme Court (would capitulation be constitutional?) down to the Joint Chiefs of Staff. A glance at the history of, say, the Equal Rights Amendment or the SALT II treaty indicates the complexities such a major issue would involve. And, of course, an inconsistent or partial capitulation would be the most dangerous of all. If we were down to our last two nuclear submarines, for example, and then changed our minds about surrendering, our opponents would be strongly encouraged to make a preemptive attack. For the United States, attempting a policy of capitulation would be a formula for disaster.

It is not realistic, then, to strive for a final "solution" to the problem of war. Instead, we should set our sights on a plan to minimize the probability of major nuclear war.

Where does the risk of major nuclear war come from? How would such a war begin? The answer we are accustomed to hearing is that nuclear holocaust, because it would be so obviously destructive, could not be a rational act of policy on either side. It therefore would come about only through some type of "accident."

This view is sound in a rough sort of way; however, if we are not careful about the meaning of "accident," we shall be led quite far astray. In our usage of this term there is a tendency to equate "accidental"—meaning "by chance"—with "unintentional"—meaning "undesired."

For example, if Johnny throws a rock at a beehive but fails to outrun the swarming bees, he is likely to tell his mother that the bee stings were an "accident." What he means, of course, is that they were undesired or unhoped-for. But they were not chance bee stings—that is, unrelated to any action that Johnny took. The very fact that he ran away after throwing the rock reveals that *he knew* bee stings were not chance events. He knew they were causally related to throwing rocks at beehives. He simply underestimated the risks: he miscalculated.

In studying how wars begin, scholars have discovered that many were unintended; that is, the aggressor did not want war and did not believe his action would start one. For example, the First World War could be called unintended in this sense. In planning action against Serbia, neither Austria nor her German ally desired a major war. Furthermore, the dominant leaders in both countries thought it unlikely that Russia would come to the aid of Serbia and that it was therefore relatively safe to go ahead with hostile action. They were wrong. They miscalculated. Russia did care enough about Serbia's independence to go to war to protect her. It was this initial Austrian move and Russian reaction that, given the mobilization patterns and alliance systems, triggered World War I.

A more recent example of an unintended conflict was the war in the Falklands. The Argentinians did not desire war and thought it unlikely that landing their troops in the Falklands would produce it. All sorts of clues and indicators suggested to them that Great Britain would acquiesce.[1] They were wrong. They underestimated the British reaction.

Hearing about so many of these "unintended" wars, the spectator might easily conclude that the lesson of history must be that wars are generally "accidental." In this way, a critical logical slip deflects his attention from the real problem to a secondary issue. World War III, he concludes, will come about as a result of some human or technical error: a misinterpreted blip on a radar screen; a careless sergeant who elbows the wrong button in a missile command post; a berserk submarine commander; and so on.

Such human and mechanical malfunctions are indeed worri-

some, and systems to limit such dangers are unquestionably a
military necessity. However, it does not seem that the lessons of
history suggest danger from this quarter. War is indeed often
unintended or unexpected, but I doubt that it has ever been accidental. Aggressors have repeatedly been surprised by the consequences of their actions; they have miscalculated on innumerable
occasions. But war never engulfed them while they were sitting
quietly under a tree, minding their own business. In each case,
they acted. The national leadership took a conscious step that they
knew would involve significant injury to their opponent. They
simply underestimated the consequences.

It is this type of error that the lessons of history warn us about:
wars that begin because an aggressor underestimated the defender's ability and/or willingness to resist. One of the striking
statistics of war is how often the nation that starts it fails to accomplish its aim — or loses outright.[2] For example, in 1885 Serbia
attacked Bulgaria and was defeated in a month. The Austro-
Hungarian empire, as noted above, initiated World War I by its action against Serbia; it was defeated and dismembered in the end.
The Second World War was begun in the West by Hitler's invading
Poland. He lost. It was begun in the East by the Japanese bombing
of Pearl Harbor. They lost too.

Since that time, the pace of wars of miscalculation has, if anything, picked up. We have, for example, the Korean War. The
North Koreans invaded South Korea; they were repulsed and their
army decimated. The 1967 Arab-Israeli war is another example.
Egypt's Nasser triggered it by blockading the Israeli entrance to
the Gulf of Aqaba; in the ensuing war Egypt lost territory and
Nasser was humiliated. And, as mentioned earlier, the 1982
war in the Falklands fits the same pattern. The Argentinians
began with an invasion of British territory; in the end they lost
the war, suffered heavy casualties, and their leader resigned in
humiliation.

One sometimes wonders, looking at all these errors of judgment,
whether there ever has been a war of *calculation;* that is, a war in
which the aggressor did not grossly underestimate the willingness
and ability of the defender to fight. In fact there are a number of
doubtful cases, but at least one really clear one: the Spanish-
American War. In invading Cuba, the United States (the ag-

gressor) was correct in expecting a short war and a relatively cost-less victory.

How is it that nations so frequently miscalculate? One would think, on a matter so serious as war, that they would study the odds with a little more care. Wars of miscalculation ought, one supposes, to be rare. Instead, these types of conflicts are common-place: aggressors often lose the wars they initiate. Anyone who wants to prevent war must come to grips with this elementary datum.

As we look into these many wars of miscalculation, we typically find that the miscalculation begins with the defender. It is the de-fender who sends out false signals about his future conduct. He lies, in effect, about what he can do and will do in the event of ag-gression. The aggressor believes the lies. He goes ahead and vio-lates the defender's rights or territories. The defender, it turns out, will not allow it; and war begins.

Defenders "lie" to potential aggressors in many ways. One of the most obvious is a policy of appeasement—that is, giving up rights or territories to the aggressor (or his allies) without a fight. Such behavior encourages the aggressor to believe that the de-fender is timid (or places a low value on the type of thing being given away). Hence the aggressor comes to expect no response to his next thrust. The role of British and French appeasement in bringing on World War II is the classic case, but only one example among many.

For example, prior to World War I, Russia had appeased the Austro-Hungarian empire in the Balkans. When Austria annexed Bosnia-Herzegovina in 1908—a violation of the great-power status quo—Russia, the aggrieved party, failed to react. Even at the time, experienced observers realized that this appeasement sowed the seeds of a miscalculation. The Russian ambassador to France, Nelidov, expressed the issue clearly:

A public exposure of this kind to our weakness has made a most painful impression upon our friends and must encourage our opponents to pre-sent the most impossible demands to Russia in the firm conviction that we shall yield.[3]

His prediction came frighteningly true a few years later. Austria did make an "impossible demand" (the subjugation of Ser-bia) in the firm (but mistaken) "conviction" that Russia would yield.

Another way in which defenders often lie to potential aggressors is by disarming—or by failing to increase their arms to keep pace with the aggressor. Again, World War II is a classic case, with Great Britain, France, and the United States failing to match the output of German and Japanese arms production. But many other examples can be found. The drastic U.S. demobilization in the late 1940s certainly encouraged Stalin and the North Koreans in undertaking the invasion of South Korea. "If the United States intends to fight for the defense of South Korea," they had to ask themselves, "why has it not maintained the forces to do so?"

The same theme enters into the war in the Falklands. The inadequate and deteriorating arsenal of Britain played a role in encouraging the Argentinians to invade. It seemed that Britain did not have sufficient forces to fight in the Falklands even if it wanted to. One observer noted the critical absence of the large-deck aircraft carrier in the British navy: "If Britain had had even one, it is entirely possible that Argentina would not have invaded the Falklands."[4]

Defenders also lie to potential aggressors by sending signals of an urgent desire for peace. These signals may be contained in official diplomatic communications that plead for negotiations in the face of intransigence; in presidential declarations about the horrors of war and the necessity for avoiding it; in campaign pledges by politicians to "deliver" peace; in citizen expressions of pacifism like demonstrations and referenda in favor of disarmament. A potential aggressor reads such signals to mean that the defender is so anxious to avoid war that he will not resist the next advance. The route to avoiding a war of miscalculation, then, is for defenders not to lie about their ultimate intentions and capabilities. They should adopt a policy of containment—a policy of checking aggressors promptly, of keeping well-armed, and of being willing to face the prospect of war. In other words, they should follow the ancient dictum: "If you desire peace, prepare for war."

This should be the U.S. policy toward the Soviet Union to limit the danger of major war. The Soviet Union and its associated states are clearly the aggressors on the world scene; we must contain this constellation of forces in the interest of peace.

There are those who deny this point and insist that the United

States is the aggressor. The refutation of this position requires either an extensive, systematic analysis of possession in international affairs,[5] or a commonsense glance at the map of the world. If we are so aggressive, why are they doing all the taking?

Containment policy[6] is often disparaged because at any instant it will typically seem unnecessary. Many people reason that since nuclear war is not about to break out tomorrow, no particular policy is needed to preserve peace, and certainly not a strenuous, war-like one. But it is not tomorrow that we should be concerned about. Tomorrow has, for most practical purposes, already happened; it is the culmination of decades of conduct. What one is trying to shape with a containment policy is the more distant future. The policy is aimed not at the Soviet Union and United States of today, but at possible transformations of these countries in the future.

Imagine, for example, that a handful of restless Soviet colonels stage a revolt, massacring the existing Kremlin leadership. What kind of world would this arrogant, resentful clique behold? Would they see a cowering United States offering them, in effect, the globe on a silver platter? Or would they see an opponent whose courage and capabilities dictated a policy of caution on their part? The day after these colonels take over it will be too late to redefine their perceptions. It will be too late to tell them that we really are tough, that our appeasements were merely "creative diplomacy" and our disarmament resolutions nothing but demagogic games. If they are to believe that we are resolute and capable, we will have to have been resolute and capable all along.

It is a grave error to be so impressed by the present that one cannot imagine a future that departs from it. Transformations, either sudden or gradual, are always possible. A nonaggressive power may grow cautiously aggressive; a cautious aggressor may develop into a reckless aggressor. Appeasement encourages this evolution; containment inhibits it.

It is not only a transformation of our opponent that we must prepare for. Our policy must also anticipate possible changes in our own attitudes.

It is strange how little the writings and theories about foreign policy take into account the fact that people can become angry. Perhaps this gap exists because anger is considered unseemly;

theorists are reluctant to recognize its existence lest they be
thought to condone it. But foreign affairs are not a matter of eti-
quette. If we are to survive we must have a realistic understanding
of ourselves. The foundation of this understanding is that we—
the American people, American congressmen, American presidents—can be made angry.

Once we do become angry, our estimate of the costs and benefits
of military action shifts profoundly. We become willing to take
steps that the aggressor, who cannot grasp our change in mood,
will not anticipate. Examples of this kind of change include the
American war-to-the-finish reaction to the bombing of Pearl Harbor. The Japanese realized that the United States would have the
upper hand in a protracted conflict; they had pinned their hopes
on our losing our will to fight and agreeing to an early settlement.[7]
Even a rather minor incident like the Iran hostage seizure illustrates how public—and presidential—anger might flare up in
reaction to certain types of affronts abroad. T-shirts saying "Nuke
the Ayatollah" quickly sold out on New York's Sixth Avenue; fifty-
four congressmen called for "military operations against Iran" if
the hostages were not released.[8]

A foreign policy that makes no allowance for one's own anger is,
ultimately, a foreign policy of deception. The opponent is given the
forebearing posture for so long that he becomes unable to conceive
of anything else. He becomes unable to anticipate a violent reaction in response to an act of aggression. In this way a miscalculation is born. A policy of containment avoids this danger; in effect,
one puts a little bit of one's potential anger into each day's actions
so that opponents correctly anticipate future responses.

The point may be well illustrated with an analogy from child-
rearing. One school of thought holds that parents should never
strike their children. What proponents of this view never allow for
is the angry parent. Through undisciplined misbehavior, a child
may drive the parent to a violent reaction that might be far more
damaging than scores of routine bottom-paddlings. One of my colleagues, a believer in avoiding physical punishment of children,
broke his son's front tooth in such a violent reaction.

In other words, the policy of never striking children is really not
that at all. The proper description of this policy is: never hit your
children until they make you so angry that you forget about the

policy. The opposite approach, of spanking children more or less all along as they misbehave, is a policy for never getting truly angry. Their misbehavior being curbed in the early stages, the children never drive the parent to the breaking point.

As things stand, it is not clear that we can recommend one of these child-rearing methods over the other. Each has different costs and benefits and suits different kinds of parents. But suppose the cost of parental anger were raised enormously. Suppose all parents had little nuclear warheads pinned to their lapels like hand grenades, and they could pluck them off and hurl them at misbehaving children in a moment of rage. In this very, very dangerous context, would it make sense to base a policy of child-rearing on the assumption that parents would never get angry?

In the final analysis, a policy of containment is necessary to keep the Soviets from misbehaving so badly that *we* lose our tempers.

Human Rights

The preceding defense of forward resistance to Soviet expansion made no explicit assumption about Soviet goals and values. Even if the Russians were out to save the world, a policy of resisting them at every turn would be defensible — although morally confusing. A potentially aggressive power, even a "good" one, should be restrained in the interest of avoiding the fatal miscalculation that could produce major war.

As it happens, there is no moral confusion for us to worry about. The Soviet Union's goals are not "good" by any stretch of the imagination. In fact, these goals are so bad that thwarting their implementation stands as the second major objective of U.S. foreign policy.

Communist regimes inspired by the Soviet Union practice the extensive abrogation of all types of freedom: political, intellectual, cultural, religious, social, and economic. Since human beings do not willingly accede to this enormous loss of freedom, Communist regimes must resort to considerable coercion and terror. The cruelty of this policy of suppression is characteristically justified as an unfortunate by-product of the construction of utopia. Yet the irony of this contention is itself cruel, for the nations where Communism has triumphed are particularly backward—backward in ideas, in art, in science, even, especially, backward in economic production and standards of living.

It surely should be our objective—insofar as we care about the fate of human beings around the globe—to check the spread of these dismal tyrannies.

One notes that certain non-Communist dictatorships have occasionally matched the Communists in brutality and backwardness. One thinks of Idi Amin in Uganda, or the rule of the Ayatollah in Iran. But such tyrannies have been *sui generis,* an outgrowth of local circumstances and individual personalities. They were not inspired from abroad; they were not implanted with foreign assistance; and they do not serve as an example to others.

The Communist challenge to freedom, on the other hand, is pervasive and predictable. Communist dictatorships are inspired and aided by the Soviet Union and its allies. Each one that comes into existence serves as both an example to be emulated and as a physical base for the implantation of more tyrannies of the same type. Furthermore, what non-Communist rulers and regimes may become is an open question. Some may allow considerable freedom; others may be more or less dictatorial. We cannot tell beforehand. The outcome of a Communist takeover, on the other hand, is predictable. One of the few truly dependable generalizations in international affairs is that the level of brutality in a country goes up when Communists take over. Virtually every side-by-side and before-and-after comparison supports this point: South Korea and North Korea; Batista's Cuba and Castro's Cuba; South Vietnam (pre-1975) and North Vietnam; South Vietnam pre-1975 and South Vietnam post-1975; West Germany and East Germany; and so on.

Another deplorable but dependable generalization is that Communist tyrannies, once established, are particularly long-lived. Indeed, since Soviet troops prevent them from dying a natural death, we cannot even say for sure that they are not immortal.

For these reasons, a nation with humanitarian goals but limited resources should concentrate on anti-Communism: holding back the Soviets; holding back their allies; and keeping countries from falling under their sway. In the world today, anti-Communism is the number one human rights policy.

The Opposition to Containment

In its broad outlines, the policy the United States should follow toward the Soviet Union is a simple one, and easy to defend. The posture of containment is both practical and morally defensible. It fuses into one position our desire for peace and our concern for human dignity around the globe.

As evidence of its soundness, we need but note that it has been the cornerstone of U.S. foreign policy for over three decades. In March 1946, before George Kennan penned the "X" article, Harry Truman was practicing containment by blocking the Soviets in Northwestern Iran. And long after Kennan had all but repudiated his stance, American presidents were still following containment —in Vietnam, in North Yemen, in El Salvador.

Perhaps the most remarkable testament to the wisdom of this doctrine is the extent to which it has been embraced by its critics, once those critics held power. In television debates, candidate John F. Kennedy declared that little bits and pieces of real estate like Quemoy and Matsu were not worth challenges to the Communists. A few months later, as president, he was heading to the brink of war over a place called Laos and declaring, in connection with another bit of real estate, "Ich bin ein Berliner."

Jimmy Carter's conversion was at least as dramatic. He began his term in office by declaring that he had transcended the "inordinate fear of Communism" of prior administrations. Three years later, after noticing the Soviet subjugation of Afghanistan among other things, he found a fear of Communism to be justified. He began his term by pledging to withdraw U.S. troops from South Korea; two years later he was pledging *not* to withdraw U.S. troops from South Korea.[9] And the lag between the enunciation of an anti-containment stand and its reversal grew progressively shorter as the Carter administration matured. By the end of the term, the interval was down to less than two weeks. For example, on 5 December 1980 the Carter administration cut off aid to El Salvador, angered by the killings of four American religious workers. The aid—the symbol of the U.S. commitment to the defeat of the Communists—was reinstated on 17 December, in spite of U.S. left-wing and media protests that nothing had been done to solve the crime.

If containment is the right policy, tried and endorsed by all U.S. administrations, what is the problem? Let's simply close ranks and pursue this posture year in and year out, quietly and persistently.

We all know it has not worked that way and is not about to work that way. Containment policy, in its day-to-day application, carries with it an enormous potential for opposition. The general lines of this policy are not criticized, and the theory behind it is seldom challenged. But each time we move to particulars, there looms the threat of a tremendous, crippling domestic opposition. This opposition, actual or potential, today stands as an almost insuperable barrier to the proper management of containment. Were there a viable alternative, I would immediately urge its adoption.

But there appears to be no alternative. Containment stands as the only safe long-run principle of conduct in a dangerous era. We have to try to make it work. We have to understand the underlying cause of domestic opposition to containment and devise strategies for coping with it. The challenging foreign policy problem of the era is not what to do about the Soviets. The answer is simple, almost inescapable. The real conundrum is how to keep the domestic opposition from undermining containment.

Almost all public policy questions, foreign or domestic, raise two types of considerations: those that are noticeable at first glance, and those that are indirect or hidden from immediate view. Typically, these types of considerations lead in opposite directions; that is, if the immediate impulse suggests that we do X, the consideration of indirect effects will suggest that we not do X. Containment policy in particular sets up a number of dramatic clashes between immediate and hidden considerations. After all, if one desires peace, what, at first glance, should one prepare for? Peace, of course. One should make concessions to aggrieved nations; one should forswear war as an instrument of national policy; one should set aside the implements of war as evidence of one's pacific aims. Yet, as I explained above, the adoption of such policies toward potential aggressors would be likely to exacerbate the danger of major war. Both theory and experience show this to be true. But neither the theory nor the experience is apparent *at first glance*. The connection between a policy of appeasement and the onset of major war is indirect, and the historical record documenting this connection is hidden from immediate view.

As a result, it is first impressions that dominate the public debate on war and peace. Even our vocabulary becomes twisted around to reflect this superficial perspective. Those who urge disarmament, appeasement, nuclear freezes, and the like are called "pacifists" even though, in this context, they are encouraging aggressors and therefore increasing the likelihood of war.[10] And those who help deter the attack of potential aggressors—such as soldiers and weapons manufacturers—are called "warmongers." The Nobel Peace Prize goes to diplomats who sign peace treaties, not to the generals who compel aggressors to want peace.

The public debate on war and peace in this country can be characterized as follows:

In the middle of the room is a control panel. It has a big green button labeled "WORLD PEACE" and a big red button labeled "WORLD WAR." An official is walking up to the console and is reaching out to press the red button. Concerned citizens rush in and attempt to drag his arm away from the red button and guide it toward the green button. He resists. There is much pushing to and fro.

From the perspective of the outraged citizens, the struggle is a simple moral crusade. They want peace, and their first glance at the control panel told them how to get it. To their way of thinking, the official who wants to push the red button either is illiterate or actually desires war.

In fact, the official wants world peace just as much as the citizens. He happens to know, however, that the control console has been miswired; world peace has been hooked up to the red button and world war is connected to the green button! How does this official explain his case—especially if the citizens are unable or unwilling to go behind the control panel and study the wiring? The answer is, as a practical matter, that he cannot *explain* it to them.

The practice of containment involves not only preparing for wars, but sometimes also fighting them. Deterrent threats are never absolutely credible; now and again opponents will test areas of weakness. The challenge may require an American military response and, hence, the loss of American lives. Once again, the immediate reaction will contradict containment policy. The costs and horrors of war will be visible at first glance. Our own sacrifices will be painfully documented on television; the injury we do to opposing forces and bystanders, and the moral dilemmas inherent therein, will stare us in the face. The benefits of fighting—such as a reduced probability of future aggression and a reduced likelihood of major nuclear war—will be completely hidden from view.

In the realm of human rights, we again encounter a tension between first impulses and long-run considerations. As I said above, Communist regimes represent the most consistent threat to human rights in the world today. This position, however, emerges only if one adopts a long-range, historical perspective. From a short-run, immediate perspective, it will often seem unjustified.

Few of us ever know about the degree of human rights violations abroad from our own experience. Instead, we are dependent on second- and third-hand reports, mainly from the media. Almost inevitably, the worst human rights violations will escape contemporaneous media coverage. Where terror and brutality have greatest sway, observers are terrorized into silence, liquidated, or simply excluded. In order to evaluate the severity of oppression in these cases, one has to engage in a process of inference and deduction long after the crime—when most findings have lost their news value.

The more dramatic and publicized reports of human rights violations will come from societies where repression is only moderate: reporters are allowed in, picture-taking is possible, local citizens are not too terrified to talk to foreign observers, and so on. Furthermore, it is only in the freer regimes where newsworthy acts of opposition—demonstrations, guerrilla movements—are likely to occur. A thoroughly ruthless police state would have eliminated such opposition before it had a chance to show itself.

As a result of these reporting biases, the media are likely to portray many non-Communist regimes as greater violators of human rights than Communist ones. For example, in reporting on human rights violations in South Korea and North Korea, papers like *The New York Times* and *The Washington Post* give over one hundred times as much coverage to South Korean transgressions! As another illustration, in 1977 when the Communist regime in Cambodia was murdering its people on a scale unparalleled in modern times, these two newspapers gave over twice as much coverage to human rights problems in Chile, and over ten times as much coverage to such problems in South Africa.[11]

A thoughtful observer will understand these biases and can reason past them to a sound overall judgment. But anyone reacting to first impressions from the mass media will be profoundly swayed. The proposition that Communist regimes are the worst violators of human rights will not seem at all credible, and the policy of protecting human rights by containing Communism will seem to be unfounded.

A perspective born of immediate impressions also ignores the future. An impulsive reaction is present-oriented; it focuses on *now*. The problem this creates is a familiar one. There will be some degree of human rights violation in almost any country, and especially in a country threatened by Communist takeover. The first impulse is to end the violations at whatever cost, or to disassociate ourselves from them. One sees brutality in a South Korea, or a South Vietnam, or an El Salvador and concludes that these countries are unworthy of our support. The issue of future brutality after a Communist takeover is overlooked.

Actually, it is not quite correct to say that the future is overlooked. What happens is that the impulsive mind convinces itself that the present is about as bad as anything could be and rationalizes that any change will be for the better. History generally discloses the absurdity of such rationalizations, but the error goes on being repeated. For example, at the fall of Cambodia to the Communists in April 1975, *The New York Times* carried a story in its "News in the Week in Review" section with this headline: "Indochina Without Americans: For Most, a Better Life."[12]

Such temporocentrism inevitably undermines a human rights policy. The impulsive approach fails to weigh future dangers accurately; it results in a human rights policy of fits and starts. For example, George McGovern led a moralistic crusade to get the United States out of Southeast Asia in 1973. At that time, a first glance told him that fighting involved suffering on our part and inflicting suffering on others; what the Communists might do to people if they won was not a consideration. In 1978, what Communists do when they win became apparent (and the pain of U.S. military involvement was out of sight). Now the senator found the idea of fighting in Southeast Asia attractive:

It would seem to me that [now, if ever, there is] a case where the international community has a good reason to ask itself, "Do we sit on the side-
lines and watch an entire people slaughtered, or do we marshal military
forces and move in quickly to put an end to it?"[13]

Notice, incidentally, how McGovern assumed that this future military involvement in Southeast Asia could be painless and surgical
("move in quickly")—another illustration of how the impulsive
mind, overpowered by the evils of the moment, tends to blot out
both past experience and realistic assessments of the future.

That an individual such as George McGovern might embarrass
himself in such flip-flops is of little consequence. When this type of
inconsistency characterizes a foreign policy, however, the outcome
will be tragic. A nation that follows the course of impulse winds up
with a contemptible human rights record, and flirts with the disaster of total war.

Toward a Policy of Rhetorical Simplicity

Impulsiveness—the tendency to react to first impressions on
public policy questions—has several causes. First, the most obvious cause is inattention. If we take only one glance at a topic,
almost inevitably we shall have a shallow, superficial view. Most
citizens most of the time do take time only for a first glance at
foreign policy issues; therefore, the populace in general may be
said to impart an impulsive orientation to policy.

The second cause follows from the first: the need to appeal to an
inattentive audience. In a free, democratic society, there are a
number of occupations where success depends on mass popularity.
These include jobs in politics and journalism (especially electronic
journalism). To succeed in these fields, one must, to a large extent,
repeat what the audience expects to hear. Since the mass audience
has adopted the impulsive view, it follows that politicians and journalists will be encouraged to adopt a similar perspective. Those
who do not tend to be weeded out.

The degree to which the public "forces" its servants to echo its
view may change over time. In the United States, the problem
seems to have worsened, especially since the mid-1950s. Getting
ahead in journalism and politics has increasingly depended on ap-
pealing to distant mass audiences.[14] As a result, personalities

highly responsive to first impressions have grown more numerous in these fields. Impulsiveness in foreign policy judgments, then, is not confined to the general public. It afflicts large segments of the elites responsible for shaping opinion and deciding policy.

Although impulsiveness comes in several forms, the basic approach to combating it is the same: set up a countervailing opinion "field." The challenge to containment policy comes from first impressions, immediate emotional reactions, the propaganda efforts of the opposing side, and the effects of our own media. If a containment policy is to be sustained, there has to be an active campaign against this challenge.

The type of campaign is set by the nature of the task. Since the opposition to containment measures is founded on superficial, immediate stimuli, the countervailing effort must work at the same level. This is not to say that reason, careful analysis, and exhaustive scholarship should not play a role in foreign policy. To the contrary, a foreign policy must be based on the highest-quality argumentation possible. But when it comes to defending this policy to a mass audience, weighty tomes and intricate scholarship are out of place. The tide of impulse is an essentially unreasoning, emotional, almost physical force. If it is to be deflected, it will take an emotional, almost physical counterforce. In other words, the campaign to protect a policy of containment must resemble, to a considerable degree, an advertising campaign.

Such a campaign has been lacking in U.S. foreign policy for about two decades. This lack justifies the contention that the United States does not really have a foreign policy. The actual responses have been, from Johnson to Reagan, from Vietnam to El Salvador, in the containment mold. But there has been no campaign of mass persuasion to go with these measures. An analogy would be Bristol Myers' developing and manufacturing a new cough syrup, yet omitting to publicize it—except perhaps in a reference in the quarterly report to stockholders. We would say that a company operating this way has not really decided whether it is marketing the cough syrup or not.

Let me give a small illustration of what we are up against. Over the past two or three years, the defense budget has been in the news. Time and again, when defense spending is mentioned in the media, this parenthetical remark is inserted: "the largest peacetime defense budget in history." In terms of nominal dollars, the claim is correct. But the use of nominal dollars is misleading. Given the effects of inflation and economic growth, the same claim could be made about almost every government expenditure. It is almost certain, for example, that the current federal expenditure on refinishing floors represents the "largest floor-waxing budget in history."

This piece of mindless journalism on the defense budget is not without consequence. It obscures, indeed reverses, the real and relevant comparisons about the U.S. defense budget. These points are that as a proportion of GNP and as a proportion of the U.S. federal budget, defense spending has declined dramatically over the past dozen years; and that relative to the unflagging Soviet effort, U.S. defense spending has declined alarmingly. The slogan about U.S. defense spending being a "peacetime record," relentlessly repeated, leads the impressionable to suppose that defense budgets are "too high" and that anyone who urges more defense spending is practically out of his mind. Thus, for example, one cartoonist has depicted a grotesquely fat boxer, labeled "Defense," gorging himself with food. This cartoonist succumbed to the prevailing view concerning U.S. defense budgets; and so did the entire committee of distinguished journalism experts that decided to give him a 1982 Pulitzer Prize for drawing it.[15]

In devising a campaign of mass persuasion, it is important to decide which themes are central and to leave aside points that may contradict this basic message. The American position, I would argue, should stress freedom—not just political freedom, but freedoms of religion, of travel, of artistic expression, and so on. Economic freedom—the freedom to work, to buy and sell, to own, to produce articles of value to others—is particularly important. Unfortunately, it goes almost entirely unheralded in official U.S. messages. It is economic freedom (often referred to by the incredibly misleading term *capitalism)* that accounts for the material prosperity of the West.

Our position should be, and our propaganda should declare, that we are crusaders for freedom *of all types.* Non-Communist dictatorships generally allow four or five of, say, seven basic freedoms; it is because Communists threaten all seven that we oppose their conquest of free world countries.

One theme it is inadvisable to stress is "democracy"—that is, the use of elections to select public officials. There is no necessary or empirical connection between the use of elections and the preservation of freedom. Electoral processes have often produced tyrants (Hitler being an obvious example). And it is not true that unelected personnel are necessarily "dictatorial." A few years back, we had both a president and a vice-president who had not been popularly elected (Ford and Rockefeller). Following our current foreign policy, we should have cut off aid to ourselves. But nobody claimed that, as a result of bypassing the electoral process, we were plunged into a dark night of civil liberties repression. In fact, all the charges about repression were directed against the previous incumbent (Nixon)—who had been popularly elected by the largest margin in history!

If we do not moderate our emphasis on elections, both our policy and our public arguments will become confused beyond repair. To be for freedom and against Communism is clear and consistent. To be for freedom, against Communism, and for elections leads to a muddled and incoherent posture. Are we supposed to approve of an elected Communist about to snuff out liberty (e.g., Allende in Chile)? Are we supposed to become enemies of a free, prosperous, but nondemocratic regime (e.g., Hong Kong)? Are we permitted to come to the aid of an unelected ruler who is besieged by Communist forces (e.g., former president Duarte in El Salvador)?

In the final analysis, it is freedom we really care about—not methods of leadership selection. Our policy and our policy rationale should reflect this basic concern.

Improving Persuasion: An Illustration

There are various degrees of thoroughness in publicizing a foreign policy stance. At one extreme, one can set up a huge Ministry of Propaganda, put loudspeakers on every street corner, and compel all public officials mechanically to repeat a militant government line.

Generally when someone stresses the publicity aspect of foreign policy, his critics have some such caricature in mind. My recommendation is much more modest. I am merely urging that administration officials be aware of domestic opinion and that they make a greater effort to have an impact on it. Let me illustrate.

On my desk is a copy of the prepared statement of a U.S. assistant secretary of state before a congressional committee in February 1982. The assistant secretary was urging U.S. opposition to the Communist guerrilla movement in El Salvador. The words he chose to express this opposition were the following:

> For most of its life as a nation, our country has faced no threat from its neighbors. But unless we act decisively now, the future could well bring more Cubas—totalitarian regimes so linked to the Soviet Union that they become factors in the military balance and so incompetent economically that their citizens' only hope becomes that of one day migrating to the United States.
>
> If we do not sustain the struggle now, we shall fall back into that terrible vicious circle in which in Central America the only alternative to right-wing dictatorship is left-wing dictatorship.[16]

How useful is this material for influencing the impressionable? What effect will it have on the bored congressman? Will it blunt the zeal of a journalist who has fallen in love with the Salvadoran guerrillas at first sight? Does it stand a chance of being a twelve-second clip on the nightly TV news?

Look at the second sentence. It is forty-eight words long and takes eighteen seconds to say out loud. It also contains four separate ideas, none of which is developed, illustrated, or emphasized. We notice, also, that the word *Communism* is avoided (as it is avoided in the entire statement).

If this official had realized that his most important job was projecting pro-containment opinions for the impressionable, he would not have been content with such murky language. He would have broken down the passage into separate ideas. Each idea would be expressed in short, pithy sentences, and then illustrated and documented. For example, one of the ideas contained here is "Communism creates refugees" (or "Communism is the greatest producer of refugees in the world today"). This point would then be documented with statistics about refugees from Communist countries, from Cuba, from South Vietnam, and so on. In a similar fashion, the idea that "Communism causes poverty" should be compactly expressed and documented (food rationing in Cuba, etc.).

The second paragraph about dictatorships illustrates how careless argumentation can unwittingly undermine the containment position. The statement implies that non-Communist ("right-wing") dictatorships are as bad as Communist ("left-wing") dictatorships, and that U.S. policy is to oppose both equally. Once this idea has been drummed into the heads of the impressionable, what happens to support for containment policy? Time and again, to resist a Communist advance, we shall have to support a regime that is, or is thought to be, a "dictatorship." The assistant secretary is convincing the impressionable that it is illogical and immoral for the United States to help such regimes. He is thus fostering *his own opposition* when he goes back to plead for support for any non-Communist regime thought to be less than a perfect democracy — *including El Salvador!*

This passage equating Communist and non-Communist dictatorships should not have appeared in the statement. It is misleading in suggesting that Communist and non-Communist dictatorships are equally undesirable, as well as destructive to containment policy.

The United States government has several hundred officials constantly making public statements on foreign policy subjects: assistant secretaries, press secretaries, public information officers, ambassadors — even a president. Such statements are important in shaping public opinion on foreign policy. Generally speaking, they have been ineffective — and often even counterproductive — in their support for the containment position. By devoting more care to their construction and implications, the officials could make these declarations play a much more positive role.

Objections to a Policy of Rhetorical Simplicity

The idea that we should pay more attention to a simple campaign of justifying containment policy has its opponents. Perhaps the most tireless foe of "liturgical anti-Communism," as he sarcastically calls it, is Henry Kissinger. Indeed, for Kissinger, refraining from criticism of Communism and the Soviet Union was the essence of "détente." This policy had no apparent consequences for what we *did:* under it, we were still supposed to contain Communism. The policy was about what administration officials *said.* And it still lives on today. The assistant secretary quoted above had problems making an effective anti-Communist statement partly because he was adhering to the unwritten policy of not making any derogatory reference to "Communism."

Kissinger's position obviously contradicts the requirements of a mass persuasion campaign. When President Ford, on Kissinger's publicly emphasized advice, refused to meet with Russian dissident Alexander Solzhenitsyn in July of 1975, the message went out that our own president thought the Russians were okay and that opponents of the Soviets, like Solzhenitsyn, were distasteful nuts. How could Ford and Kissinger then marshal support to oppose the Russians—to resist, for example, the Communist advance in Angola a few months later? The answer is, they couldn't and they didn't.

As one looks more closely into how and why Kissinger and others have adopted détente as a rhetorical posture, one encounters a number of misconceptions. First, Kissinger accepts the existence of a stereotype: the wild-eyed anti-Communist. What characterizes this sort of person is not his dislike of Communism—all of us, including Kissinger, dislike it—but the dogmatism of his approach. In particular, such people first, refuse to negotiate with or even "recognize" Communists under any circumstances, and second, yearn for a speedy and final reckoning with Communism; that is, they are eager to begin World War III regardless of the cost. Kissinger refers to these people as "conservatives"; he apparently believes they are as numerous and as threatening to sound policy as the appeasement-oriented liberals:

> Conservatives saw in foreign policy a version of the eternal struggle of good with evil, a conflict that recognized no middle ground and could end only with victory. . . . Regard for the purity of our ideals inspired conservatives . . . to put Communism into quarantine: There could be no compromise with the devil.[17]

> Conservatives at least remained true to their beliefs. They wanted no truck with Communism whatever the tactical motivation. They equated negotiations with Moscow with the moral disarmament of America.[18]

To be sure, in a nation of 200 million there must be some adherents to any conceivable doctrine. But as a practical matter, there simply are no such people in or near the seats of power. *No one* is against ever negotiating with the Russians. (Of course, we all dispute about when to do it and what to give away.) And *everyone* recognizes the common interest both powers have in avoiding nuclear holocaust. *No one* is in favor of pushing the "war" button as soon as possible (the presumption that some people *are* traces, in large part, to the red button/green button misunderstanding explained above).

The Eisenhower-Dulles administration—to take the best example of an apparently hard-line regime—was not against negotiating with Communists. They negotiated an armistice with Communists in Korea, as well as the Austrian neutrality treaty with the Russians—not to mention Geneva (1955) and Camp David (1959), and the informal nuclear test ban.

Kissinger was eager not to become identified with the hard-liners. The studious avoidance of anti-Communist rhetoric seemed the obvious way to distance himself: if you don't talk like a wild-eyed anti-Communist, then nobody can accuse you of being one.

This tactic did not work. In spite of all his efforts to talk mildly about the Soviets, Kissinger found himself reviled by the Left as a warmonger. The anti-containment forces, anxious to believe that reckless aggressors controlled U.S. policy at the highest level, were bound to pin the "wild-eyed anti-Communist" label on any prominent advocate of containment.

A second error underlying détente language and symbolism stemmed from a misunderstanding of the opposition to containment policy. Kissinger and others have supposed that by adopting parts of the platform of anti-containment forces, these forces would be conciliated. Again, the evidence on the results of this strategy is overwhelming: it does not work. Lyndon Johnson's handling of the Vietnam War was calculated, practically day by day, to conciliate domestic opposition: the numerous bombing pauses, the refusal to mine Haiphong Harbor, and so on. Opposition to the war was not brought into the fold by these tactics. Instead it swelled to a mass movement that destroyed the entire policy.

Kissinger had the same experience. Time and again the Nixon administration would make some pro-"peace" move the opponents of the war had been urging it to make. Instead of being grateful that their advice had been taken, the anti-war forces would immediately escalate their demands and Kissinger was left tearing his hair.[19]

Adopting the tactics and rhetoric of "conciliation" will not defuse anti-containment opposition. To the contrary, it will make it worse. The first impulse in most containment issues is some variant of "be nice and they'll be nice in return." This impression can be combated only by a countervailing view to the effect that "they're not nice to begin with," or "they want what they shouldn't have."

Any administration that uses appeals for negotiations and "peace" moves as a public relations ploy is only fueling its own opposition. It reinforces that first impression, that being nice to enemies is the road to peace. As a result, the movement demanding that we cease resisting our enemies grows even more convinced of its rightness.

Crusades based on first impressions are not rational or responsible. They respond to the prevailing field of images, symbols, and slogans. Any statesman who thinks he can make a "deal" with the tide of impulse fails to understand the problem.

"Speaking Out" vs. Rhetorical Simplicity

At the beginning of the Reagan administration, several officials voiced rather stern remarks about the Soviet Union and related Cold War issues. The reader might wonder if these officials were actually applying the policy of rhetorical simplicity advocated here, and if so, whether that policy succeeded.

It is useful to treat these questions in reverse order. First, on the issue of success, it must be recognized that a policy aimed at shaping the climate of opinion will never have a clear or certain test of success. Any given effort will have but an infinitesimal impact on opinion. Furthermore, many other forces are always at work shaping opinion. It is, as a practical matter, impossible to separate out the impact of this speech or that declaration on the prevailing congressional or journalistic mood.

We can be clear about one point, however: with a policy of rhetorical simplicity, one cannot employ public reaction to the statements themselves as a measure of success or failure. The essence of this policy is to introduce ideas or impulses that contradict the anti-containment perspective. Naturally, those subject to this perspective will object—even as their own opinions are being transformed (ever so slightly) by what they are objecting to.

It is therefore inappropriate to say that the rhetorical approach of the early Reagan administration—whatever it was—"failed" because critical letters appeared in *The New York Times*. Adverse comment would be an inevitable by-product of even the best-conducted campaign in support of containment policy.

As it happens, however, what emerged in the first months of the Reagan administration was not a rhetorical *policy* of any kind. What was to be said was not collectively planned beforehand; instead, certain officials simply spoke out independently. As the Reagan administration found out, there are weaknesses in this freewheeling approach.

For example, in March 1981, testifying before a congressional committee on Central America, Secretary of State Alexander Haig said that the Soviet Union had a "hit list" for the takeover of Central America.[20] First of all, the use of this phrase made the secretary seem simpleminded, equating the conduct of world politics with a television crime drama. Secondly, it appeared to be a concrete claim, but Haig could not document it by producing a captured "list" or any such thing. Thus the secretary seemed to be making an "irresponsible" claim, which created credibility problems for him. In general, analogies, metaphors, and similes cause problems in mass communication. The speaker is trying to say that "X is like a Y in one respect," but impressionable listeners often interpret such statements to mean "X *is* a Y: the same in all respects."

A process of collectively reviewing language beforehand does more than clean up word choice—it keeps in focus the aims of language. A policy of rhetorical simplicity has a definite purpose: to blunt the anti-containment tide of images and slogans, and to support the pro-containment position. Nothing belongs in public pronouncements that contradicts or detracts from this purpose. When public officials speak off the cuff, this rule is often violated. For example, they may attack their domestic critics. When Lyndon Johnson jabbed at the "nervous Nellies" opposing his Vietnam policy, he did nothing to change the climate of opinion on containment policy; he simply irritated his critics.

In the early days of the Reagan administration, several media flaps grew out of this type of needless irritation. Speaking before a group of conservatives, National Security Advisor Richard V. Allen called "outright pacifist sentiments" in Western Europe "contemptible."[21] He got cheers from the conservative audience, which already supported containment, but only resentment from the pacifist-leaning groups he should have been trying to influence.

Another problem arose when Richard Pipes, on the National Security Council staff, insulted West German Foreign Minister Hans Dietrich Genscher as one disposed to yield to Soviet pressure. Naturally, the State Department had to make amends. But Haig did not discreetly disavow the remarks; with a rhetorical immaturity of his own, he declared himself to be "especially outraged" by Pipes's references.[22] In this way, Haig dramatized and further publicized the very statements he wanted ignored.

In the same Reuters interview, Pipes declared that "Soviet leaders would have to choose between peacefully changing their Communist system in the direction followed by the West or going to war. There is no other alternative and it could go either way."[23]

The remark was, first, unjustifiably dogmatic ("no other alternative") and therefore projected simplemindedness. Secondly, it had an *anti-containment* thrust. It needlessly fanned the fear of war that underlies the impulse to appease; it implied that there was no positive course for the United States, like a containment policy, to limit the danger of war. Finally, coming from a policymaker, the statement appeared to be a threat: the Soviet Union must change its internal system or the United States will undertake a preemptive war. It was this last overtone that made it necessary for the White House to repudiate what Pipes had said: "The views expressed do not represent administration policy."[24]

What we see in such episodes, then, is the exact opposite of any kind of language policy. Officials in the early Reagan administration did not agree beforehand on what to say and how they would deal with the reactions (and misquotes!) their declarations would provoke. Instead, they sallied forth independently, like *vaqueros,* each whirring his own *bola* over his head, without regard for the purposes — or safety — of his colleagues.

The President's Role

It is clear, then, that a coherent and effective campaign of justification is an essential component of containment policy.

Without it, the climate of opinion will be anti-containment. The first impulse will be to press for "peace," to appease, to do nothing and hope for the best. The views of the impressionable will sway with this impulse, undermining, in fits and starts, an orderly policy for limiting the danger of major war and for sustaining human freedom against the tide of tyranny.

In a well-ordered administration, this publicity campaign would receive more attention than anything else. Deputy secretaries of defense would weigh the nuances of slogans more carefully than the payloads of cargo planes. Presidential task forces would spend weeks hammering out the logic and language of the public relations campaign to support a particular containment policy action. No administration could hope to explain how the control panel is hooked up and why the red and green buttons have been mislabeled. But if it keeps saying "green means war," it can succeed in cross-pressuring the impulsive citizens into a neutral, possibly even thoughtful, state of mind.

In such campaigns, the president plays a vital leadership role. He can, by announcements and by appropriate policy moves, create, for a time, the dominant impulse. The impressionable react well to leadership; when someone stands up and announces "Hey, let's do this!" their first impulse is to go along.

Recent administrations have apparently not understood this helpful fact. They have preferred to let sleeping dogs lie, hoping that if they downplayed the issue, their opposition would dissipate. Johnson tried to soft-pedal Vietnam; Carter downplayed the issue of Soviet troops in Cuba; Reagan refuses to raise the issue of Nicaragua.

But our system does not function well in free-fall, with no one leading and no one insisting; opinion becomes molded by journalists quoting journalists. Dramatic presidential action is a tremendous resource for creating a pro-containment field. Of course this resource can be overused. But if my reckoning is correct, it has been over a decade since it has been used at all.

It is important not to exaggerate what an appropriate public defense of containment could do. It would be too much, for example, ever to expect a *New York Times* headline on the eve of Communist victory somewhere to predict the future correctly: "Indochina Without Americans: For Most, Terror and Tyranny."

But a persistent campaign of justifying containment in clear and simple terms would create a countervailing climate of opinion. Journalists could no longer be so wholeheartedly anti-American. The headline might then read: "Indochina Without Americans: For Most, a Question Mark." Thus, bit by bit, the wave of self-righteous opposition to containment would slacken, and a safe and humane policy option would be open to us.

IV

Conclusion

11

AARON WILDAVSKY

From Minimal to Maximal Containment

Assuming that the Soviet Union poses a danger to American security, containment is one alternative in a very short list of possible responses to this problem. The possibilities are:

1. *Accommodation.* Let the Soviet Union and its allies expand at will. Expansion has indeed occurred, but no American government has been willing to concede this much as an overt policy.

2. *Condominium.* Divide the world (or as much of it as will permit itself to be so treated) with the Soviet Union. No American government has been (and, in my opinion, ought to be) willing to accept this proposition.

3. *End the threat.* This class of responses includes both efforts to change the Soviet Union, so it will not wish to be aggressive, and attempts to convince the Soviets that they do not need to be aggressive. The Carter administration tried the latter and, as

we saw, the Soviet Union exploited the possibility: professions of peace were met with new challenges and more arms.

4. *Containment.* If the danger is there, if the United States cannot accept the results of Soviet pressure and does not do anything to remove it, it must be contained. The physical analogy to this policy is the resistance to outward pressure. America's choice is to allow expansion, remove the pressure, or contain it by measures that are designed to resist its continuation. Therefore it is foolish to attack containment; we must rather consider and choose among its variants. Even if we had a long-term plan to end our struggle with Soviet expansionism, we would still have to use containment in the meantime.

   The important variants of containment are:

   a. *Minimal containment.* This policy necessarily rests on the hope of early change in the Soviet Union, leading it to be less aggressive. The latter hope has proved futile: in the nearly four decades since World War II, Soviet aggression has not diminished.

   b. *Fixed line at borders of Soviet empire.* No retreats, no trades. Because the Soviets have breached the line, the fixed line has become flexible, and this policy has merged with the next variant.

   c. *Fixed line around assets* (Western Europe, Israel, North America, Japan, etc.) *vital to the United States.* America will not act to repel aggression outside that line. By redefining downward what is "vital," successive losses can be tolerated so that containment becomes, in effect, a "Fortress America" policy.

   d. *Flexible containment.* All forms of containment without direct attack on Communist control of the Soviet Union. Though there is no attempt at military "rollback" on the borders of the Soviet Union, economic and political methods are used to persuade the Soviet Union to moderate its behavior within its empires.

   e. *Containment plus.* Programs to change the Soviet Union or reduce the Soviet empire can be added to any of the above containment policies. This policy has not yet been tried, although some experimentation with it has begun.

Containment is thus not a single policy, but a family of policies that lie along a continuum. At one end is *minimal containment*. Under this policy, the role of the West is purely reactive, actively defending lines after they are challenged by the Soviets or their allies. At the other end of the continuum is *maximal containment*. This policy goes beyond defense against aggression to measures aimed at persuading the Soviet Union not to undertake aggression, and to measures that weaken or limit the expansionist tendencies of the Soviet system.

There is an asymmetry in American foreign policy—widespread practice of minimal containment but little practice of maximal containment. The overwhelming stress on responding to events, rather than preventing them from occurring, gives American policy its defensive cast. Why, we may ask, has containment remained minimal rather than maximal, emphasizing reaction rather than prevention?

There are real advantages to responding after the fact as required by minimal containment. Decision-makers who act after events occur do not have to predict or guess what will happen; they already know. They do not have to persuade themselves or their people that something *might* happen. One does not have to imagine elite and popular preferences or infer aggressive intent except as these qualities reveal themselves in action. Because no one fully knows the causes of the evils that occur, or their probability, the net of prevention has to be cast wide. This may be dangerous and is certainly expensive. Thus there is one more thing to be said for a strategy of minimal containment: as the modifier *minimal* suggests, it limits the evil encountered to the case in hand. There is no need for general doctrines or for immense preparation, which, when in place, may lead to larger difficulties. When Robert Tucker writes in this volume that the United States has not done so badly with containment, he undoubtedly has in mind that America has avoided the worst even if it cannot, in the nature of things, get the best. When Ernst Haas wants to hedge his bets, he is sufficiently uncertain of Soviet intentions to keep open the possibility of moving beyond the minimal.

All of us support at least minimal containment, but several of us believe that it should be supplemented. Since minimal containment is the prevailing doctrine and practice, it has seemed to me worthwhile to spell out in some detail what a more maximal containment would be like. My purpose in editing this volume has been precisely to elucidate maximal containment as an alternative. Debate on foreign policy might then proceed by asking where, between the minimal and the maximal, Americans wish to draw the line.

Viewing containment as a consequence of a bipolar world, one in which Western Europe and Japan refuse to act as great powers, leaving the rivalry between the United States and the Soviet Union on center stage, Robert Tucker sees containment superior to withdrawal or confrontation. There are limits the Soviet Union cannot cross without a military response from the United States, but these should be severely circumscribed; Western Europe, Japan, and perhaps the Persian Gulf represent the only places in which the United States has a vital interest. For the rest, Tucker counsels patience, saying it would be unfortunate if the United States tried to speed up processes of disintegration he sees at work to weaken Soviet control over Eastern Europe and Soviet dominance in parts of the Third World.

The *selective engagement* Ernst Haas proposes is more than minimal but far from maximal containment. His aim is both to decouple the various issues of Soviet-American rivalry from one another and to make clear the minimal assets or interests that the United States considers vital enough to protect. Since there is no way of knowing how aggressive the Soviet Union will be in the future, Haas wishes the United States to maintain its nuclear deterrent (though not a war-fighting capability) and its protection for Western Europe, Japan, South Korea, and the Pacific Basin. In addition, all existing democracies should, if they so wish, be defended. Finally, countries so close to the United States that an adversary could use them to initiate hostile action, or that contain indispensable commodities, should also be protected, if necessary by force. Otherwise, Haas wishes the United States to remove itself militarily and to a degree economically from the Third World, compensating Third World governments for the loss of exports incurred by a policy of American independence. In sum, Haas would include in containment North America, Central America, the Caribbean, South Korea, the Pacific, and a number of existing democracies.

Addressing himself mainly to policy directed at Soviet influence in the Third World, Charles Wolf wants the United States to encourage selected allies to act against the Soviet use of proxies. To aid in that endeavor, the United States is to provide mobility and light weapons for these associated countries, backed up by a new logistical and planning center combining elements from the Departments of State and Defense and dispensing both military and economic aid. Extending containment to the economic sector, Wolf would have America follow a strict principle of not subsidizing the Soviet bloc—no loan guarantees, no artificially low interest rates, and no tax preferences. Taken together, Wolf's proposals extend containment to the economic realm and to parts of the Third World where alliances of associated countries may act to ward off Communist control or, when feasible, to reverse it. Though he has only modest hopes, Wolf's extended containment would include "a declaration of explicit and overt—yet selective, limited, and measured—support for genuine and legitimate movements within the Third World that seek to achieve liberation from Communist imperialism and totalitarianism, and that also seek to advance more pluralistic, open, and at least incipiently democratic forms of government." If only one Communist Third World government were to fall to democratic forces, the aura of inexorable advance would be removed from Soviet-sponsored movements.

Yet while under these proposals containment is extended geographically, it remains defensive rather than preventative. I have proposed a policy designed to "pluralize" the Soviet Union as a way of weakening its aggressive intent before it grows so threatening that all that is left to us is capitulation or nuclear war. Pluralization is to be accomplished over the decades by using political means to encourage diversity within the Soviet Union. By disseminating information, by exposing privilege, by amplifying dissent, and by otherwise giving expression to the various differences within the Soviet Union over national, ethnic, religious, gender, environmental, health, and other issues, the United States can hope if not to end then to soften the intensity of Soviet antagonism. Containment would become maximal, reaching the heart of the Soviet system, attempting to prevent hostile acts from occurring as well as coping with the consequences afterwards.

Dynamic containment, according to Max Singer, will include the use of political, economic, ideological, and military means to reduce the external Soviet empire while arms control objectives are pursued unilaterally to achieve agreements that may reduce the risk of war or the harm if war occurs. The focus is on the overall balance with the Soviet Union, so there can be both advances and retreats. Arms control is to be moved toward providing fewer offensive and more defensive weapons so that containment is not seen as leading inevitably to nuclear war.

Which would have the potential for greater public support: minimal or maximal containment? Minimal containment has the advantage of putting less strain on government authority. The interests defended, being small in number, are more likely to be regarded by the public as genuinely vital; besides, the fewer the places to defend, the fewer the actions for which support is required. Yet a policy of minimal containment might eventually reduce public support; many peripheral interests could be sacrificed, so that in the end, with so little left to defend, the whole situation might look hopeless. Mere survival, it could then be argued, might be easier to achieve by surrender.

By contrast, the views expressed by James Payne and shared by several of the authors that "anti-Communism is the number one human rights policy" might make sense out of the risks of containment. For Payne the problem with containment lies mainly in the lack of support; public support even for a policy of minimal containment is by no means guaranteed. Indeed, all the authors in this volume saw the problem of insufficient public support as critical. Payne's solution is to formulate a new rhetorical strategy to sell containment to the public.

My preference is for a policy of maximal containment. I would have the government of the United States adopt all of the policies proposed here. Containment should apply to Western Europe, Japan, South Korea, Israel, Central America, the Caribbean, the Pacific, and to existing democracies. Use of Soviet proxies should be fought by associations of Allied nations; Leninist governments should be opposed. In regard to the international economy, normal trade without subsidies is to be encouraged. Toward the Soviet Union a policy of prevention is to be pursued. By supporting efforts at internal pluralization, the United States can hope gradually to lessen the hostility of the Soviet Union. For, as Singer says, conquest by intimidation is no less (I would say more) probable than overt use of force.

People who prefer a less ambitious policy have found eloquent advocates in this volume. They can also add any of the additional elements proposed without taking all of them. Though minimal containment may need more public support than it has recently received, it needs less elucidation because by and large it has been the prevailing policy. Thus I have sought to give expression to a variety of ways for maximizing containment. My hope is that consideration of these alternatives, taken singly or as a whole, adding up to more maximal containment, will spur debate instead of drift in regard to American policy toward the Soviet Union.

Notes

Contributors

Index

NOTES

2. Aaron Wildavsky: "Dilemmas of American Foreign Policy"

1. Kenneth Waltz, "Another Gap?" in *Containment, Soviet Behavior and Grand Strategy* (Berkeley, Calif.: Institute for International Studies, 1981), p. 80.

2. George W. Breslauer, "Why Detente Failed," typescript (March 1981), pp. 16–17.

3. Waltz, p. 81.

4. Seweryn Bialer, "Soviet Foreign Policy: Sources, Perceptions, Trends," in *The Domestic Context of Soviet Foreign Policy,* ed. Seweryn Bialer (Boulder, Colo.: Westview, 1981).

5. Norman Podhoretz, "The Future Danger," *Commentary* (April 1981): 44.

3. Aaron Wildavsky: "The Soviet System"

1. Quoted from a paper prepared for the State Department by William Taubman in support of a similar position by Alexander Solzhenitsyn. See Seweryn Bialer, "Soviet Foreign Policy: Sources, Perceptions, Trends," in *The Domestic Context of Soviet Foreign Policy,* ed. Seweryn Bialer (Boulder, Colo.: Westview Press, 1981), p. 439.

2. Irving Kristol, "The Succession: Understanding the Soviet Mafia," *The Wall Street Journal,* 18 November 1982, p. 30.

3. Richard Lowenthal, "Development vs. Utopia in Communist Policy," in *Change in Communist Systems,* ed. Chalmers Johnson (Stanford, Calif.: Stanford University Press, 1970), pp. 33–116; and idem, "On 'Established' Communist Party Regimes," *Studies in Comparative Communism* (Winter 1974): 335–58.

4. Victor Zaslavsky, *The Neo-Stalinist State* (Armonk, N.Y.: M. E. Sharpe, 1982), p. 87.

5. Valerie Bunce and John M. Echols, III, "Soviet Politics in the Brezhnev Era: Pluralism or Corporatism?" in *Soviet Politics in the Brezhnev Era,* ed. Donald Kelly (New York: Praeger, 1980), p. 12.

6. See T. H. Rigby, "Politics in the Mono-Organizational Society," in *Authoritarian Politics in Communist Europe,* ed. Andrew C. Janos (Berkeley, Calif.: Regents of the University of California, 1976), p. 75.

7. Richard Spielman, "In Poland," *Foreign Policy,* no. 49 (Winter 1982–83): 33.

8. Seweryn Bialer, *Stalin's Successors: Leadership, Stability, and Change in the Soviet Union* (Cambridge, Mass.: Cambridge University Press, 1980), p. 196.

9. Robert V. Daniels, "Soviet Politics since Khrushchev," in *The Soviet Union under Brezhnev and Kosygin: The Transition Years,* ed. John W. Strong (New York: Van Nostrand Reinhold, 1971), p. 23.

10. Zaslavsky, p. 23.

11. Rigby, p. 31.

12. Philip Selznick, *The Organizational Weapon: A Study of Bolshevik Strategy and Tactics* (Glencoe, Ill.: Free Press, 1960), p. 62. See also Merle Fainsod, *How Russia Is Ruled* (Cambridge, Mass.: Harvard University Press, 1953), p. 150.

13. Bohdan Harasymiw, "Nomenklatura: The Soviet Communist Party's Leadership Recruitment System," *Canadian Journal of Political Science* (December 1969): 493–512.

14. John P. Willerton, Jr., "Clientelism in the Soviet Union: An Initial Examination," *Studies in Comparative Communism* (Summer/Autumn 1979): 181.

15. Daniels, p. 20.

16. Derek J. R. Scott, *Russian Political Institutions* (New York: Praeger, 1961), p. 171.

17. Harasymiw.

18. Bialer, *Stalin's Successors: Leadership, Stability, and Change in the Soviet Union,* p. 172.

19. Hendrick Smith, *The Russians* (New York: Ballantine, 1970), p. 391.

20. Gregory Grossman, "The 'Second Economy' of the USSR," *Problems of Communism* (September/October 1977): 25–40.

21. Henry Kissinger, *Years of Upheaval* (Boston: Little, Brown, 1982), p. 244.

22. Letter to the author dated 10 April 1983.

23. Borrowing a phrase from Gordon Tulloch, T. H. Rigby refers to

> "the 'whispering down the lane' problem—i.e., the cumulative distortion (deliberate or unwitting) undergone at each echelon by commands as they pass down and information as it passes up a hierarchy, such that the message as eventually received and applied may bear little resemblance to the message as originally sent and intended. . . . This problem tends to be particularly acute in the mono-organizational system. Hence the need for severe sanctions against misinterpreting, misapplying, disobeying, or failing to respond to commands, and against supplying misleading reports; for multiple and powerful checking mechanisms to detect such distortions; and for constant and intensive indoctrination and propaganda messages at all levels and in all divisions of the system" (Rigby, p. 63). Yet it is precisely this "common frame" that ensures self-serving, not self-revealing, reports.

24. Zaslavsky, inter alia.

25. Ibid., p. 92.

26. Ibid., pp. 117–18.

27. Ibid., pp. 33ff.

28. A summary of his conclusion in *Pravda.* Quoted in Charles T. Baroch, "The Mirror-Image Fallacy: Understanding the Soviet Union," Heritage Foundation *Backgrounder,* no. 193 (29 June 1981), p. 4.

29. Ibid. For a review of the pros and cons of independence in trade unions, see D. Richard Little, "Political Participation and the Soviet System," *Problems of Communism,* vol. XXIX (July/August 1980): 65.

30. Uri Ra'anan, "Soviet Decision-Making and International Relations," *Problems of Communism,* vol. XXIX (November/December 1980): 42.

31. Kissinger, p. 245.

32. Kenneth Jowitt, "Soviet Neo-Traditionalism: The Political Corruption of a Leninist Regime," typescript (University of California, Berkeley, 1982).

4. Paul Seabury: "Reinspecting Containment"

1. George Saintsbury, ed., "Second Letter on a Regicide Peace," *Political Pamphlets* (New York: Macmillan, 1892), p. 84.

2. George Kennan, unmailed letter to Walter Lippmann, 6 April 1948. Quoted by Eduard Mark, "Mr. 'X' Is Inconsistent and Wrong," in *Decline of the West: George Kennan and His Critics,* ed. Martin F. Herz (Washington, D.C.: Ethics and Public Policy Center, 1978), p. 160.

3. One indicator of the widespread practice of using the balance concept as an organizing principle for U.S.–Soviet political-military affairs can be seen in its adoption by the Institute for Strategic Studies (now the International Institute for Strategic Studies) in the 1960s in its annual authoritative report on the military capabilities of the powers: *The Strategic Balance.*

4. One project undertaken by Western firms during détente was of great symbolic importance. This was the Kama River Truck City, completed in the mid-1970s with massive infusions of U.S. capital and technical assistance. In 1968, when the Red Army invaded Czechoslovakia, a shortage of military vehicles had required Moscow garbage trucks to be requisitioned to accomplish the mission. This logistical impediment has now been overcome.

5. George Kennan, *American Diplomacy 1900–1950* (Chicago: University of Chicago Press, 1951), p. 118.

6. Ibid., p. 66.

7. Ibid., p. 73.

8. Walter Lippmann, *The Cold War: A Study in U.S. Foreign Policy* (New York: Harper and Brothers, 1947), pp. 15–16.

9. In 1947, Lippmann pontificated to the effect that the Western European democracies would utterly reject the logic of containment. The Europeans, he then wrote (two years before the NATO alliance was ratified),

> are no longer to be counted upon as firm members of a coalition led by the United States against the Soviet Union. We must not deceive ourselves by supposing that we stand at the head of a worldwide coalition of democratic states in our conflict with the Soviet Union.

(Ibid., p. 27.)

10. Ibid., pp. 29–30.

11. Ibid., p. 51.

12. Kennan, much later, tried to argue that his formula for containment was not military, but economic and political. Nevertheless, at the onset of the Korean War he firmly supported the use of force to respond to the attack.

13. For further details of these matters, see Kennan, *American Diplomacy 1900–1950*, p. 125.

14. A minor example of official self-deception may be seen in Washington's stolid diplomatic pursuit of "mutual balanced force reduction" in Vienna with the Soviets since 1974. This negotiation persisted even as evidence accumulated, in the European theater, of a massive Warsaw Pact arms buildup. The talks consistently belied any interest whatsoever in even merely *sustaining* their overall superiority in theater conventional weaponry.

15. Adam Ulam, "How to Restrain the Soviets," *Commentary* (December 1980): 41.

16. Kennan, *American Diplomacy 1900–1950*, p. 127.

17. Lippmann, pp. 15–16.

18. Walter Lippmann, *Essays in the Public Philosophy* (Boston, Mass.: Little, Brown, 1955), pp. 23–24.

6. Ernst B. Haas: "On Hedging Our Bets: Selective Engagement with the Soviet Union"

1. This treatment of strategies owes much to Gordon A. Craig and Alexander L. George, *Force and Statecraft* (New York: Oxford University Press, 1983), especially chs. 9 and 17. I have followed their categories rather than those chosen in John L. Gaddis's masterful *Strategies of Containment* (New York: Oxford University Press, 1983). Gaddis distinguishes between containment proper (Kennan's version), JCS–68, the new look, flexible response, and détente, and he considers all of them types of containment. He treats them as varying from each other in terms of the relative weight given to "universalism" (imposing an American-designed world order) and "diversity" (the preservation of a global balance of power).

2. The suggestion was made, according to Kissinger's memoirs, during the negotiations leading to the Basic Principles Agreement. See Alexander L. George, *Managing U.S.–Soviet Rivalry* (Boulder, Colo.: Westview Press, 1983), pp. 112–13.

3. The subtle case is made by R. Judson Mitchell, *Ideology of a Superpower* (Stanford, Calif.: Hoover Press, 1982), and by John Lenczowski, *Soviet Perceptions of U.S. Foreign Policy* (Ithaca, N.Y.: Cornell University Press, 1982).

4. Paul Seabury, "Clausewitz: Visions of a Nuclear War," *The American Spectator*, August/September 1978, p. 16.

5. For excellent examples of such analyses see Vernon V. Aspaturian, "Soviet Global Power and the Correlation of Forces," *Problems of Communism* (May/June 1980); George W. Breslauer, "Why Detente Failed," in George, op. cit.

6. Even if we and the Soviets always prefer peace to double-crossing each other on some suitably promising occasion, we can never be sure — given the technological frailties of monitoring systems and our lack of understanding each other's motives — that the other is *not* planning to double-cross us by launching a preemptive war. Hence the system of mutual deterrence is inherently unreliable even if neither side wishes to be an aggressor. The mind boggles at trying to imagine a way of persuading the adversary that the thought of a double-cross has never been entertained.

For the game-theoretic logic underlying this argument see George H. Quester, "Six Causes of War," *The Jerusalem Journal of International Relations*, vol. 6, no. 1 (1982): 1–23. On the basis of similar demonstrations (buttressed by historical examples), Glenn Snyder and Paul Diesing conclude that there are enormous variations in the way crises are structured and managed. The variation is best explained by different ways in which actors process information. Since these ways are far from uniform, past patterns provide a most unreliable guide to the future, thus suggesting the need for the invention of new ways of bargaining if crises are to be managed *(Conflict Among Nations* [Princeton, N.J.: Princeton University Press, 1978]).

7. Aaron Wildavsky: "Containment plus Pluralization"

1. See, for instance, Konstantin M. Simis, *USSR: The Corrupt Society: The Secret World of Soviet Capitalism* (New York: Simon and Schuster, 1982).

2. I associate myself entirely with James Payne's comments on elections in chapter 10.

3. Jimmy Carter, *Keeping Faith: Memoirs of a President* (New York: Bantam, 1982), p. 218.

4. When President Kennedy spoke in public, saying, "And if we cannot end now our differences, at least we can help make the world safe for diversity," he was also guilty of self-deception, for the Soviet aim is exactly a world in which it is unsafe to differ with them. (Commencement address at American University in Washington, D.C., 10 June 1963 in *John F. Kennedy, Public Papers of the President of the United States, 1963* [Washington, D.C.: U.S. Government Printing Office, 1964], pp. 459–64, quoted in William G. Hyland, "Soviet-American Relations: A New Cold War?" Rand Publication Series, R–2763–FF/RC [Santa Monica, Calif.: Rand Corporation, May 1981], p. 9.)

5. Morton Schwartz, *The Foreign Policy of the USSR: Domestic Factors* (Encino & Belmont, Calif.: Dickenson, 1975), pp. 148–49.

6. Norman Podhoretz makes the salient point: "One of the 'lessons of Vietnam' that is rarely mentioned is that public support became impossible to maintain in the absence of a convincing moral rationale for our effort there. Having, paradoxically, gone into Vietnam for idealistic reasons (in the strict sense that there was no vital geopolitical or material interest at stake, and that what we were actually trying to do was save the South Vietnamese from the horrors of Communist rule that have now befallen them), we then tried to justify our involvement in the language of *Realpolitik*. But no good case could be made in that language for American military intervention; and even if it could, it would not in the long run have convinced the American people." ("The Future Danger," *Commentary*, April 1981, pp. 38–39.)

7. For sophisticated discussions of trade policy, consult Samuel P. Huntington, "The Renewal of Strategy," in *The Strategic Imperative: New Policies for American Security*, ed. Samuel P. Huntington (Cambridge, Mass.: Ballinger, 1982), pp. 16–19.

8. See Gail Warshofsky Lapidus, "The Impact of Soviet-American Scholarly Exchanges on the USSR" (typescript, 1979, paper prepared for a joint review of the IREX programs by the Ford Foundation, National Endowment for the Humanities and International Communications Agency), for an informative discussion of the positive consequences of exchange.

9. Authors who assume that the regime has been fundamentally transformed since Stalin's time and that its prospects for stability and reform are good can usually do no more than assert that the difference is that Brezhnev allowed the outwardly conformist Soviet man to "breathe freely, live quietly, and work well," so long as he didn't meddle in things that didn't concern him, such as politics. (Jerry F. Hough, "The Brezhnev Era: The Man and the System," *Problems of Communism*, vol. XXV [March–April, 1976].) This represents a promise by the regime not to bother people who give the regime no reason to be concerned with them. KGB psychiatrists' diagnoses of dissidents confined in mental hospitals demonstrate that this is the "normal" psychology expected of Soviet subjects. The "mentally ill" dissidents are said to suffer from a form of schizophrenia because they are concerned with their own work and national politics as well—a sure sign of a serious psychological disorder! (Zhores Medvedev and Roy Medvedev, *A Question of Madness: Repression by Psychiatry in the Soviet Union* [New York: Vintage Books, 1972], provides an example of this kind of diagnosis.)

10. "Since all religion is willy-nilly a denial of Communist legitimacy, 'toleration' of it typically resembles that accorded a besieged city on which one is not ready to make the final assault" (Rigby, "Politics in the Mono-Organizational Society," in *Authoritarian Politics in Europe*, ed. Andrew C. Janos [Berkeley, Calif.: Regents of the University of California, 1976], p. 65).

11. Vladimir Bukovsky, *To Build a Castle—My Life as a Dissenter* (New York: Viking, 1979).

12. Seweryn Bialer and Joan Afferica, "Reagan and Russia," *Foreign Affairs*, vol. 61, no. 2 (Winter 1982/83): 265.

13. Ibid., pp. 265–66.

14. Alexander L. George, "Introduction," *Managing U.S.–Soviet Rivalry: Problems of Crisis Prevention* (Boulder, Colo.: Westview Press, 1983), p. 3.

8.   Charles Wolf, Jr.: "Extended Containment"

1. Michael Polanyi, *The Tacit Dimension* (New York: Anchor, 1966), pp. 3–25.

2. Olympiad S. Ioffe, "Law and Economy in the USSR," *Harvard Law Review* (May 1982): 1591, 1625.

3. *The Wall Street Journal*, 20 October 1982, p. 33.

4. See Hélène Carrère d'Encausse, *Decline of an Empire: The Soviet Socialist Republics in Revolt* (New York: Harper and Row, 1979).

5. See J. A. Hobson, *Imperialism* (New York: Gordon Press, 1975), p. 15. It is worth recalling Hobson's remark concerning the "quibbles about the modern meaning of the terms 'imperialism' and 'empire.'" Hobson's use of the term encompassed, within the British empire, areas that Britain "annexed or otherwise asserted political sway over," and he acknowledged that there is a "sliding scale of political terminology along which no man's land, or hinterland, passes into some kind of definite protectorate." A similarly elastic terminology is implied in my use of the term *empire* to refer to the various forms of political sway, influence, and "protectorate" that the Soviet Union has acquired in the past decade.

6. For a more extended discussion of some of these aspects, see my article "Beyond Containment: Reshaping U.S. Policies Toward the Third World" (pamphlet, California Seminar on International Security and Foreign Policy, Santa Monica, Calif., September 1982), pp. 1–29; and "Beyond Containment: Redesigning American Policies," *The Washington Quarterly* (Winter 1982): 107–17.

7. An example of what I have in mind is provided by the State Department's recent report to Congress, *Country Report on Human Rights Practices for 1982* (Washington, D.C.: U.S. Government Printing Office, 1983). With rare exceptions, the most egregious violations of human rights occur within Communist states. The report contrasts the more pervasive and subtle violations occurring in Communist systems with those occurring elsewhere, without thereby absolving the latter.

8. For a more complete exposition of the reasons for forging a closer link between security assistance and economic and technical aid, see my "Beyond Containment: Reshaping U.S. Policies Toward the Third World," pp. 22–25.

9. See, for example, Henry Trofimenko, "The Third World and the U.S.–Soviet Competition: A Soviet View," *Foreign Affairs* (Summer 1981): 1025–27.

10. See Daniel F. Kohler and Kip T. Fisher, *Subsidization of East–West Trade through Credit Insurance and Loan Guarantees* (Santa Monica, Calif.: Rand Corporation N–1951–USDP, January 1983), pp. 43–46. For a more complete discussion of these matters, see my testimony before the Senate Committee on Foreign Relations and the Subcommittee on International Economic Policy, *Hearings on Economic Relations with the Soviet Union,* Washington, D.C., July, August, 1982, pp. 116–25, and before the Workshop of the Senate Committee on Foreign Relations and Congressional Research Service, Library of Congress, *The Premises of East–West Commercial Relations,* Washington, D.C., December 1982, pp. 142–52.

11. During the past several decades, numerous export subsidies have been instituted by Western Europe and the United States. These subsidies distort normal commercial incentives to engage in transactions with the Soviet Union and other CMEA countries. The subsidies— many of which reflect governmental efforts to promote exports and international investment in general, rather than only to the CMEA countries—include the following: loans at preferential rates and the provision of loan guarantees; investment guarantees underwritten by government agencies; and preferential tax treatment of foreign business or personal income. These subsidies are, in the final analysis, borne by the taxpayers of the countries concerned in the form of higher budgetary or "off-budgetary" expenditures. The rules of the game proposed in the text are intended to retract these subsidies as they bear on trade with Eastern Europe and the Soviet Union. It is to be hoped that such retraction might later be extended to other areas as well.

12. Joint Chiefs of Staff, *Department of Defense Dictionary of Military and Associated Terms* (Washington, D.C.: U.S. Government Printing Office, 1979), p. 120.

13. Donald W. Moffat, *Economics Dictionary* (New York: Elsevier, 1976), p. 95.

14. Robert Loring Allen, "Economic Warfare," in *Encyclopedia of the Social Sciences,* ed. David L. Sills (New York: Macmillan Company and the Free Press, 1968), p. 471.

15. It is worth noting, as Robert Loring Allen observes in ibid. and as our European allies tend to overlook, that the very act of attempting to use persuasive "favors" may "render the initiator vulnerable. If the trade is large for the recipient, it is also large for the initiator, and the recipient under some circumstances may subject the initiator to pressure through the same relations that the initiator is employing."

16. Saul Bellow, *The Dean's December* (New York: Pocket Books, 1982), p. 63.

9. Max Singer: "Dynamic Containment"

1. In El Salvador we do *not* have what is so widely assumed: a war for social justice by "the Left" against a conservative-military government; we have instead a war started and prosecuted by truly extremist groups trying to seize power from a moderate revolutionary government that had thrown out the old regime and was making reforms, committed to free elections, and supported by the great majority of the people. (It must be said, however, that in its fight to protect the country from the unpopular insurrection, this moderate revolutionary

government has been guilty of many horrible atrocities against innocent people—although not as many as it has been accused of.)

If the basic nature of the war were correctly understood, the whole political balance on El Salvador in the U.S. (and elsewhere) would be fundamentally different. (People think Lenin is fighting the czar, not Kerensky.)

2. Doan Van Toai, "A Lament for Vietnam," *New York Times Magazine,* 29 March 1981; idem, "A Lesson from Vietnam" (with David Chanoff), *Encounter* (September/October 1982). (See also his *The Vietnamese Gulag,* forthcoming.)

3. On Communist deceit, and Western well-meaning self-deceit, see Paul Hollander, *Political Pilgrims* (New York: Oxford University Press, 1981).

4. While it is commonplace to assert that controlled war is impossible, that is a misunderstanding. What is impossible is to have confidence in advance that a war will be controlled. Let me define *controlled nuclear war.* There are two possibilities: *controlled* or *uncontrolled.* Uncontrolled is where both sides either fire all their weapons or destroy most major civilian targets. Anything else is a controlled war. At the end of a controlled war there are extensive undestroyed civilian targets and unfired weapons (or else it would be an uncontrolled war). Therefore the nature and degree of control is an important influence on the amount of damage in a controlled war. You cannot tell whether a war is controlled until it is over.

An uncontrolled war is worse than a controlled one. If we try to increase the chance that a nuclear war will be controlled, it is possible that we can succeed in improving that chance without making the war more likely.

5. Since this approach to arms control is not well known, although it was briefly and favorably discussed in Hudson Institute analyses as long as twenty years ago, perhaps I should elaborate on it a little.

A military balance like the one I am about to describe could not be reached before 1995, perhaps not before 2005, and it may not even be a meaningful possibility before 2025. But even so, it may be important for arms control decisions today.

Consider the situation after a period of ten years or so during which the U.S. and the USSR were regularly spending $50 billion per year each on strategic defenses (active and passive) and $5 billion per year on strategic offensive forces.

To give some quantitative background for these numbers, one might note that during the 1970s the U.S. bought $4 billion worth of defensive equipment and $31 billion worth of offensive. Using the same measures, the Soviets bought during that same ten years $39 billion worth of defensive equipment and $65 billion of offensive. (All numbers are in constant dollars but none of them is meaningful to an accuracy of better than, say, plus or minus 50 percent.)

The following table (in billions of 1983 dollars) gives the general pattern of change I am talking about. (The U.S.–USSR symmetry is only for convenience, not because I think that such symmetry is necessary or desirable.)

Now		Then	
United States:		United States:	
Offense	$20	Offense	$ 5
Defense	1	Defense	50
Total	21	Total	55
Soviet Union:		Soviet Union:	
Offense	$40	Offense	$ 5
Defense	10	Defense	50
Total	50	Total	55
Summary:		Summary:	
Total offense	$60	Total offense	$10
Total budget	$71	Total budget	$110

It can be seen that this example involves three changes from the current situation: decrease in offensive expenditures, increase in defensive expenditures, and equalization between U.S. and USSR overall levels. Each of these is desirable. (Equalization at lower levels would be even more desirable, *if* the new defense/offense ratio were kept. From an arms control point of view, it would be better to have a higher overall level of expenditures if that were necessary to get a higher defense percent.) The shift to a high defense/offense ratio is desirable even if there is no equalization. In most cases it is desirable for either side to shift to a higher defense/offense ratio regardless of the other side's ratio.

The strategic offensive forces include bombers, land-based missiles, sea-based missiles, or space-based missiles. Defensive forces include active air defense (against planes); active defense against missiles, whether local or area defense and however based; and passive defense—that is, measures designed to reduce the damage to people or property from weapons that penetrate the active defenses.

Despite the technological uncertainties inevitable about such a distant and complex future, I think we can reach some reasonably robust conclusions about the effectiveness of the defense in such a situation, after ten years in which it has been outspending the offense by 10 to 1, as in the second column above.

To evaluate the forces, we can estimate the expected effects of an attack by 10,000 1 MT warheads designed to produce maximum civilian damage. Many of the warheads would be needed to sop up defensive fire, or to attack defensive weapons, in order to make sure that the maximum number of weapons would get through to the hypothesized civilian targets, according to the offense calculations. (If no more than $50 billion had been spent on offensive forces during the previous ten years, then a 10,000 1 MT weapon attack would be a pretty big attack, probably using a fairly high percentage of the force. It doesn't seem likely that in such a world the defense would have to cope with an attack ten times as big.).

We need to consider two cases: a no-warning case, in which there is an attack out of the blue during which all the big cities are hit simultaneously; and a warning case, in which there is perhaps half an hour from when the first weapons are exploded over the U.S. to the time when many hundreds of weapons land on cities, so that most of the defending urban population has tens of minutes to get to shelters.

The best way to describe this situation is by a table of probable fatalities that can be summarized in the following way. For the *warning case,* where most city people hear about the war thirty minutes or more before a bomb falls on them, so that most could get to shelters (maximum distance to a city shelter would be less than a mile — average distance, 1/2 mile): (i) a 10 percent chance of fewer than a million fatalities (if the offense works poorly and the defense works well); (ii) perhaps a 40 percent chance that only 100 weapons get through and that they kill 2–4 million people; (iii) a 40 percent chance that 500 weapons get through and kill 10–15 million people; and (iv) a 10 percent chance that 2,500 or more weapons get through and kill 50–60 million people. (This fatality estimate is based on the assumption that the shelters would be designed to be hard enough and separated enough so that each 1 MT weapon would kill, on the average, 20,000 people, which is a very feasible shelter system design objective — see below.)

The passive defense measures that would have been included in the pre-war defense effort will preserve the ability to restore the economy from the effects of the 100 and 500 penetrating weapons cases, regardless of warning. If 2,500 1 MT weapons are delivered against cities and 50–60 million people are killed, there would be a chance that reorganization after the attack would require outside help, and economic recovery might take a decade.

Attacks in these size ranges have been extensively evaluated, and it is possible to have reasonable confidence in the general understanding of the damage and economic recovery problems (particularly if 10 billion dollars had been spent in the previous ten years to reduce the most critical recovery problems).

Specifically we can have substantial confidence in saying that for an attack of 2,500 1 MT weapons that kills 50−60 million people in thirty days, the overwhelming share of the harm from the attack would be these prompt fatalities and, to a much smaller extent, the direct and immediate property damage. Secondary harms, from fallout if the weapons were groundburst, from "ecological" effects, and from economic costs of disorganization, etc., would be much less important than the deaths. Of course the secondary and indirect damage from the smaller attacks would be very much smaller.

In the *no-warning case,* in which most of the weapons land on cities within the first fifteen minutes or so, three to five times as many people would be killed. Property and environmental damage would be about the same, although relative to the human damage it would be much smaller.

These two cases might be compared to the current situation. Today the Soviet Union could with high confidence deliver 10,000 MT on U.S. cities and value targets, probably killing over 150 million Americans and causing so much damage that no basis for reorganization and recovery could be seen. The best course for the survivors might be to try to move elsewhere.

The main reason for confidence that these kinds of estimates are roughly correct is that a large share of the effectiveness of defense comes from what it accomplishes before the war. If you have a certain offense force budget and there is no defense to contend with, you might be able to buy 1,000 1 MT warheads and the means to deliver them with high confidence. But if the defense has spent three times as much money as your offensive force budget, you will have to divert so much of your money and available payload to systems intended to make sure that you will be able to deliver *something* through the defenses that the maximum blow you would deliver, even if the defenses failed completely and your penetration systems worked perfectly, would probably be less than the equivalent of 500 1 MT weapons. (That pre-war reduction of the attack resulting from measures to defeat defense is called "virtual attrition.")

The one calculation that is most reliable is the ability of shelters to limit fatalities if there is time for people to get to them. Although the attacker can destroy any shelter he hits, he can destroy it only once no matter how bad the defense is. Since shelters would hold less than 20,000 people each, he could kill no more than 20,000 with each warhead, even if they were 100% accurate and reliable and if the shelters were somewhat weaker than they were supposed to be. The shelters only have to be good enough so that if a bomb explodes over one shelter it will destroy only that shelter and not the set of shelters closest to it.

(Much of New York City is so densely populated that it would require much more money or time to give it the same level of protection as other cities. If not it would suffer a higher number of fatalities for each 1 MT weapon than most of the country.)

For example, consider a shelter system designed to limit casualties in the sheltered population to 20,000 for each MT equivalent delivered, with a maximum population density of 10,000 people per square mile. The current population distribution is:

Density	Millions of People	Requirements
Well over 10,000/sq. mi.	7	Would need special arrangements.
About 10,000/sq. mi.	12	OK. Shelter hardness: 100 psi.
Well under 10,000/sq. mi.	125	OK. Shelter hardness: 30−80 psi.
Under 1,000/sq. mi.	85	OK. No blast shelter required.

So with this system, there would be about 7 million people (5 million of them in New York City) who would have to be moved or otherwise specially protected. Shelters can be designed to provide the levels of hardness required by this system with a reasonable degree of confidence and without excessive cost, and any mistakes probably wouldn't result in failure of the whole system—much more likely they would increase fatalities by only a small fraction of the sheltered population.

Therefore, if the existence of the defense can force the offense to reduce the amount of megatonnage launched against cities, and if the defense can shoot down even a modest share of the weapons launched, and if the specific characteristics of the defense prevent the offense from delivering most of his weapons on the cities simultaneously without warning, so the cities are given even thirty or forty minutes' warning (from the first explosions), the shelters can be counted on to protect most people, not reliably but in the sense that there will be many fewer people killed by each bomb than there would be if there were no shelters so that only the first few weapons could kill very large numbers of people. (A reasonable approximation is that 20,000 people would be killed for each 1 MT bomb for the first 2,500 bombs, plus the unsheltered and those in any defective shelters hit; 10,000 people per bomb for the next 5,000 bombs; and 5,000 people per bomb for the next 10,000 bombs.)

6. This point is explained in my article "A Non-Nuclear, Non-Utopian World," *Arms Control and Disarmament*, vol. 3 (London: Pergamon Press, 1968). A similar point is discussed in Herman Kahn, "Nuclear Proliferation and Rules of Retaliation," *Yale Law Journal* 76 (November 1966), and in Herman Kahn and Carl Dibble, "Criteria for Long Range Nuclear Control Policies," *California Law Review* 55 (May 1967).

10.   James L. Payne: "Foreign Policy for an Impulsive People"

1. General Vernon Walters, the American emissary to Argentina during this period, reported that the Argentinian leaders were convinced that Britain would not act, and they could not be told otherwise. A major cause of this expectation, he reported, was their perception of the British domestic political scene. Many top Argentinian officials had lived in Britain and had been impressed by the magnitude of "pacifist" forces, as seen in many demonstrations to "ban the bomb," etc. They assumed that this anti-war sentiment would inhibit action by the British government (speech and discussion, Texas A&M University, 28 September 1982).

2. In one tabulation of fifty nineteenth- and twentieth-century wars, the authors found that initiators lost in sixteen cases (32 percent of the time). See J. David Singer and Melvin Small, "Foreign Policy Indicators: Predictors of War in History and in the State of the World Message," *Policy Sciences* 5 (1974): 282.

3. Luigi Albertini, *The Origins of the War of 1914*, translated and edited by Isabella M. Massey, 3 vols. (London: Oxford University Press, 1952), vol. I, p. 257.

4. Damian Housman, "Lessons of Naval Warfare," *National Review* 34 (23 July 1982): 896.

5. See James L. Payne, *The American Threat: National Security and Foreign Policy* (College Station, Tex.: Lytton, 1981), chapters 4 and 5.

6. On three points, my conception of containment policy may differ from other presentations. First, I do not assume any certain change in the Soviet Union as a result of containment. The Soviet Union may "evolve" into something nicer over the course of containment, but this transformation is neither promised nor required by the policy as I conceive of it. Second, as used here, containment policy includes resistance in marginal, Third World places. Some, including George F. Kennan, have suggested that we need defend only "heartlands," especially Western Europe and Japan, and that we can let the rest of the world go down whatever drain it wants to. This selective containment policy turns out to be unworkable—as even Kennan discovered when South Korea was invaded. See Payne, pp. 213–19, for a review of this problem.

Finally, containment policy remains applicable as long as the Soviet Union has allies that engage in aggression. For some, including Kennan, only the presumed "monolithic" nature of Communism in the early days made containment necessary. After dissention appeared in the Communist world in 1957–62, Kennan felt containment should have been abandoned. See George F. Kennan, *Memoirs 1925–1950* (Boston: Little, Brown, 1967), pp. 366–67. The Communist unity issue, however, is largely a red herring. From the viewpoint of both deterrence (demonstrating will) and protecting one's interests, the organizational unity of opponents is irrelevant. For example, is Cuba a "friend and ally" of the Soviet Union or a "puppet"? The point is academic. Cuba tests U.S. will and furthers Soviet aims just as much either way.

7. See Masanori Ito, *The End of the Imperial Japanese Navy* (New York: MacFadden-Bartell, 1965), pp. 28, 32, 175; David Bergamini, *Japan's Imperial Conspiracy* (New York: William Morrow, 1971), pp. 810–12; Nobutaka Ike, ed., *Japan's Decision for War: Records of the 1941 Policy Conferences* (Stanford, Calif.: Stanford University Press, 1967), p. 282.

8. *Keesing's Contemporary Archives*, 25 April 1980, p. 30208.

9. For an account of this fascinating 180-degree turn, see Payne, pp. 243–50.

10. The consistent role of "pacifism" as a force for war arises from the fact that these movements always arise in the wrong place at the wrong time. The comprehensive generalization is this: a country pluralistic enough to allow a peace movement is too pluralistic to be an aggressor.

In its typical application, this hypothesis points to dictatorships as nonpluralistic aggressors that do not allow domestic peace movements to undermine their aims. They will face defensive democracies which, being pluralistic, do allow peace movements. Since these movements encourage the aggressor to be more assertive, they invite his aggression and hence war.

This pattern has been repeated about a dozen times in the past half-century, the most recent case being the war in the Falklands. There was no "peace" movement in Argentina, the aggressive dictatorship; the "peace" movement in defensive, democratic Britain played an important role in luring the Argentinians to believe that Britain would not respond to their invasion of the Falklands (see note 1).

The above generalization will also cover the case when a democracy is the aggressor. If there is enough sentiment for aggression in a democracy, then a peace movement won't be permitted (or won't be fashionable). For example, the United States was the aggressor in the Spanish-American War. But there was no peace movement in, say, 1897, crusading against U.S. involvement in Cuba. Such a movement would have had to adopt the shockingly unfashionable position that it was all right for the Spaniards to do what they wished in Cuba (concentration camps, massacres, etc.). The tide of impulse at this point was all for aggression and making war.

Much later, "anti-imperialism" and "pacifism" became fashionable—after the need for it had passed. William Jennings Bryan, for example, was one of the more prominent leaders of the "anti-imperialism" forces after 1900; but when the Spanish-American War began, he rushed to be among the first to volunteer to fight it.

We thus reach the dismal conclusion that pacifist movements will probably never arise when and where they are needed to prevent war—that is, in the camp of the aggressor. Instead, they will arise in the society of the defender, and hence contribute to war.

11. In 1977, *The New York Times* ran 48 rights-related stories on South Korea and 0 on North Korea; in 1980, it ran 154 such stories on South Korea and 2 on North Korea. For *The Washington Post*, the parallel figures were 21 and 1 for 1977, and 84 and 0 for 1980.

For the two papers combined, the 1977 stories touching human rights were: Cambodia, 44; Chile, 106; South Africa, 485. See Accuracy in Media, *AIM Report 8* (no. 3), February–I, 1979, p. 3; *AIM Report* (no. 6), March–II, 1982, p. 3.

12. *The New York Times*, 13 April 1975, IV, p. 1. The story was filed from Phnom Penh by Sidney H. Schanberg.

13. United States Senate, Subcommittee on East Asian and Pacific Affairs, Committee on Foreign Relations, *Indochina*, 95th cong., 2nd sess. (1978), p. 24.

14. For documentation of this type of change for the U.S. House of Representatives, see James L. Payne, "The Changing Character of American Congressmen: Some Implications for Reform," paper delivered at the meeting of the Midwestern Political Science Association, 1977; idem, "The Personal Electoral Advantage of House Incumbents, 1936–1976," *American*

Politics Quarterly 8 (October 1980): 465–82; idem, "The Rise of Lone Wolf Questioning in House Committee Hearings," *Polity* 14 (Summer 1982): 626–40.

15. The drawing was by Ben Sargent and appeared in the *Austin American-Statesman.*

16. Thomas O. Enders, "The Case for U.S. Assistance to El Salvador," *Department of State Bulletin* 82, no. 2060 (March 1982), pp. 61–62.

17. Henry Kissinger, *Years of Upheaval* (Boston: Little, Brown, 1982), p. 239.

18. Ibid., p. 240.

19. See, for example, Henry Kissinger, *White House Years* (Boston: Little, Brown, 1979), pp. 1010–14.

20. *The New York Times,* 19 March 1981, p. A1.

21. *The New York Times,* 22 March 1981, p. A1.

22. *The New York Times,* 20 March 1981, p. A3.

23. *The New York Times,* 19 March 1981, p. A8.

24. Ibid.

CONTRIBUTORS

ERNST B. HAAS is Hobson Research Professor of Government at the University of California, Berkeley, where he has taught since 1951. A specialist on international relations theory, international organizations, and processes of international collaboration, he was director of Berkeley's Institute of International Studies from 1968 to 1973. He also headed a Rockefeller Foundation–sponsored research project on international scientific and technological regimes from 1974 until 1979, and chaired the university-wide committee that resulted in the creation of the Institute on Global Conflict and Cooperation in 1982. His most recent book is *Scientists and World Order* (1977).

JAMES L. PAYNE, professor of political science at Texas A&M University, has also taught at Johns Hopkins, Wesleyan, and Yale Universities. His most recent book is *The American Threat: National Security and Foreign Policy* (1981).

PAUL SEABURY is professor of political science at the University of California. His various writings on international politics and U.S. foreign policy include *The Rise and Decline of the Cold War* (1965) and, with Aaron Wildavsky and Edward Friedland, *The Great Detente Disaster* (1975). He currently serves as a member of the President's Foreign Intelligence Advisory Board.

MAX SINGER is president of the Potomac Organization and co-founder and former president of the Hudson Institute, and has been director of the World Institute in Jerusalem. The results of his policy research have appeared in a number of reports and articles, and he is currently finishing a book called *The Edifice of Error,* about the perspectives of the Club of Rome and *The Global 2000 Report.*

ROBERT W. TUCKER, Burling Professor of International Law and Diplomacy at the Johns Hopkins School of Advanced International Studies, is also president of the Lehrman Institute. His latest book (with David C. Hendrickson) is *The Fall of the First British Empire* (1982).

CHARLES WOLF, JR., is dean of the Rand Graduate Institute and director of the Rand Corporation's research program in international economic policy. He has written extensively on economic development, foreign policy, international economic policy, and relationships between economic and national security issues.

AARON WILDAVSKY is professor of political science and public policy at the University of California in Berkeley. He is the author of *Risk and Culture: An Essay on the Selection of Technological and Environmental Dangers* (with Mary Douglas, 1982), *The Nursing Father: Moses as a Political Leader* (forthcoming, 1984), and many other books and articles.

INDEX